The Political Economy of Underdevelopment and Poverty in Nepal

This book argues that mainstream economics cannot explain the underdevelopment and poverty of Nepal, nor can it be explained in terms of economics alone or capital inadequacy even, as is conventionally believed. The author asserts that Nepal's underdevelopment, in spite of its huge resource potential and the advantages of a small nation needs to be located in the nature of the state, which has been shaped by the collusion of interest among politicians, mafias and the resulting bureaucracy over the last two-and-a-half centuries, triggering rampant corruption and the growth of crony capitalism.

The book presents a critical and radical analysis of factors that have kept Nepal in a state of underdevelopment and poverty, with a huge section of historically marginalized and excluded people in underprivileged and deprived socio-economic conditions, despite six decades of planning, seven decades of dependence on foreign aid, and numerous political regime changes, from the Rana regime for over a century from 1846 to 1950 through to the republic regime from 2007 onwards.

To support this argument, the book delves into an exploration of growth performance in Nepal, government attempts at poverty alleviation, inflow of foreign aid and its effects on the economy and the nature of the state, with a focus on Maoists' ten-year rebellion. Each chapter presents the existing picture and examines the possible reasons for the failure in achieving the desired results. A comparative analysis of Nepal's position with respect to the South Asian Association for Regional Cooperation (SAARC) countries is also presented in a number of chapters.

The audience for the book will be students, academics and researchers, and within Nepal itself, intellectuals, politicians development practitioners and officials of the ministries, the National Planning Commission, the central bank and other banks and financial institutions.

Sri Ram Poudyal, former Professor of Economics, Tribhuvan University, Nepal was a Member of the Board of Directors of Nepal Rastra Bank, the Central Bank of Nepal.

Routledge Studies in Development Economics

173. **Digital Financial Inclusion and Regulation**
Ogochukwu Monye

174. **Household Demand for Consumer Goods in Developing Countries**
A comparative perspective with developed countries
Eliyathamby A. Selvanathan, Saroja Selvanathan and Maneka Jayasinghe

175. **Unlocking Private Investment in Sustainable Infrastructure in Asia**
Edited by Bhajan Grewal, Nella Hendriyetty, Iskandar Abdullaev, Chul Ju Kim, Naoyuki Yoshino and Eisa Khan Ayoob Ayoob

176. **The Political Economy of Bilateral Aid**
Implications for global development
Peter Blunt with Cecilia Escobar and Vlassis Missos

177. **Development and Economic Growth in India**
Drivers for Indian states
Biswa Swarup Misra

178. **Towards a Sustainable Economy**
The case of Bangladesh
Edited by Moazzem Hossain, Qazi Kholiquzzaman Ahmad and Mazharul M Islam

179. **Development as Swaraj**
Towards a sustainable and equitable future
Sumanas Koulagi

180. **The Political Economy of Underdevelopment and Poverty in Nepal**
Sri Ram Poudyal

For more information about this series, please visit: www.routledge.com/Routledge-Studies-in-Development-Economics/book-series/SE0266

The Political Economy of Underdevelopment and Poverty in Nepal

Sri Ram Poudyal

Routledge
Taylor & Francis Group
LONDON AND NEW YORK

First published 2023
by Routledge
4 Park Square, Milton Park, Abingdon, Oxon OX14 4RN

and by Routledge

605 Third Avenue, New York, NY 10158

Routledge is an imprint of the Taylor & Francis Group, an informa business

British Library Cataloguing-in-Publication Data
A catalogue record for this book is available from the British Library

Library of Congress Cataloging-in-Publication Data
Names: Poudyal, Sriram, author.
Title: The political economy of underdevelopment and poverty in Nepal / Sri Ram Poudyal.
Description: Abingdon, Oxon ; New York, NY : Routledge, 2023. | Series: Routledge studies in development economics | Includes bibliographical references and index.
Identifiers: LCCN 2022046516 (print) | LCCN 2022046517 (ebook) | ISBN 9781032417981 (hardback) | ISBN 9781032418001 (paperback) | ISBN 9781003359777 (ebook)
Subjects: LCSH: Poor--Nepal. | Poverty--Nepal. | Economic development--Nepal.
Classification: LCC HC425.Z9 P673 2023 (print) | LCC HC425.Z9 (ebook) | DDC 362.5095496--dc23/eng/20230118
LC record available at https://lccn.loc.gov/2022046516
LC ebook record available at https://lccn.loc.gov/2022046517

ISBN: 978-1-032-41798-1 (hbk)
ISBN: 978-1-032-41800-1 (pbk)
ISBN: 978-1-003-35977-7 (ebk)

DOI: 10.4324/9781003359777

Typeset in Bembo
by SPi Technologies India Pvt Ltd (Straive)

Contents

Figures

Tables

Author's Notes

An idea was haunting me for over a decade that there should be a book on Nepal's development with a critical analysis of the factors that have kept the country underdeveloped and poverty-stricken despite six decades of development planning and an increasingly large amount of foreign aid inflow every year. By now, there are several books being written on Nepal's development focused on different aspects of the economy, but they present a contemporary picture from the neo-liberal lens and do not go deeper to explore the root causes of the persistence of underdevelopment and poverty.

The book argues that mainstream economics cannot explain the underdevelopment and poverty of Nepal. Neither can the underdevelopment of Nepal be explained in terms of economics alone, not even of capital inadequacy, as it is conventionally believed. It argues that Nepal's underdevelopment needs to be located in the nature of the state which has been shaped by the collusion of interest among the politicians, bureaucracy and the political and business mafias, irrespective of the type of regime. The country witnessed regime changes since its emergence as Nepal in 1769 – from the Shah (monarchy) regime of 77 years (1769–846) to the autocratic Rana regime of 104 years (1846–950); from the Rana regime to the monarchy-dominated regime of 10 years, with a brief spell of democracy; from democracy to the king-led, single-party Panchayat regime of 30 years (1960–90); from the Panchayat regime to the multi-party democratic regime with a constitutional but powerful monarchy for 16 years (1990–2016); and from a democratic regime to a federal democratic republic in 2008. But there was no fundamental departure in policies and programmes for transforming Nepal from an economically backwards to a more prosperous nation and freeing the poor, deprived and disadvantaged people from systemic suppression and exploitation. Based on the experience of teaching post-graduate students of economics at Tribhuvan University for over three decades and as a working researcher and with an insider view from my brief stint as chief economic adviser to the prime minister and two finance ministers in the post-republic era, I have tried to analyze the underdevelopment of Nepal with a political economy perspective with my limited knowledge on the subject. I must emphasize that this study is by no means exhaustive, but it attempts to offer a political economy insight into the factors that have locked the Nepalese economy in a state of low-level-equilibrium trap and growing inequality and poverty of the mass.

Chapter 1 explains that the adoption of economic planning for development in Nepal since 1956 has not led to higher growth and industrialization as in Russia, China, Korea and even India. The chapter presents the targeted growth rate and achievement of each plan and shows that none of the plans has met the growth target and other sectoral targets. An exponential trend is also fitted to gross domestic product (GDP) for pre-liberalization and post-liberalization periods to assess whether liberalization has led to higher growth. Comparison of Nepal's growth rate, per capita gross national income and GDP per capita growth is also made with South Asian Association for Regional Cooperation (SAARC) countries and China, the United States and the United Kingdom. The chapter examines the progress status of National Pride Projects which have been the priority projects of the government that are considered crucial for the country's development. Also examined in the chapter are the explanations offered for the failure of planning in terms of a lack of natural and human resources, and decade-long internal conflict from 1995 to 2006 and political instability. But these do not appear to be valid explanations. The chapter explains that these are planning machinery and planning systems which have made planning a failure, which in turn are the manifestations of the nature of the state and the interplay of self-interest between different classes. The chapter examines the lacunas and contradictions of the Fifteenth Plan and ends with the suggestion of the need for a stronger planning commission.

Chapter 2 analyzes the poverty rate and its geographical variation by region, ecological belt and district on the basis of data published by the National Planning Commission in 1977, Nepal Rastra Bank in 1984/5, the World Bank Nepal in 1991 and the Nepal Living Standards Surveys in 1995/6, 2003/4 and 2010/11. Estimates made by other organizations such as OPHI and ICIMOD in 2017 are also analyzed and compared with the government estimates. The chapter compares Nepal's poverty rate with other SAARC countries and presents the failure of SAARC in the reduction of regional poverty. Two major factors that have contributed to intensified poverty of the poor, i.e., demolition of squatters' settlements and COVID-19 pandemic, are also examined. The chapter questions the authenticity of government statistics showing a decline in the poverty rate from 41.5 percent in 1995/96 to 18.7 percent in 2017/18 and labels this illusionary because of focus on the aggregate figure, use of unrealistic poverty line, neglect of mountain and remote hill districts, false claim of poverty reduction as the fruit of democracy and liberalization and worsening income inequality. The chapter analyzes the neo-liberal social and political explanations of poverty in Nepal and draws attention to the knowledge gap in poverty analysis in Nepal.

Chapter 3 analyzes the trend in foreign aid inflow in Nepal and its composition by type, source and sectoral allocation. A review of previous studies on foreign aid is made to ascertain whether aid has helped to boost Nepal's economy and produced other beneficial results. The chapter explains that despite noticeable expansion of road infrastructure due to foreign aid, this has not led to increased production as expected. The national debate sparked off by the Millennium

Challenge Corporation's $50 million grant is examined in terms of its connection with the US Indo-Pacific Strategy and National Security Strategy highlighting the implications of Nepal's diplomatic relations with the United States and China. The chapter examines technical assistance that has spanned to politics, parliament, local development, foreign affairs, judiciary and defence and raises doubt whether this has contributed to institution building, capacity development and sustainability. Nepal's dependence on foreign aid is examined in terms of government fiscal behaviour, financing of development plans, foreign debt servicing and influence in policy formulation. Also examined in the chapter are donor concerns in enhancing aid effectiveness through high-level forums and conferences and the compliance of promises and declarations made by them. The chapter ends by discussing country examples of exit from aid and examining the likelihood of Nepal to exit from aid.

Chapter 4 explains that the roots of Nepal's underdevelopment need to be located in the nature of the state that evolved in different political regimes, i.e., the Shah regime, Panchayat regime (1960–90), democracy period (1990–2006) and republic era. An examination of configurations of class in Nepalese society is also presented to provide an overview of how different classes/castes have emerged and developed and controlled the state power. The chapter explains that the political parties and their leaders spent the post-democratic period in political wrangling for power and wealth, consequently giving rise to political instability, high-level corruption and politicization of bureaucracy. The chapter also analyzes the political scenario after Maoists, which fought the "People's War" for ten years (1995–2006) and eventually overthrew a nearly two-and-a-half-century monarchical system and converted Nepal into a federal republic with an inclusive parliament through a proportional election system. The chapter explores the reasons for the declining political influence of Maoists after the Constituent Assembly Election of 2008 and discusses the merger of Maoists and UML after the first general election of 2017 and demerger after three-and-half years. The merger of the two parties produced a nearly two-thirds majority in the parliament with KP Oli as prime minister. The chapter examines the events that led to the displacement of the Oli government by NC president Sher Bahadur Deuba as prime minister of a four-party coalition in June 2020. The chapter also critically examines the much-pronounced slogan of 'economic prosperity and socialism-oriented economy' of the Nepal Communist Party when it was in power and shows that clandestine decisions made by the then prime minister contributed to fostering of crony capitalism instead of socialism. The chapter ends with an assessment of the possibility of altering the nature of the state through another revolution. The concluding chapter presents a discussion on future challenges confronting the Nepalese economy in terms of both political and economic challenges.

The completion of the book took a long time because of my desire to incorporate newer developments emerging in the country, which witnessed a fluid political situation after the restoration of democracy in 1990, and my engagement in advisory responsibilities in addition to teaching. Completing the book was often challenging, frustrating and at one point in time when the book was in the last stage of completion, I was haunted by the spectre of it not seeing the light of day. But somehow it did not succumb to that misfortune and is now in the hands of intelligent readers who have the right to question the development discourse of the country for a better future. It is up to them to judge whether I have been able to give them a recipe to their satisfaction to some extent in the debate and discussion of Nepal's development dilemma.

Foreword

Nepal has been languishing in a vicious cycle of underdevelopment and poverty for the past two-and-a-half centuries. This is the outcome of not a single factor but of a multitude of factors associated with the nature of the state and socio-economic structures that were instituted and sustained for the continuance of the political regimes that emerged in different eras of Nepal's history. With many countries swept by waves of democracy in the 1940s and 1950s, Nepal also witnessed this wave, but the December 1960 royal coup d'état terminated the infant democracy when it needed to be groomed and institutionalized. The palace was never happy with the democracy because it was dictated by the compulsion to revive the monarchy that was made powerless by the Ranas for 104 years. The fledgling democracy was attacked for not even delivering four important achievements in four years and was branded with such features as selfishness, greed and jealousy. By mobilizing some opportunist leaders of the Nepali Congress, King Mahendra sabotaged democracy on 15 December 1960 and announced a new political system in the form of 'Partyless Panchayat Democracy', which was justified as matching to the Nepalese soil and cultural tradition. But the democracy was a suppressed democracy which deprived people of fundamental rights and freedom to speak or express their views that were critical of the Panchayat system. The system was a 'rule of the minority' and was basically meant for strengthening the absolute power of the monarchy with the king as the sovereign ruler and supreme authority of Nepal over all three organs of the state. The system, which was virtually guided by the king, promoted limited pro-palace people and the bourgeoisie class in military, bureaucracy and diplomatic services for strengthening the monarchy's domination in the political, economic and social structures of the country. Not only were people discriminated against by caste, ethnicity, sex, language, religion, occupation, political or other opinions, etc., and in access to rights, public services and opportunities but also excluded and restricted in social and occupational mobility. On the other hand, socio-cultural and ethnic diversities of the country manifested in terms of different customs, culture, values, dress, language, religion, caste and ethnicity were camouflaged under a single connotation, such as national dress, national language and Hindu kingdom. Likewise, the regime alienated the terai (Madesh) from mainstream development, despite its significance as 'granary of the country', and neglected the Madeshi people in education, employment and other opportunities. The Madeshi people were not even identified as Nepalese citizens.

The consequences of these actions were increasing inequalities, vulnerability and poverty and accentuation of rich-poor, rural-urban, hill-terai, upper caste-lower caste and gender divide in political, economic and social spheres. When the Panchayat system was introduced, the ruling king claimed that the system would deliver economic development in one decade that took centuries to achieve for the developed countries. But the expected level of development was nowhere seen even after two-and-a-half decades and another promise was made in 1985 to lift the country to the 'Asian Standard' in 15 years. But this also did not go beyond royal political rhetoric. The regime continued to produce five-year plans in succession, but the actual economic performance always lagged far behind the plan targets. The regime promoted the recruitment of Gorkha warriors in the British and Indian armies for earning foreign exchange. This stripped Nepal of some of its ablest young men who could have been used for the expansion of the productive capacity of the country. The regime also relied more on foreign aid rather than the mobilization of domestic resources, which increased the country's vulnerability to external influences and interferences.

People's suffocation, deprivation and hardships under the autocratic Panchayat rule for three decades gradually culminated and reached to climax in the form of a 'people's national movement' under the initiation of democratic, as well as left political forces, civil societies and professional organizations in April 1990 which succeeded in overthrowing the Panchayat regime and restoring democracy for the second time. However, the Nepali Congress and left parties failed to foresee the dangers of retaining a monarchy as the constitutional head of the state, which seized power in 2005 and squashed democracy. The parties also failed to visualize the consequences of the non-execution of the Mallick Commission report to punish the atrocities committed by the leaders and authorities of the Panchayat regime on flourishing reactionary and pro-feudal elements always bent upon maintaining the status quo. The democracy was applauded by the people for some time, but soon frustrations started to build up owing to the nonfeasance of governments and political wrangling for power, while the people languished in unemployment and poverty. The democratic polity was not inclusive to represent the voices of the unheard mass – the poor, ethnic and deprived communities left isolated and neglected for centuries. On the contrary, it served the interests of the ruling and bourgeoisie classes and created business-politician nexus at all levels of the bureaucratic hierarchy for meeting the financial needs of politicians, particularly in elections. The consequence has been the growth of corruption, rise of crony capitalism, failure to develop a sustainable domestic economy and increase in social and economic oppression of the poor and deprived communities.

The Nepali Congress majority government constituted after the first democratic election made a departure from state-directed to market-directed development under the rubric of 'economic reforms'. These reforms consisted of liberalization of trade and industrial policy, privatization of public enterprises, financial sector liberalization and liberalization of foreign direct investment that were justified as transitions to higher growth, efficient economy and increased inflow of foreign investment. But the outcome was a stagnant and inefficient economy, increased import dependency, widening trade deficit, financial disorder, etc.

Furthermore, the democratic governments institutionalized a culture of foreign employment of Nepalese youths with government stimulus to manpower agencies to recruit and export labour in Gulf countries, Malaysia and other countries for lessening the unemployment problem and earning foreign exchange. This has converted the vast tract of fertile agricultural land into barren land and combined with low government priority to agricultural development, the country, once an exporter of rice, has since for many years been depending on an increasingly larger volume of rice import for meeting domestic requirements. It is not only that the import dependency has increased but also the dependency on foreign aid has enlarged owing to the government's tendency to evade tough decisions for mobilizing domestic resources even to meet the regular expenditure. All these fostered a pattern of development based not on our needs, problems, resource potentials and experience but based on borrowed ideas, concepts and policies. Moreover, the government's intention of not hurting the nexus of privileged classes by introducing redistributive policies kept intact the socio-economic structure of domination, suppression and discrimination. The democracy was used by the ruling parties and their leaders for promoting their own class interests, leaving a vast oppressed, marginalized and deprived majority to fend for themselves. Certainly, this was not the outcome expected of the democratic polity, and frustrated millions were no longer passive but were seeking another political solution which they found in Maoists' 'People's War'.

It is hard to deny that politics has a decisive role in economic development. But politics cannot be imported like other inputs of growth; it has to be set within the country by the effort of its own people. It was precisely with the objective of altering the political system of Nepal, which had been under the control of a hereditary monarchy for nearly two-and-a-half centuries, and ending all forms of feudalism and discrimination of people in terms of caste/ethnicity, religion, gender and property that the Maoists initiated the 'People's War'. The 'People's War' was carried for a decade by the heroic acts of thousands of warriors, many of whom sacrificed their lives for the good of the country, and eventually, after a decade, a new political era was heralded in Nepal's history. No one can deny that it was the Maoists' war that led to the abolition of the monarchy, transformed Nepal into a federal democratic republic and instituted inclusive state structures and governance from the central to the local level. The achievements are there to be seen by everyone – representation of various caste and ethnic groups, Dalits and marginalized communities and women in the federal as well as provincial parliaments, municipalities and rural municipalities and in all constitutional bodies. Moreover, women now make up a third of the federal and provincial parliaments. So far, our efforts have concentrated on safeguarding a new constitution and secular state and institutionalizing federalism in order to not lose the unique and historical accomplishments earned after over 60 years of political struggle and armed insurrection. We needed federalism and a secular state in order to promote national unity, institute a system of governance that empowers local bodies to engage in development activities based on their needs and priorities, deliver public services at people's doorsteps and accommodate diverse religion, caste/ethnicity, culture and opinion. Therefore, the party could not initiate radical policy initiatives in the direction of transforming the semi-feudal socio-economic structure to a more dynamic, vibrant and equitable economy. This requires a relatively longer duration of the party holding the rein of government, but we have not yet been provided this opportunity by the people. We are longing for this opportunity to build a prosperous Nepal and make the Nepalese people happy based on the foundations of our abundant resources and most valuable asset, the youths and socialism-oriented development that fosters an egalitarian society.

Over the years, a number of books have been written by different scholars on Nepal's development/underdevelopment, but this book by Sri Ram Poudyal is a rather unique book in the sense of presenting a comprehensive enquiry into the nature and causes of underdevelopment of Nepal which is away from the mainstream discourse or political thinking. This study attempts to explain the persistence of underdevelopment and poverty in the backdrop of the nature of the state, political wrangling for power, dependence on foreign aid and politics – bureaucracy – business nexus for bribery, which has become so rampant and larger than ever, giving rise to the growth of crony capitalism rather than 'economic prosperity and socialism' that was promised by the Nepal Communist Party government headed by KP Oli during 2018-2021. The book rightly conveys that Nepal's economic backwardness as it exists today cannot be explained in terms of economics alone, not even of structural factors or political stability/instability factors but in a broader politico-economic framework and also in the structure and attitude of authorities of the government in legislative and executive organs and the bureaucracy. A small, beautiful country with a vast potential of natural as well as human resources, Nepal would have become an advanced country with an egalitarian society had the politics and bureaucracy been attuned and sincerely committed to resolving the obstacles in the process of development, poverty reduction and non-partisan delivery of government services without any overt or covert personal interest. The author argues that for this to happen, there is a need for alteration of the nature of the state that transfers power from the ruling classes to the working classes through the socialist revolution but doubts whether this would happen in the foreseeable future.

I would say that the book exhibits a high degree of academic as well as empirical underpinnings and thoughtful insights and think that no serious reader of Nepal's economy can afford to overlook the book. It is my hope that politicians, planners and policymakers, development partners and academics/researchers of Nepal will benefit from reading the book for retrospection to set a new trend for the future. It is a valuable contribution to the debate on the nature and causes of the underdevelopment of Nepal.

Puspa Kamal Dahal (Prachanda)
Chairman, Maoist Centre and Prime Minister of Nepal

Acknowledgements

I take this occasion to salute thousands of heroic warriors who fought and surrendered their lives under the leadership of many visionary political leaders at different phases of history to change Nepal's political system for the better and particularly the Maoist 'Peoples' War' that led to transformation of Nepal from a nearly two-and-a-half-century-long feudal monarchical system to a federal democratic republic. The Maoist 'People's War' carried out over a decade could not, however, achieve its goal of seizure of power for the socialist transformation of the country for its true development. It was judged that the democratic revolution was completed and the socialist revolution would be achieved through parliamentary struggle which, however, seems uncertain as the political development and election results of the recent past show.

As it would be almost impossible to acknowledge all the leaders under whose direction the historic 'People's War' was executed, culminating in a great force that dismantled a nearly two-and-a-half-century unitary monarchical system and converted Nepal into a federal democratic republic with an inclusive political system, I would fail in my duty if I do not mention the names of Chairman of Maoist Centre Puspa Kamal Dahal 'Prachanda', the legendary figure and supreme commander of the 'People's War'; Dr. Baburam Bhattarai, then vice-chairman of the party; and Barsha Man Pun, Standing Committee member who played an instrumental role in carrying the rebellion forward. This is because I had the privilege of spending some months with them in an advisory role when they were prime ministers and finance ministers of the government of Nepal and also because they had given me immense affection, support and thoughtful inspiration. I owe a great debt to these three towering leaders, and I remain forever grateful to Chairman 'Prachanda', who contributed an insightful foreword adding substantial value to the book.

For about three decades, a team of academics and researchers, including myself, was associated with the 'Centre for Policy Studies and Rural Development' for undertaking a wide variety of research works and integrating academics with research. The initial team included Mukunda Sharma, the late Harish Chandra Acharya, Bal Krishna Sharma, Chitra Kumar Gurung, Jamal Devi Shrestha, Phanindreshwor Paudel, Bam Dev Sigdel, Narayan Khadka and Bikash Wagle. The late Harish Chandra Acharya, a man of simplicity and thoughtful dealings, played an instrumental role in the growth of the Centre in the formative years.

With the passage of time, all except a couple of members discontinued their association with the Centre due to death, health problems, migration and personal reasons, but it was sustained with the unbreakable support and unstinting effort of Dr. Bam Dev Sigdel, Hari Shankar Bhattarai and Prakash Basnet. Also, the association of Sudip Pandey and Bhanjakaji Bajracharya with the Centre cannot be forgotten. I sincerely thank them all for their effort to keep alive the Centre. The research discussions in the Centre have been helpful in influencing my thinking when this book was being written.

In preparing the book, I have been helped by many persons, but I should make special mention of Neil Robertson for stimulating academic discussions for years, Gajanand Agrawal for econometric estimation; Hari Shankar Bhattarai for reading the draft, offering useful comments and helping me in all matters; and Prakash Basnet for providing technical support. I would like to express my sincere thanks to them all. I wish to offer my heartfelt thanks, as well, to my colleagues and friends: Ram Mani Pokhrel, former ambassador to Belgium, Er. Rajeshwar Sharma, Dev Raj Adhikari, chairman, University Grants Commission, Chandra Kanta Poudel, former member National Planning Commission, the late Baburam Shrestha, B. K. Man Singh, Narayan Shrestha, advocate and Opendra Sharma for their invaluable support and cooperation.

Writing a book requires an insatiable quest for reading, creative thinking, devotion and, above all, peace of mind. All these require an enabling family environment, which I could enjoy due to the care, concern and tolerance of my spouse Pabitra Poudyal. The book required of me many hours of solitary confinement, and I have been sustained in this strenuous task throughout by her, to whom I dedicate this book. I was fortunate to have all the affection from my daughters Supriya and Sumita and son-in-laws Anuj Dhungana and Dr. Rabin Bhandari who always took care of my overall concerns and health problems, while son and daughter-in-law Suraj and Sangita helped in household matters. I would also like to thank Anita Adhikari and Sharad Wagle for their concern and support to us.

I am highly thankful to Routledge, Taylor and Francis Group, for bringing this book to the light of the day. Also, I express my sincere thanks to the editorial staff at Routledge and most of all to Kristina Abbots, senior editor, who tirelessly supported me in the refinement and publication process of the book and Melissa Levine for her excellent copy-editing of the book. In addition, I am thankful to Christiana Mandizha, assistant editor, at Routledge and Suba Ramya, project manager at Straive for her kind cooperation and facilitation in getting the book published. Finally, my thanks go to Andy Humphries for introducing me to the editors at Routledge. All the errors and omissions are, however, my own responsibility.

Sri Ram Poudyal
Kathmandu, Nepal

1 Persistence of Underdevelopment

1.1 Explanation of Underdevelopment

The Nepalese economy is characterized by the persistence of underdevelopment and poverty. The situation has been described as 'retarded development'[1] or 'misguided development'[2] or 'failed development'[3] depending very much on one's ideological persuasion and political perceptions about the dialectics of underdevelopment of Nepal. In 1971, the United Nations (UN) identified Nepal as one of the least-developed and poorest countries in the world, characterized by deplorable economic and social conditions, demanding serious attention. A report by Asian Regional Team for Employment Promotion (ARTEP) in 1974 stated bleakly, 'Nepal is poor and is daily becoming poorer' (ARTEP, 1974). The situation was even more alarming in 1980 as documented by Blaikie et al., reflecting a state of crisis fundamentally rooted in the failure of productive forces to grow (Blaikie et al., 1980). In terms of the Human Development Index (HDI), Nepal's score of 0.378 in 1990 was the lowest among the South Asian Association of Regional Cooperation (SAARC) countries (UNDP, 1990). The lowest position remained unchanged in 2000 with HDI of 0.446. In 2010 and 2015, Nepal's HDI at 0.529 and 0.558, respectively, were lower than all the SAARC countries but slightly higher than Pakistan (UNDP, 2016). Nepal Human Development Report of 2009 also depicts the persistence of low HDI in Nepal, 'Nepal's HDI was the lowest of the five countries of SAARC in 2005. This has persisted in the last three decades – with the exception of 1990 and 1995, when Nepal ranked just above Bangladesh' (UNDP/Nepal, 2009: 32). In a similar vein, the Asian Development Bank in 2009 stated, 'Nepal's economic growth during the last five decades has not been very impressive when compared with that of other South Asian Countries. The growth rate has been even more modest when considered in per capita terms' (ADB/DFID/ILO, 2009). The 2014 World Development Report, like the past reports, listed Nepal in the category of 'Low-Income Countries' in terms of gross national income (GNI) per capita (World Bank, 2014). Nepal's GNI per capita at US $700.00 in 2012 was only 1.4 percent of the GNI per capita income of the United States, which is considered a model for emulation by the Nepalese middle class and elites. Compared to Japan, another model country for emulation, Nepal's GNI per capita was only 1.5 percent in the same year. Nepal's relative position did not change even after five years. In 2017, even though Nepal's GNI per capita

DOI: 10.4324/9781003359777-1

increased to US $800.0, this was only 1.4 percent of GNI per capita of the United States and 1.7 percent of Japan's GNI per capita (World Bank, 2018). All these substantiate that the deplorable economic condition of the country has been a persistent phenomenon over half a century, and Nepal's lowest position in the global setting is not the phenomenon of a couple of years or even a decade, but a feature carried over the past several decades. What prevails in Nepal now after six decades of development efforts and expenditure of billions of rupees is the persistence of underdevelopment and deepening of inequality between a tiny, privileged class and a large, dispossessed majority.

This deplorable state of affairs is, however, overshadowed by using the euphemistic epithet 'developing', implying that the country is making efforts to develop, but the success has been poor due to constraints basically lying within the broad parameters set by mainstream development economics. For a long period of time and even now, Nepal's natural disadvantages, such as its landlocked position, limited resource endowments, small size, rugged terrain, long and porous border with India, adverse weather conditions, rapid population growth and capital shortage, were offered as explanations to the slow pace of development. These explanations are blindly copied from the World Bank reports produced from time to time to assess the economic situation of Nepal as a prelude to extending its aid supposedly to bridge the resource gap in accelerating growth and development. These reports are replete with sentences such as 'efforts to develop the economy of Nepal take place against the background of severe physical, institutional and economic obstacles. The severity of these constraints is quite evident from the slow progress in almost all sectors during the 30 years since the country began to modernize its economy. Meanwhile rapid population growth has made it increasingly difficult for the country to break out of a low- level equilibrium trap' (World Bank, 1983: 1); 'few countries, however, began their development as late and with such a meagre resource base endowment – a situation compounded by Nepal's land-locked location, rugged terrain and weak institutions' (World Bank, 1989: ix–x); 'limited natural resource endowments and a high rate of population growth averaging 2.6 percent per annum over the past decade contributed to extensive poverty with some eight million people – about 43.0 percent of the population – presently living in absolute poverty'. (World Bank, 1992: 1). The rulers from 1951 unto 1990 often blamed the Rana regime of 104 years (1846–950) as an exploitative regime that perpetuated economic backwardness and inequality. After the restoration of democracy in the country in 1991, successive governments formed through the electoral process often blamed the totalitarian Panchayat regime of three decades (1961–90) for the underdevelopment and distortions in the economy, which constrained their efforts to develop the country. The Panchayat regime was also charged with breeding a highly inefficient economy and corrupt and lethargic bureaucracy preoccupied with personal benefit at the cost of public resources. The politicians of the Panchayat regime were also blamed for amassing personal fortunes out of state properties and propping up foreign aid without which they thought that the country could not be developed. Such explanations have been forwarded many times by the ruling politicians and their henchmen in the post-democracy period to disguise their failure to develop the country. The governments formed between 1995 and 2007 lambasted the Maoist insurgency of a decade (1995–2005) for the poor economic performance of the country. Although it cannot be denied that these factors have made the task of development quite difficult, they cannot be taken as sole alibis for the government's failure to develop the country.

With regard to capital shortage, as we explain in Chapter 3, Nepal did not have the problem of capital shortage from the 1960s with foreign assistance pouring into the country from all parts of the world for almost every activity. The natural constraints need to be taken as 'given' or the 'context' within which the country needs to chart out its contours of development. Smallness is not itself a bottleneck but offers an advantage of efficient management and effective communication and coordination of policies between the centre and the districts, not so easy in large countries, such as India and China. Smallness as a constraint has been refuted by many small countries in the world, smaller than Nepal, which have made remarkable progress. Breiding (2019) explains that small countries are better placed than their large counterparts to address the issues of governance, inequality, unemployment, quality of life and delivery of services. He describes that the smaller countries such as Switzerland, Singapore, Ireland, Israel and some Scandinavian nations have made a virtue out of their small size and developed at least one unique quality that has made them economically prosperous and better educated, more egalitarian and wealthier populations. Contrary to what is presumed in any discussion of the problems of development faced by landlocked states, there is no near axiomatic correlation between a country's landlocked position and its economic underdevelopment. Although there is no denying the fact that the limitations arising out of landlocked geography affect the process of growth, it is not the sole barrier to achieving rapid progress. The four landlocked states of Western Europe (Switzerland, Austria, Luxembourg and Czech Republic) are among the most developed and prosperous countries listed in the group of 'most liveable' countries by the Human Development Report of 2004. Similarly, seven landlocked states of Asia that were part of the former Soviet Union are well placed above other Asian landlocked states which come at the very bottom of HDI listing, and even some African landlocked states are not at the rock bottom, as is Nepal, by any indicator of economic and social development (UNDP, 2004). Collier (2008) argues that landlocked geography is not always a handicap, as countries can benefit from the growth spills over of their neighbours.

> We found that in general all countries, landlocked or not, benefitted from the growth of their neighbour: growth spills over. The global average was that if a country's neighbours grew by an additional 1.0 percent, the country grew at an additional 0.4 percent … for the landlocked the spillover is not 0.4 percent but 0.7 percent. … If you are coastal, you serve the world; if you are landlocked, you serve your neighbours.
>
> (pp. 56–57)

But Nepal failed to orient its economy to maximize growth spills over from its fast-growing two large neighbours: China and India. This failure reflects the continuation and perpetuation of a historically manifested semi-feudal politico-economic structure that retards the development and expansion of the productive base of the economy.

In Nepal's history, the Rana regime of 104 years (1846–1951) can be considered as internal colonialization that inhibited the forces of growth and modernization. It is true that the Rana regime did not lay the foundation of development and the system was virtually engrossed in expropriation and appropriation of maximum surplus for its self-aggrandizement. But this does not also offer the sole explanation of the development of underdevelopment in Nepal in the later phases of history. Nepal's underdevelopment and poverty cannot also be linked to colonization because it had never ever been subjected to colonial domination. The country has remained a sovereign nation ever since King Prithivi Narayan Shah, king of Gorkha, annexed several petty states into one territorial jurisdiction under the name Nepal in 1769. The link between colonization and underdevelopment is, however, extremely tenuous because colonization has also led to startling development in some countries. The examples of Hong Kong, which was a British colony from the Second World War until 1998, and the two tigers of East Asia, Taiwan and South Korea, which were the colonies of Japan before the Second World War, refute the hypothesis that colonization retards development. In India, though colonization retarded the cotton industry, it stimulated development through the exploration of mines and the development of physical infrastructure, particularly the railway network and education base. Saunders argues,

> Even some Marxists accept that the net effects of colonization on economic development have been more beneficial than harmful and quotes Bill Warren, "Direct capitalism, far from having retarded or distorted indigenous capitalist development that might otherwise have occurred, acted as a powerful engine of progressive social change".
>
> (Saunders, 1998: 34)

Although Nepal remained a sovereign nation, the geographical constraints (about 1,600 km open border with India and access to sea only from India) and India's desire for political, economic and security hegemony over Nepal has made the country a semi-colonial appendage of India. As Bhattarai says, 'The semi-colonial mode of integration with India since the British Colonial period has imposed on the space economy all the disadvantages of colonialism with none of the "advantages", e.g. those deriving from productive investment of capital' (Bhattarai, 2003: 45). Thus neither mainstream development economics nor any other apologetic discourse provides a logical explanation to Nepal's retarded development and the growing poverty of the masses. Studies undertaken to explain the development problems of Nepal have also been mainly replete with the mainstream diagnosis, and as Bhattarai says, '[These studies] continue to lack an objective and holistic approach and fail to locate the basic malaise in the internal and external relations of production' (Bhattarai, 2003: ix).

Neo-classical economics does not recognize Nepal's peculiar characteristics shaped by geo-strategic location, socio-economic structure and nature of the state and considers the prevailing social and economic order as the ideal one and argues that whatever imperfections and hurdles are there, these can be corrected through injection of more capital and appropriate state policies. These theories also assume that the state functions to promote the benefit of all sections of the society. Had the neo-classical economics worked, six decades of development planning and state policies would have made a fundamental transformation of the Nepalese economy. But the economy is still languishing in the persistence of underdevelopment and deepening dichotomy between a small affluent group and the large mass of the population, with a large majority deprived of living a life with human dignity. This raises some serious questions. Can the underdevelopment of Nepal be explained in isolation without enquiring into the nature of the state, class structure, power relations and the way the government functions? Can Nepal's underdevelopment be seen independently of its peripheral status in the global capitalist system, particularly of Indian interest and interference? These are serious questions and cannot be dismissed as unimportant, irrelevant or merely ideologically motivated, as seems to be the general thinking of mainstream economists in Nepal. What we attempt here is to offer an explanation of the persistence of underdevelopment, poverty and economic inequalities in Nepal from the political economy perspective drawing upon the Marxian approach, howsoever inadequate.

1.2 Strategy of Development

The definition of what development means has undergone a paradigm change, and the analysis of how to achieve it and what factors promote or inhibit it has also been changing. For a long period of time, the bourgeois economists equated economic development with economic growth or the growth of gross domestic product (GDP), which was considered a necessary concomitant to poverty reduction and the increase in people's welfare. The assessment of development was made on the basis of indices such as the rate of growth of GDP and per capita GDP, as these provided aggregative measures, which could be quantified, and movements which could be analyzed and compared among nations. Although so popular with the UN agencies and the World Bank, such indices do not reveal the structure or dynamics of an economy. Measurement of the level of development by per capita income would have placed Kuwait at a higher position than United States and Venezuela at a higher position than Romania and Japan six decades ago, as Amin mentions,

> [I]n Kuwait the product per head in 1960 ($3,290) was greater than in the United States ($3,020) and in Venezuela it was higher than in Romania or Japan ($780 against $710 and $660, respectively) and Gabon today approximately the same level as that of France in 1990.
>
> Amin (1976: 292)

Development in this sense of higher per capita income automatically meant capitalist development without concern to income inequality among the citizens is out of context in the bourgeoisie development discourse. Capitalist development implied incessant economic expansion through accumulation, involving in the process the use of modern technologies and a shift away from an agrarian to a modern industrial society. The issue of distributional justice is assumed away by saying that 'if we take care of growth, equity will take care of itself through trickle down effects'. The main thrust of bourgeois development economics lies in its emphasis on capital accumulation for economic development. The capitalist sector is propagated as the engine of development in a dual economy, as it is the sector that is capable of self-expansion. As the capitalist sector expands and accumulates, it will impinge on the production relations in the pre-capitalist sector, ultimately annihilating it. As the entire economy comes within the orbit of capital, there will be a full transformation from pre-capitalism into capitalism and dualism will cease to exist (Sanyal, 1988). The strategy of economic development projected and propagated by Nepalese policymakers and planners is basically derived from this theoretical postulate. The results of pursuing this strategy are often slow growth, regional disequilibria, inequality, unemployment, dependence on foreign countries and specialization in the production of primary products and poor education and poor health conditions for a large majority of people. Such outcomes are, however, taken as symptoms of underdevelopment or as deviations from the ideal which would vanish with higher economic growth and modernization. Attention is focused on symptoms of underdevelopment rather than on the basic structural elements, which keep underdeveloped countries locked in the vicious circle of underdevelopment. The capitalist process of development, because of its inherent polarizing character, has reinforced the capital-pre-capital dualism rather than annihilating it.

For a long period of time, mainstream economists treated Nepal's underdevelopment as a low rate of growth of GDP or low per capita income in comparison to developed countries. A doyen of bourgeois economists, Paul Samuelson, for example, says, 'A less developed country is simply one with real per capita income that is low relative to the present-day per capita incomes of such nations as Canada, the United States, Great Britain and Western Europe generally' (Samuelson, 1970: 741). A critique of growth-focused strategy emerged within the bourgeois discourse on economic development, and it was increasingly realized that growth alone would not lead to a rise in the living standards of people. In 1972, Dudley Seers made a shift away from the conventional definition of growth by asking three questions about a country's development: What has been happening to poverty? What has been happening to unemployment? What has been happening to inequality? If all three of these have become less severe, then this would be a period of development for the country concerned. If one or two of these central problems have been growing worse, especially if all three have, it would be strange to call the result 'development', even if per capita income has soared (Seers, 1972: 3–4) Sen goes a step further and defines 'development as freedom' that consists of five distinct freedoms: political freedoms, economic facilities, social opportunities, transparency guarantees and protective security (Sen, 2000: 10). But in a society with different class hierarchies and power relations, there is no guarantee that any expansion of the individuals' freedoms would enable all to utilize freedom for their welfare. Besides, Sen's work glosses over international power relations and world development agencies that produce and reproduce underdevelopment in poor countries. On the other hand, the Marxian theory in contrast to neo-liberal theories of development/underdevelopment posits underdevelopment in terms of the production system, relations of production and exploitation of labourers by the capitalists and imperialist exploitation of the colonies. Dissenting with the index of per capita income as a measure of development, Szentes, a Marxian economist, says,

> The index of per capita national income is not consistent with the dynamic approach. It glosses over the conditions of the production, distribution and utilization of the national income – i.e. the very factors that are of decisive importance from the point of view of internal possibilities and limitations of development. Under what production relations, in what social and economic sectors and branches is the national income produced, who gets hold of it, and for what purposes is it utilized?
>
> (Szentes, 1976: 24)

The situation of economic underdevelopment in Nepal is conceptualized as being the consequence of lagging behind in the development of productive forces due to interplay of certain growth inhibiting or limiting factors, particularly capital. Relying on the neo-classical theory, it was accepted that if there was no capital, there would be no investment and no growth. Furthermore, capital was postulated as providing a 'Big Push' to jump from an economically backward stage to a developing stage (Rodan, 1943) and also to get out the vicious circle of poverty (Nurske, 1953). The circular causation of poverty is tersely stated, 'because it is poor, the country does not develop, because it does not develop, it remains poor' (Gill, 1963: 28). The critical importance of capital in determining the rate of growth was reinforced by the Harrod–Domar model which postulates the rate of growth as being a function of rate of capital formation and the capital-output ratio (Domar, 1946; Harrod, 1948).

Assuming that the capital-output ratio is a fixed coefficient, which cannot be changed in a short time span, the rate of growth virtually becomes a function of capital. The model is extended to show that a poor country growing at a rate dictated by the quotient of savings rate and capital-output ratio (s/c) would witness an increase in its growth rate from s/c to (s + f)/c as a result of foreign capital inflow indicated by f, expressed as a fraction of Gross National Product (GNP). In the two gap models, foreign aid is perceived as a means of bridging the savings gap (the shortage of domestic savings to finance the required investment) or the foreign exchange gap (the shortage of foreign exchange to pay for necessary imports), thereby permitting fuller use of domestic resources and continuation of development (Chenery and Strout, 1966; McKinnon, 1964). All these constructs assume investment or the rate of accumulation of capital as the prime determinant of economic growth and totally ignore labour, the relations of production and the contradictions in production relations. Neo-classical growth theories of later genres (Solow, 1956, 1957), however, treat labour, natural resources and technical progress as equally important as capital investment for growth. The major flaw of the neo-classical growth theories is that

> they digress from capitalist relations of production, which determine the goal of production, profit as the driving motive of accumulation, and ignore the contradictions of capitalism which cause imbalances between the different spheres of production, and completely leave out of account the class content of the categories.
>
> (Ryndina, 1984: 182)

The Nepalese planners fully subscribed to the neo-classical capital-centred development and relegated all other constraints as being merely the manifestations of capital shortage. The Harrod–Domar model was used as the framework of the planning exercise, as this provided a logical basis for making a desperate plea for an increasingly larger amount of foreign aid to meet the resource gap of the targeted growth rate. The planning exercise basically hinged on fixing the desired growth rate and working backwards to estimate the investment requirement on the basis of the presumed capital-output ratio and to estimate the size of foreign aid required given the domestic savings rate. The transformation of the Nepalese economy from a traditional to a modern society was envisaged as passing through five stages, as postulated by W. W. Rostow, viz., the traditional society, the pre-conditions for take-off, the take-off, the drive to maturity and the age of high mass consumption (Rostow, 1960). These (capitalist) stages of growth were forwarded as an alternative to Marxian stages of growth, which also postulated five stages – namely, slavery, feudalism, capitalism, socialism and communism. A careful analysis of these two theories of stages of growth shows that Rostow's traditional society is the same as the Marxian stage of feudalism, whereas the rests are totally contrasting.

In Nepal's context, an American adviser named William O. Thweatt, who was in Nepal in 1959, analyzed the process of development from the perspective of Rostow's stage theory of growth. On the basis of guesstimates of the national income in Nepal (1954–60) and the capital requirements during the 'pre-conditions' and the 'take-off' stage, Thweatt presumed the Nepalese economy fully entering into the pre-conditions stage in the 1960s, readiness for the take-off by 1970 and entering the period of take-off in the next two decades (Thweatt, 1961). The take-off is meant to be the crucial stage of growth defined as requiring (i) a rise in the rate of productive investment from say 5.0 percent or less to over 10.0 percent of national income, (ii) an industrial revolution characterized by rapid expansion of one or more manufacturing sectors (leading sectors) with a high rate of growth and (iii) an institutional framework leading to modernization of the economy and realization of external benefits. The Nepalese planners also grafted these concepts and continued doing so, employing the same instruments, mechanisms, stimuli and organizational structures as those of capitalist countries or as suggested by the Western advisers. But the outcome has been abysmal – the country would have attained the take-off stage by the end of the 1990s as postulated by Thweatt, but three more decades have elapsed, and the take-off is going even farther.

Development does not seem to occur mechanistically as a result of investment, nor does the development of agriculture and industry in itself solve the problem of poverty when prevailing political and socio-economic structure and production relations, which produce various manifestations of inequality and constantly aggravate it, are preserved and reproduced. As Dostovalov says,

> [T]he main cause of poverty does not lie simply in the backwardness of agriculture, which itself is a derivative of the socio-economic conditions inherited from the colonial past. Poverty and underdevelopment like unemployment, exploitation and inequality are necessary attributes of capitalism that will be reproduced in ever new forms while it exists.
>
> (Dostovalov, 1984: 204)

Another component of the development strategy followed by Nepal was the adoption of the mixed economic system and emphasis on import substituting industrial development. India too had adopted the mixed economic system after its independence from British colonial rule with centralized planning. A component of the mixed economic system was the emphasis on industrial development which was to be carried out through public and private sectors. Industrial development was taken as the vehicle to get the country out of the vicious circle of backwardness and catch up with the high living standards of industrialized countries. The development of the manufacturing sector was seen to have spillover effects on the rest of the economy through backwards and forwards linkages leading to the transformation of agriculture into a highly productive sector. Industrialization was also seen as providing the escape from the economic dependence on developed countries through self-sufficiency in various consumer as well as investment goods. In view of the constraints operating in the economy, the state took the lead in the process of industrial development through the creation of public-sector enterprises in areas where the private sector was not to be trusted and where it was not willing to invest. The state had to perform the role of Schumpeterian entrepreneur, as the private sector was at a nascent stage, the capital market was virtually non-existent and infrastructural facilities were not adequately developed. So the periodic plans demarcated what the government would do and what the private sector was required to do.

The third component of the development strategy was import substitution as a vehicle for industrialization because India as well as other Asian and Latin American countries had patterned their industrialization on the import substitution strategy (ISI). There were two main approaches to import substitution. India adopted the approach of the 'basic industries' first strategy, concentrating on the substitution of imports of a core of capital goods industries such as industrial machinery, chemicals and heavy equipment. This was justified by its huge size and the industrial development strategy of foregoing consumption in the early years to generate resources for the production of capital goods (machines to build machines, to build fertilizer plants, to build consumer goods industries) for much higher consumption in the future. The other approach was to focus on industries producing consumer goods that replaced imported goods or carried out assembly of imported materials and gradually worked backward to basic industries. This was the strategy of industrialization adopted by most Latin American countries from the 1930s until the late 1980s. But by the start of the '70s, the ISI started to falter, and the possibilities for further import substitution had disappeared, causing a slowdown of industrial growth, decline in employment growth and worsening of income distribution. Nepal also started the process of import substituting industrialization by erecting heavy tariff walls with a nominal rate of protection ranging between 23.2 percent and 105.0 percent on third country–sourced imports and between 11.2 percent and 50.0 percent on Indian-sourced imports from the 1960s till 1980s (Maxwell Stamp, 1991) for substitution of imported consumer goods by domestic production. Contrary to general expectation that essential imports would be substituted by domestic production, industrial units that produced nonessential goods, such as cigarettes, beer, alcohol, soft drinks, confectionary and synthetic textiles and industries based on screw-driver technology having hardly any value added domestically, such as electronics, galvanized iron sheets, bitumen and barrel, were established. Despite stringent licensing policies for such industries, entrepreneurs were able to start such industries by influencing politicians and bureaucracies through rent seeking. A number of import substituting industries groomed under the 'infant industry' argument started crumbling in the face of stiff competition from imported goods with the initiation of economic liberalization and privatization policies from the late 1980s.

1.3 Planning and Development

Many South East Asian and other countries, including Russia, China and Korea, have achieved substantial economic progress through state planning. Planning was most successful in the post-war and post-independence periods when there was a desperate need for reconstruction and revival of war-devastated and regime-ruined economies all over the world. Presenting a summary sketch of effectiveness of planning, Field says,

> Planning enjoyed its Asian heyday in the post-war and post-independence periods, when it was applied to reconstruction and basic industrialization. Even Pakistan, where economic growth has generally been fitful, implemented two highly successful plans in the 1950s, which were then taken by South Korea as a model for its planning exercise after 1960. The 1950s also saw India growing steadily at 3.8 percent under a planned regime and China achieved an average 8.9 percent rise in national income under its First Five Year Plan, from 1953 to 1957. The biggest successes for planning were South Korea and Taiwan.
>
> (Field, 1995: 49)

As illustrative examples, it would be worthwhile to briefly present the achievements made by Russia, China and Korea through state planning.

1.3.1 Soviet Union

Various studies have documented spectacular economic advancement made by the Soviet Union since the victory of the October 1917 revolution and through the adoption of planning. It was the first country in the world to start planning as early as 1928 and during 1928–40, the GNP growth rate averaged 5.8 percent per annum.[4] Mandel documents the transformation of the USSR from a backward and essentially agricultural country to an industrial country through overall planning, placing it ahead of Britain and Germany in some industrial products by 1965. The Soviet Union was

> the second industrial power in the world, in particular for basic raw materials, electric power and machine-tools, its output of which exceeds the combined output of Britain and Germany. The USSR possessed in 1953 a stock of 1,300,000 machine tools of all kinds, double what it had before the war, whereas the second capitalist power, Britain, had in 1950 only 880,000. The American stock amounted at the same period to 1,800,000 superior in quality to the Soviet ones.
>
> (Mandel, 1974: 557–8)

Writing on Soviet achievement Devine says, 'Historically it made possible in three decades, interrupted by the unprecedented destruction wrought by the Nazi invasion, the transformation of the Soviet Union from a backward society with an underdeveloped economy into one of the world's two super powers' (Devine, 1988: 59). The Soviet achievement was reflected in terms of (i) rapid industrialization based on domestic resources, (ii) full employment during a decade when the west had plunged into the Great Depression with massive unemployment, (iii) spectacular progress in education and health and (iv) highly egalitarian (compared to the rest of the world) distribution of income and wealth was something unparalleled in the world (Chandra, 2004). The development regime in the Soviet Union consisted of a centrally determined system of production, consumption and utilization of surplus which together determined the course of the economy oriented towards the desired direction of development for the economy as a whole or for a particular industry or sector. Production was organized and coordinated within an administrative hierarchy with targets fixed at the centre and passed down through the intermediate level of hierarchy to the individual enterprises (Devine, 1988). The individual enterprises estimated the inputs required by them to fulfil the output targets set for them and forwarded the information back to the centre through the hierarchy. The planning authorities drew up the material balances plan consisting of estimates of the potential availability of goods or services (output, imports and stocks) and estimates of use. This provided the planning authorities with a flexible framework for modifying targets in order to maintain a balance between estimated availability and estimated use. Along with output targets, enterprises also set financial targets as a part of a financial plan for the whole economy consistent with the physical plan based on the material balances. There was also an incentive system for the enterprises in the form of bonuses varying with the progress made in the fulfilment of output targets. Chandra attributes the success of Soviet planning to the 'core' of the Soviet economic system, which consisted of

> (i) state ownership or control of most productive enterprises; (ii) central planning of production and allocation of goods and services at state determined prices; (iii) a subsidiary role for money, banking and finance with primacy assigned to production targets in physical units; (iv) price control and supply restrictions on domestic trade, except for foods produced on the collective farmers' plots; (v) freedom (not unfettered) of workers to choose their jobs; and (vi) state monopoly over foreign trade and transactions.
>
> (Chandra, 2004)

At the top of these, there was a very strong state and a committed bureaucracy with accountability to the public. The Soviet impact on non-socialist countries between 1947 and 1991 was so pervasive that the United States had to radically alter its own policies towards its allies to foster their economic development and make them less susceptible to communist influence (Chandra, 2004). The spectacular Soviet achievement had some costs too in terms of control of individual freedom, forced collectivization, arbitrary decision-making, inefficiency and waste, shortage and lack of consumer satisfaction. But this was the price to be paid for rapid growth, regional development, full employment and increase in the standard of living of the people.

1.3.2 China

China too was able to transform her backward, low growth economy into a high growth and more egalitarian economy through administrative command planning. Before the communists swept to power in 1949, China had all the classic symptoms of economic backwardness: political corruption, social debility and class exploitation, economic stagnation, negligible technical change and heavy demographic pressure. But within two decades after the communists came to power, Chinese industry was transformed into a highly advanced stage capable of producing aircraft, ships, electrical generators, locomotive cargo ships, etc., and China ranked in the status of the world's major military powers in terms of launching of satellite communication and explosion of atomic and hydrogen bombs (Xing, 1999). The high growth rate of the Chinese economy during the three decades of the communist regime (1952–78) and its ranking among the top ten countries in the world concerning the absolute level of GNP, industrial production, power generation and production of crude oil, chemical fertilizers, coal, cement and clothing were made possible due to central planning of the economy. Not only was the economic growth rate higher than that of developed countries during the period but also the inter-provincial and inter-rural inequalities were significantly reduced through state-guided market intervention. A comparison of Chinese and Indian development performance also shows China's impressive performance on all fronts, even though both countries had central planning with state-led industrialization. China and India had many similarities in their 'initial conditions' with regard to levels of living, wide geographic variations and economic, as well as social diversities, when they got political freedom at about the same time (1949 and 1947), but since then, China's achievements have significantly surpassed that of India. During 1980–93 GDP, grew in China at 9.6 percent per annum compared to 5.2 percent in India. The growth of per capita income was 8.2 percent in China while it was 3 percent in India. Exports in China grew at 11.5 percent, but the growth of Indian exports was 7.0 percent per annum. In terms of HDI, China ranked 34th against India's rank of 63rd (Khandwalla, 1999). There is substantive evidence that China has outperformed India in every respect with little hope left for catching up in the near future (Nagraj, 2005).

1.3.3 South Korea

South Korea is cited as a role model to be followed by underdeveloped countries in implementing economic reform for industrialization and growth. South Korea had gone through the agony of partition in 1945, following the Second World War and war with North Korea between 1950 and 1953, which disrupted its economy by causing massive damage to infrastructure, destruction of almost two-thirds of productive capacity and killing of one million people. In the post-Korean war period (1953–61), the annual growth of per capita GDP was only 1.0 percent, and exports constituted only 5.0 percent of GDP by 1961. The economy was characterized by a huge savings-investment gap, balance of payments deficit, virtual absence of manufactured exports and high rate of poverty. In 1960, South Korea had the same level of income as India and Pakistan, but by 1995, its income level was 25 times that of India and Pakistan (Desai, 2005: 290). But in the next 30 years from 1961 onwards, Korea was able to transform itself from one of the poorest countries to an industrialized country, establishing itself as 'the miracle on the Han River'. It has become the home for world-famous brands from cars to smartphones and fashions. It was not that Korea was exceptionally endowed with natural resources, but it was the ambitious planning and government interventions under the direction of President Park Chung Hee in the early 1970s that pushed the economy into a high growth trajectory, resulting in spectacular economic achievement. The concerted planning efforts led to significant diversification and deepening of the export and industrial structure, making Korea a growth pole in steel and ship building as well as in electronics on par with Japan (Hasan, 2007). Assessing the Korean economic performance, the United Nations Development Programme (UNDP) Human Development Report of 2016 stated,

> The Republic of Korea has travelled a highly successful path of human development over the past six decades. And the major drivers behind the country's sustained trajectory of high human development include successful land reforms, rural development, extensive human resources development and rapid equitable economic growth. Export orientation, sustainable domestic resource mobilization with strong redistribution policies, and public infrastructure development also played major roles. Needless to say, effective institutions and governance were also key.
>
> (UNDP, 2016)

Obviously, the achievements made by these countries through planning were shaped by their setting and a complex mix of political, economic, social and institutional factors, generalization for any individual country may not be justifiable. But lessons can be drawn and applied with suitable adjustments to the country-specific socio-economic and political circumstances.

1.4 Planning and Growth Performance in Nepal

Over six decades have passed since Nepal adopted planning for development. The First Plan was started five years after the overthrow of the despotic Rana regime of 104 years in 1950. An outline of the First Plan was hurriedly prepared in 1955 for presentation in the 1955 Colombo Plan meeting to appeal for foreign assistance for Nepal's development. A more detailed framework was prepared in 1956 and was implemented for a period of five years ending in 1961. However, it was not a plan in the sense of constituting an internally coordinated set of targets and investment decisions. The First Plan was followed by a Three-Year Plan (1962–5) after a delay of one year to resolve the organizational problems witnessed in the First Plan and to reorganize planning in accordance with the partyless Panchayat regime that King Mahendra announced in 1960 after a coup d'état of first democratically elected government which had prevailed for 18 months.

The performance of the First Plan was poor both in financial and physical terms. The actual expenditure was about Rs. 220.0 million as against the targeted outlay of Rs. 330 million, and the achievement remained far short of physical targets in all except the education and health sectors. The Second Plan (1962–5) was focused on establishing data and information bases on various sectors and conducting surveys of natural resources for building the foundation of a long-term plan of 15 to 20 years. The next four plans (Third to Seventh plans), which were of five-year durations each, were executed during the Panchayat regime under the direct rule of absolute monarchy. However, when the Eighth Plan was to begin in July 1990, the democracy movement instigated in the early 1990s eventually forced King Birendra to abolish the Panchayat regime and restore multiparty democracy. Hence, the Eighth Plan could not take off in 1990 because of the political change, and, consequently, two years were without plans. The Eighth Plan (1992–7) was launched in 1992, but with a major departure from the past in development paradigm from a state-controlled economic regime to that of a liberal, deregulated and market-guided regime. The Ninth Plan (1997–2002) and the Tenth Plan (2002–7) followed the pattern of the Eighth Plan with hardly any new innovative exercise, and by the time the Eleventh Plan was to be initiated from mid-July 2007, a radical political change occurred in the country. The change was the overthrowing of a two-and-a-half-century monarchical system and the transformation of Nepal from a unitary state to a federal democratic republic. This was made possible by an alliance between the Communist Party of Nepal (Maoist), which had waged the People's War for a decade (1995–2005) against the repressive state and the feudal monarchical system which perpetuated and protected an oppressive socio-economic order and the seven political parties, which had been side-lined by King Gyanendra through a political coup on 1 February 2005. Following a 12-point agreement between the warrior force and parties on 17 November 2005, an aggressive national movement was launched in April 2006 for the restoration of democracy, election to the Constituent Assembly (CA) and writing of a new constitution. Gyanendra was eventually forced to reverse his coup d'état and restore the parliament. Furthermore, the monarchy was abolished, and the country was declared the sovereign people's (democratic) Republic of Nepal in 2008. The four plans (2007–19) initiated after this political change were of three-year duration, while the Fifteenth Plan started in mid-July 2019 after the general election of 2017 was of five-year duration.

1.4.1 Objectives of Plans

The Nepalese plan documents list a set of objectives, which are almost repetitive between different plans and reveal the same pattern as the previous ones. The overriding objective of all the plans has been increasing production, although in the later plans, social objectives were also articulated. From the Fifth Plan (1975/6–1979/80) onwards the objectives have remained almost the same and they look very much like the ones listed in the previous plans. In the earlier plans, import substitution, self-reliance, dominant role of the public sector and encouragement of the private sector were stressed. However, the Eighth Plan (1992/3–1996/7) made a shift from the controlled economic system of the Panchayat regime towards a free-market-oriented and liberal economic system. The plan had the principal objective of sustainable economic growth along with poverty alleviation and reduction of regional imbalances. The Ninth Plan (1997/8–2001/2) listed poverty alleviation as its main objective and laid emphasis on high and sustainable growth rates and trickle-down effects. The Tenth Plan (2002/3–2006/7) had poverty reduction as the only objective, with a focus on four strategically important areas – namely, high, sustainable and broad-based growth; improvement in the access and quality of infrastructure, social and economic services in the rural areas; targeted programmes for social and economic inclusion of the poor and marginalized communities; and good governance to improve service delivery, efficiency, transparency and accountability. The plan was also named the Poverty Reduction Strategy Paper (for meeting the International Monetary Fund (IMF) conditionality of a soft loan.)

The Three-Year Interim Plan (2007/8–2009/10) set a long-term vision of building a 'Prosperous, Modern and Just Nepal' through the development of all regions and inclusive growth. The plan had the objectives of supporting the establishment of peace through relief, reintegration and reconstruction and reducing existing unemployment, poverty and inequality in the country. It also emphasized supporting poverty alleviation and the establishment of lasting peace through employment-centred inclusive and equitable growth. The Three-Year Plan (2010/11–2012/13) embraced the long-term vision of transforming Nepal from a least-developed country to developing country status within two decades while making it a prosperous, peaceful and just nation. The plan had also the goal of achieving Millennium Development Goals by 2015, creating dignified and gainful employment, reducing economic disparity, achieving regional balance, improving the living standards of the general public and reducing poverty to 21.0 percent through sustainable development. The Thirteenth Plan (2013/14–2015/16) had the objective of bringing about a direct positive change in the living standards of the general public by reducing the economic and human poverty prevalent in the nation. This plan also had a target to upgrade Nepal from a least-developed to a developing country status by 2022. The Fourteenth Plan (2016/17–2018/19) set a growth target of 7.2 percent per annum and a long-term goal of upgrading Nepal to a middle-income country status by 2030. The Fifteenth Plan (2019/20–2023/4) aims at making Nepal a developing country in the first three years (by 2022) elevating it to a middle-income country by 2030, and to a developed country status in a time span of 25 years or by 2045. The plan aims at freeing all people from absolute poverty and achieving UN sustainable development goals. The objectives of the Nepalese plans can be broadly summarized as follows:

i ***To achieve an increase in production***: This is the so-called growth objective, which is quantified in terms of an annual growth target of GDP in all the plans except the first two plans. The target growth rate has all along been around 5.0 percent with slightly higher rates in the latter plans. The Third Plan had the target of doubling the national income within 15 years, which was pronounced by the king. In the Ninth Plan, the growth target was set at 6.0 percent, the highest ever from the past. The Tenth Plan also envisaged a 6.2 percent average growth rate in the normal case and 4.3 percent in the lower case. The plan also set a long-term growth target of 8.3 percent to be achieved by 2016/17. The Three-Year Interim Plan as well as the Three-Year Plan had set a growth target of 5.5 percent on average per annum during the respective plan periods. The Thirteenth Plan had a growth target of 6.0 percent per annum for the period 2013–16. The Fourteenth Plan had a growth target of 7.3 percent per annum. The Fifteenth Plan has a growth target of 9.6 percent per annum and aims at touching double-digit growth (10.3 percent) in the last year of the plan (2023/24).

ii ***To increase employment***: Although stated in different ways, an increase in productive employment has been another important objective in all the plans. The Second Plan underscored the necessity of providing employment to additional 150,000 persons every year resulting from population growth and also the underemployed in the agricultural sector. The Fourth and Fifth Plans laid emphasis on the maximum utilization of manpower resources. The Sixth Plan regarded an increase in productive employment opportunities as necessary from the point of view of equitable distribution of national income and production. The Seventh and Ninth Plans also listed an increase in productive employment opportunities as one of the major objectives. The Tenth Plan laid emphasis on enlarging employment opportunities and widening the access to means and economic achievements for women, Dalits, people of remote areas and poor and backward groups through various programmes. The Three-Year Plan executed in the new political set-up reiterated employment-oriented, pro-poor and broad-based economic growth. The Fifteenth Plan also shows high concern for growing unemployment and underlines the need to discourage foreign employment by generating domestic employment. The plan aims at expanding productive and dignified employment opportunities within the country and making foreign employment organized, dignified and safe. The specific targets consist of reducing the unemployment rate from 14.5 percent to 6.0 percent, increasing the labour force participation rate from 38.5 percent to 48.5 percent and increasing the share of formal sector employment from 36.5 percent to 50.0 percent.

iii ***To reduce poverty***: The issue of poverty reduction started to figure prominently as one of the major objectives of Nepalese plans, particularly since the Eighth Plan. In the Sixth Plan, the need to reduce poverty alleviation was embedded in the form of fulfilment of basic minimum needs. At the end of the Sixth Plan, a 15-year plan under the rubric of 'Programme for the Fulfillment of Basic Needs' was introduced aimed at removing poverty and attaining the Asian standard of living by 2000 AD. The Eighth Plan listed poverty alleviation as one of the three principal objectives. The Ninth Plan made poverty alleviation its main objective and targeted to reduce poverty from 42.0 percent to 38.0 percent by the end of the plan period. The Tenth Plan targeted to reduce poverty to 30.0 percent. The Three-Year Interim Plan laid emphasis on establishing peace and reducing poverty and inequality in the country. The Three-Year Plan had a target of reducing poverty to 21.0 percent and the Thirteenth Plan targeted to reduce it further to 18.0 percent by July 2016. The Fourteenth Plan aimed at reducing poverty to 17.0 percent. The Fifteenth Plan has the target of reducing poverty to 11.0 percent by the end of the plan period and abolishing poverty in the country by 2042/3.

1.4.2 Growth Performance

If the effort to development were to be equated to 'planning', Nepal would have been on a higher growth trajectory and alleviated poverty of the masses by now. However, the reality has been exactly the opposite. The planners and policymakers claim that Nepal has progressed much compared to the situation prevailing prior to the initiation of planning. They, however, seem to forget that comparison with very low initial base does not truly reflect the achievements of the plans, and some of these changes would have taken place anyway without any plan. On the other hand, comparison of actual performance with the plan targets shows dismal performance. The growth performance has almost consistently been short of targets in all the plans with the exception of the Sixth Plan (Table 1.1).

The government makes a self-confession of low growth performance over a span of 25 years from the Third Plan to the Seventh Plan. It says,

> During the period between 1964/5 and 1989/90 the average annual growth rate in GDP was 3.4 percent, whereas the growth rate in per capita income was a mere 0.8 percent. In absolute terms, per capita income reached Rs. 1,605.0 in 1989/90 as compared to Rs. 1,304.0 in 1964/5. Thus in a period of 25 years the increase in per capita income was merely Rs. 301.0 at 1974/75 prices. As a result of low growth of per capita income, Nepal happened to stand low even among the poorest nations of the world.
>
> (NPC, 1992: 2)

This statement of the government makes it apparent that the economy was virtually stagnant during three decades of the Panchayat regime under the direct rule of the king. The Eighth, Ninth and Tenth Plans, which were implemented in the post-democracy period, also failed in achieving the targeted growth rate. The scenario has not changed even after the country became a federal republic in 2008 (Table 1.1).

The special target of the Thirteenth Plan of graduation to a developing country status by 2022 was deemed unachievable in 2018. The threshold for graduation to a developing country status required per capita income of US$1,242.0 averaged over three years and double that (US$2,284.0) for upgradation to a middle-income country status. In 2017, Nepal's per capita GNI was estimated at US$862.0, and attaining US$1,242.0 by 2022 was considered impossible. However, in terms of HDI and Economic Vulnerability Index (EVI), Nepal qualified for graduation in 2015 with HDI of 68.7 and EVI of 26.8 (threshold of greater than 66.0 and less than 32.0, respectively). But the failure to achieve the per capita income threshold was taken as a 'blessing in disguise' as it enabled the government to make a plea in the UN Office of the High Representative for the Least-Developed Countries, Landlocked Developing Countries and Small Island Developing States to defer Nepal's graduation. As a least-developed country, Nepal would continue receiving 136 different types of assistance from developed countries as well as from multilateral organizations like the World Bank and the Asian Development Bank. Such assistance includes a large amount of foreign aid in the form of grants, concessionary loans, customs-free or low-customs access to foreign markets, technical assistance for trade improvement, etc. However, all such facilities will end once the country is upgraded to developing country status in 2026, as decided by the 76th Session of the UN General Assembly held on 11 November 2021. Neither the government nor the National Planning Commission (NPC) seems to be working out a plan to cope with the situation of increased competition in its exports, heavy cuts in access to priority markets and reduction in foreign aid after upgradation to developing country status.

A simple graphical presentation of Nepal's year-to-year growth rate of GDP in constant and current prices during the period between 1964/5 and 2017/18 does not show a stable pattern (Figure 1.1 and Annex 1). In some years, the growth rate peaked at a high level but then dropped to a low level in the subsequent year. The main reasons for each peak appear to be the growth of the agricultural sector and the low or negative growth rate in the preceding year. For instance, in 1981/2, the growth rate was 8.3 percent, but in the preceding year, it was negative

Table 1.1 Target Growth Rate and Achievement in Different Plans

Plans	*Period (FY)*	*Growth Target (Basic Price) (Percent)*	*Specific Targets*	*Achievement (Percent)*
Third	1965/6–1969/70	4.7	Doubling of national income in 15 years	2.2
Fourth	1970/1–1974/5	4.0		2.2
Fifth	1975/6–1979/80	4.0 (max.) 5.0 (min.)		2.2
Sixth	1980/1–1984/5	4.3	Fulfilment of the minimum needs of the people	4.4
Seventh	1985/6–1989/90	4.5	Attainment of Asian Standards by 2000 AD	4.8
Eighth	1992/3–1996/7	4.8		4.9
Ninth	1997/8–2001/2	6.0	Long-term growth target of 8.3 percent by 2016/7 and poverty reduction from 42 percent in 1996/7 to 10.0 percent within the next 20 years	3.6
Tenth	2002/3–2006/7	6.2 (normal case) 4.2 (lower case)	Poverty reduction to 30.0 percent	3.4
Interim Plan (Three Year)	2007/8–2009/10	5.5	Reduction of unemployment, poverty and inequality and making improvements in people's living conditions	4.5
Three-Year Plan	2010/11–2012/3	5.5	Poverty reduction to 21.0 percent	4.0
Thirteenth Plan	2013/14–2015/6	6.0	Poverty reduction to 18.0 percent Upgrade Nepal from a least-developed to a developing country status by 2022	2.9
Fourteenth Plan	2016/17–2018/9	7.3	Upgrade Nepal to a middle-income country status by 2030. Poverty reduction to 17.0 percent	6.8
Fifteenth Plan	2019/20–2023/4	9.6	Upgrade Nepal from least-developed to a developing country status by 2022. Poverty reduction to 9.5 percent	−2.4 (2019/20) 3.8 (2020/1) 5.5 (2021/2)

Source: Plan Documents, National Planning Commission, Government of Nepal. Economic Survey, 2021/22, Ministry of Finance, Government of Nepal.

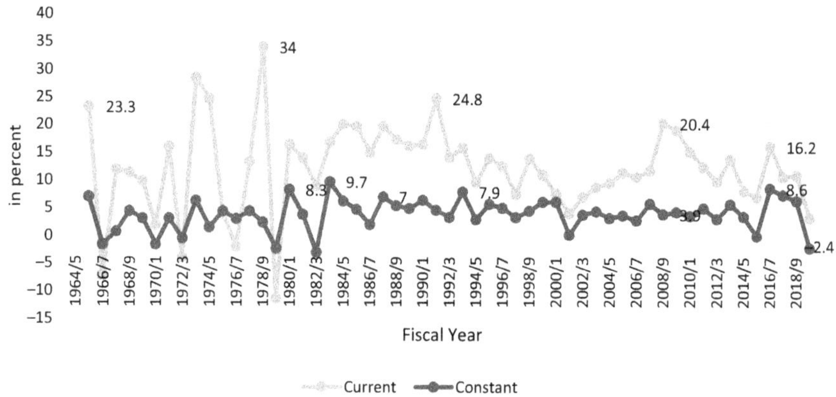

Figure 1.1 Growth Rate of GDP.

(−2.3 percent). Similarly, in 1983/4, the growth rate peaked at 9.7 percent, but in the preceding year, it was negative by 3.0 percent. Another growth peak (8.3 percent) was witnessed in 1993/4, but that was due to the revised series of GDP. The growth rate in 2016/17 was 8.6 percent, the highest in the last two decades, but this growth occurred due to zero growth in 2015/16, which was a catastrophic year. The year witnessed a 7.8 magnitude earthquake on 25 April 2015, with the death of 9,000 people and the destruction of more than 600,000 homes in Kathmandu and outside districts. The economic adversity due to the earthquake was compounded by an undeclared Indian blockade for four months, starting from 23 September 2015, that paralyzed trade, industry and people's livelihoods. In 2019/20, the growth was again negative by 2.1 percent owing to the effects of the COVID-19 pandemic, which disrupted production and supply chains and halted foreign employment and tourist inflow in 2020. The erratic pattern of GDP growth over the years fundamentally reveals a serious ineptitude of rulers of Nepal at different historical epochs to build a sustainable productive structure that could sustain the high growth rate achieved in some years and place the Nepalese economy on a higher growth trajectory.

An exponential trend fitted to real GDP data for the period from 1964/5 to 2017/18 yields a growth rate of 4.1 percent. The trend growth rates of the three sectoral divisions of the economy broadly comprising primary, secondary and tertiary sectors for the period are 2.7 percent, 5.7 percent and 6.8 percent, respectively. The trend equations were also fitted by bifurcating the entire period into two sub-periods – 1964/5 to 1990/1 and 1991/2 to 2017/18 in order to assess the growth performance of the economy during the authoritarian Panchayat regime of three decades (1960–91) and democratic period (1992–2017). Furthermore, starting in the Eighth Plan, Nepal officially altered its development strategy from a state-dominated controlled regime to a liberal market-oriented regime. We, therefore, examine the issue of whether any significant change in the growth of the economy and its sectors can be observed between pre-democracy/pre-liberalization and post-democracy/post-liberalization periods.

The estimate for the two sub-periods yields a trend growth rate of 3.3 percent for the pre-democracy period and 4.2 percent for the post-democracy period. The estimates of trend growth rates of the three sectors for pre- and post-democracy periods show 2.3 percent and 3.1 percent for primary, 5.5 percent and 4.2 percent for secondary and 5.9 percent and 6.9 percent for the tertiary sector. Data availability allowed an estimation of the trend growth rate of the manufacturing sector for the post-democracy period, and the trend growth rate turns out to be only 1.9 percent. This means that the manufacturing sector, which is one of the major commodity-producing sectors, grew at a snail's pace despite the pursuit of liberalization and a market-directed regime in the last two-and-a-half decades. The estimated equations read as follows (Table 1.2):

The democracy period shows a higher growth rate (4.2 percent) compared to that of the Panchayat regime (3.3 percent). In terms of sectoral growth rate, the Panchayat regime shows higher growth for the secondary sector (5.5 percent), while the democracy period shows higher growth for the primary and tertiary sectors. Apart from before and after estimation, a more rigorous empirical analysis was carried out to assess the impact of economic liberalization policies initiated after 1991/2 on growth rate by estimating the Lucas growth model used by the authors of a World Bank study for India (Kappel, 2004) in Nepal's context for the entire period (1964/5 to 2017/18) and for the period after economic liberalization in 1990/1. For the entire period, the estimated equation reads as follows:

$$\begin{aligned} \log \mathrm{GDP}_t &= 1.657 + 0.856\ \log \mathrm{GDP}(t-1) + 0.006t \qquad (1.1)\\ &\qquad (2.65)\ \ (15.45) \qquad\qquad\qquad (2.76)\\ R^{-2} &= 0.998, \quad \mathrm{DW} = 2.38, \quad F = 17{,}045.39 \end{aligned}$$

(Note: Figures in parentheses show t values. The estimates are statistically significant at a 5.0 percent level)

The estimate over the entire period yields a trend growth rate of 4.4 percent per annum, which is almost the same as the exponential growth rate. Following the World Bank study, an additional time trend was introduced for the post-liberalization period (1990/1 to 2017/18) to examine whether the Nepalese economy witnessed a higher growth rate due to economic liberalization policies that started in the 1990s. The estimated equation reads as follows:

$$\begin{aligned} \log \mathrm{GDP}_t &= 1.542 + 0.866\ \log \mathrm{GDP}(t-1) + 0.006t + 0.000\text{time trend} \qquad (1.2)\\ &\qquad (1.83)\ \ (11.68) \qquad\qquad\qquad (2.25)\quad (0.21)^{*}\\ R^{-2} &= 0.998, \quad \mathrm{DW} = 2.4, \quad F = 11{,}145.85 \end{aligned}$$

(Note: Figures in parentheses show t values. The estimates are statistically significant at a 5.0 percent level except those marked by an asterisk)

Table 1.2 Trend Growth Rate ($y = a_o e^{a1t}$)

Period	*1964/5 to 2017/8 (N = 54)*			*1964/5 to 1990/1 (N = 27)*			*1991/2 to 2017/8 (N = 27)*		
	a_0	a_1	R^{-2}	a_0	a_1	R^{-2}	a_0	a_1	R^{-2}
GDP	11.334 (654.1)	0.041 (74.88)	0.991	11.4364 (595.7)	0.033 (27.22)	0.966	11.31 (514.8)	0.042 (79.87)	0.998
Primary	10.986 (891.8)	0.027 (69.34)	0.989	11.046 (687.0)	0. 023 (22.59)	0.951	10.824 (713.5)	0.031 (85.27)	0.996
Secondary	8.798 (209.9)	0.057 (43.37)	0.972	8.786 (170.3)	0.055 (17.21)	0.919	9.494 (90.37)	0.042 (16.49)	0.912
Tertiary	9.386 (284.8)	0.0068 (65.48)	0.988	9.491 (214.5)	0.059 (21.51)	0. 947	9.374 (85.65)	0.069 (26.31)	0.964
Manufacturing							9.762 (117.1)	0.019 (10.59)	0.867

Note: Figures in parentheses are t values. The estimates are based on data at factor cost of the variables at the 2000/1 price. Composition of sectors: Primary – agriculture and forestry, fishing, mining and quarrying. Secondary – manufacturing, construction, electricity and gas. Tertiary – wholesale and retail trade, hotels and restaurants, storage and communication, financial services and social services.

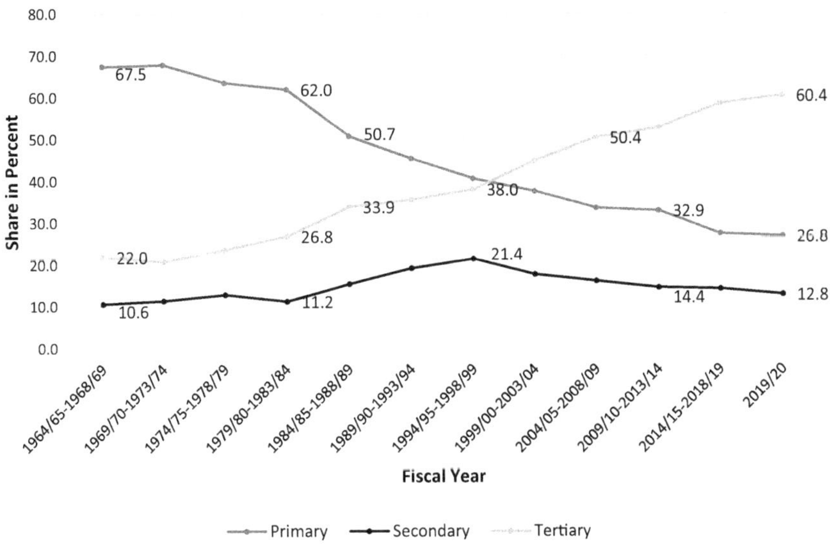

Figure 1.2 Composition of GDP by Three Broad Sectors (Economic Survey, Different Years, Ministry of Finance, Government of Nepal).

The value of the coefficient of additional time trend is zero and also not significant, which implies that the trend growth rate in the post-liberalization period is not higher than before liberalization. The new trend growth rate is 4.3 percent per annum, which is the same as the one estimated without an additional time trend (Equation 1.1).

The sectoral composition of GDP shows a decline in the predominance of the primary sector and an increase in the share of the tertiary sector over the last five-and-a-half decades. As a percentage of GDP, the share of the primary sector was between 68.0 percent to 64.0 percent till 1974/5 and 1978/9, but declined steadily in each successive five-year period and dipped to 27.4 percent during 2014/15 and 2018/19. On the other hand, the share of the secondary sector remained largely stable, but that of the tertiary sector increased steadily from 22.0 percent during 1964/5 and 1968/9 to 58.5 percent in the last five-year period. Within the services sector, faster growth was observed in wholesale and retail trade, hotels and restaurants, banks and financial institutions, real estates and education and health.

The relatively higher growth rate of the tertiary sector and an increasingly larger share in GDP suggest that whatever GDP growth has occurred in the last two decades has been substantially on account of faster growth of the services sector. The material commodity-producing sectors have witnessed no acceleration in their growth rates and neither have their shares in GDP increased. The most crucial sector in Nepal is still the primary sector, which provides livelihood to about three-fourths of the working population of the country, a proportion that has changed only marginally over the years, even though the share of the primary sector in GDP has constantly declined in each decade starting from the 1970s. This means that the agricultural sector has an acute problem of disguised unemployment, which is accentuating year after year with labour productivity being very low or almost zero, and consequently, living conditions of agriculture-dependent households are harsh.

Nepal's growth scenario gives a jolt to the received theories of structural transformation of economies as well as the experience of countries that industrialized during the second half of the 19th and the first half of the 20th century. These theories postulate that (i) initially the share of the agricultural sector in both output and employment is overwhelmingly large; (ii) as development proceeds, the share of the manufacturing sector in output and in employment rises while that of the agricultural sector decreases; and (iii) at a higher stage of development, the share of the industrial sector in both output and employment declines, while that of the services sector increases (Nayyar, 2013). This suggests that services sector growth occurs in the last phase of the transformation of a country from a traditional to a modern stage. However, in the case of Nepal, neither of the last two propositions holds true. First, the contribution of agriculture to GDP has declined substantially from about 68.0 percent in the 1970s to 34.0 percent in the recent decade, but this has not been followed by increases in the share of the manufacturing sector in output and employment. And the increases in the contribution of the services sector in output and employment have not occurred consequent to growth in the manufacturing sector. Moreover, the decline in the share of agriculture to GDP has not occurred due to a slower rise in the demand for food as compared with other goods and services or the use of modern farm technologies resulting in an increase in food production per hectare and per worker. The decline was mainly due to the heavy exodus of youths from the rural areas for gainful employment in Gulf countries and other destinations, leaving vast tracts of cultivable land barren. Second, the rapid growth of the tertiary sector was mainly due to economic liberalization policies of the past three decades which opened many service sector activities, such as banking and finance, airlines, education and health, to the private sector and the growth of real estate business rather than due to growth in commodity-producing sectors.

1.4.3 Nepal's Growth Performance Compared to SAARC Countries

In the SAARC region, Nepal's economic growth performance has remained miserable all throughout the years from 1965 and onwards except in 2017, 2018 and 2019. Real GDP growth in 2017 was 7.9 percent, the highest over the last five decades, but this emanated from the low base of 0.6 percent growth in the preceding year due to the devastating earthquake of 2015 and trade disruption at the southern border with India. Nepal's growth rate was slightly higher than that of Bangladesh during 1965–80 and 1980–90 and the same during 1990–2000, but from 2012 and onwards, Nepal lagged far behind Bangladesh with the exception of 2017 (Table 1.3). On the whole, India remained a higher performer in the region all through the period, almost comparable to China except for a few years. However, in 2020, the growth rate of all but Bangladesh, Pakistan and China was

Table 1.3 Average Annual Growth Rate of GDP of SAARC Countries and China (in Percent)

Country	*1965–80*	*1980–90*	*1990–2000*	*2000–10*	*2012*	*2013*	*2014*	*2015*	*2016*	*2017*	*2018*	*2019*	*2020*
Bangladesh	1.7	4.3	4.8	5.9	6.5	6.0	6.1	6.6	7.1	7.3	7.9	8.2	2.4
Bhutan	–	–	–	–	5.1	2.1	5.8	6.6	8.1	4.7	3.1	5.5	−6.8
India	3.6	5.3	6.0	8.0	5.5	6.4	7.4	8.0	8.3	6.8	6.5	4.0	−8.0
Maldives	–	–	–	–	2.5	7.3	7.3	2.9	6.3	7.2	8.1	7.0	−32.0
Nepal	1.9	4.6	4.8	3.8	4.4	3.5	6.0	4.0	0.4	9.0	7.6	6.7	−2.1
Pakistan	5.2	6.3	3.7	5.1	3.5	4.4	4.7	4.7	5.5	5.6	5.8	1.0	0.5
Sri Lanka	4.0	4.0	5.3	5.6	9.1	3.4	5.0	5.0	4.5	3.6	3.3	2.3	−3.6
China	6.8	9.5	10.3	10.8	7.9	7.8	7.4	7.0	6.8	6.9	6.7	5.9	2.3
Low-Income Countries	4.9	6.1	3.4	5.5	2.7	6.2	5.9	1.9	3.6	4.4	4.5	4.1	0.9

Source: Figures up to 2000–10 are from World Development Report, various years, and from 2012 and onwards from World Development Indicators, 2020, The World Bank, Washington.

negative, with Nepal witnessing a −2.1 percent growth rate mainly due to economic disruption caused by COVID-19.

The picture appears highly dismal if we compare the GNI per capita of Nepal with SAARC countries, not to speak of China, the United Kingdom and the USA. Nepal was the only SAARC country with the lowest per capita income all through the years from 1962. The increase in per capita income was staggering over the years; it took a decade to double the per capita income of US$70 in 1970 to US$140 in 1980, and the addition in per capita income in 2000 compared to 1990 was only US$20. From 2000 to 2010, the increase was US$310. Almost all SAARC countries registered a decline in GNI per capita in 2020 due to the effects of the COVID-19 pandemic.

The World Bank uses GNI per capita as the main indicator to categorize countries among low-income, lower-middle-income, upper-middle-income and high-income groups. The GNI per capita thresholds are revised each year on July 1. The update of 1 July 2019 categorizes countries with per capita GNI of less than US$1,026 as low income, between US$1,026–3,995 as lower middle income, between US$3,996–12,375 as upper middle income and higher than US$12,375 as high income, which does not, however, reflect the impact of the COVID-19 pandemic. Nepal had crossed the low-income nation status in 2018 with GNI per capita of US$1,120 against the low-income threshold of less than US$996 but was deferred till 2026. Even though the GNI per capita of 2019 (US$1,230) places Nepal in the category of lower-middle-income countries, that is just crossing the threshold (US$1,026), and in terms of development performance, the country still lags far behind compared to India, which continues to be a lower-middle-income country with GNI per capita US$2,120 in 2019, while Sri Lanka climbed the upper-middle-income groups.

Compared to the United States, which is considered a model for emulation by the Nepalese middle class and elites, Nepal's GNI per capita was only 1.5 percent of US GNI per capita in 1962 and was almost the same at 1.6 percent even after five-and-a-half decades in 2015 and 1.9 percent in 2019.

The average per capita income masks the deplorable living conditions of a large majority whose income has been at the bottom of the poverty line. Furthermore, the capital-centred development strategy followed over the years favoured certain regions and groups unequally resulting in a few enclaves of growth amidst stagnating, backwards and primitive vast hinterlands, particularly the Karnali region and other remote backwards hill, mountain and some terai districts. The movement of capital, labour, educated and technical manpower and services from the stagnating to expanding areas in a cumulative manner further reinforced and accentuated the dualism that was there at the start of the development process itself in the form of hill-terai, rural-urban, rich-poor and upper caste-lower caste, male-female contradictions. Although some spread effects might have been transmitted to the hinterland in the form of increasing outlets for agricultural products, and production of raw materials for the growing industries in the centres, these have remained very weak in countervailing the strong backwash effects (Myrdal, 1972). Within the rural-urban dualism, the rich-poor and the upper caste–lower caste polarization was exacerbated by the extractive political and economic institutions that

Table 1.4 GNI Per Capita of SAARC and Other Countries (Atlas Method Current US$)

Country	*1962*	*1970*	*1980*	*1990*	*2000*	*2010*	*2015*	*2016*	*2017*	*2018*	*2019*	*2020*
Bangladesh	–	–	230	320	440	800	1,220	1,370	1,520	1,750	1,940	2,010
Bhutan	–	–	–	560	700	2,040	2,520	2,650	2,800	2,970	3,140	2,860
India	90	120	270	380	440	1,220	1,600	1,680	1,820	2,010	2,120	1,900
Maldives	–	–	–	–	2,240	6,600	8,070	8,600	9,210	9,670	6,830	–
Nepal	50	70	140	210	230	540	890	880	990	1,120	1,230	1,190
Pakistan	90	170	320	400	480	970	1,260	1,310	1,400	1,480	1,410	1,280
Sri Lanka	–	170	280	460	870	2,410	3,760	3,810	3,870	4,040	4,010	3,720
China	70	120	220	330	940	4,340	7,940	8,270	8,740	9,600	10,390	10,610
UK	–	2,480	9,530	18,530	29,230	41,740	44,340	42,940	41,280	41,740	42,130	–
USA	3,280	5,230	13,380	24,060	35,960	48,990	56,740	57,270	59,460	63,510	65,910	–
LMIC	–	132	421	520	588	1,657	2,119	2,129	2,175	2,290	2,360	1,110
LDC (UN Method)	–	-		292	299	790	1,007	997	1,009	1,063	2,201	1,075

Source: World Development Indicators, 2020, The World Bank, Washington.

concentrated power in the hands of a limited bourgeoisie class, political leaders and bureaucrats.

The periodic plans from 1992 until the initiation of the Fifteenth Plan had to muddle through an unstable political environment due to frequent changes in government. Despite this, in a Westminster-style democracy, as practiced in Nepal and other South Asian countries, the prime minister, as head of the government, is immensely powerful. He holds the supreme authority to govern, discipline his ministers and direct bureaucracy to execute government policies and programmes with rationality and consistency and take actions against non-execution of his orders. Almost every prime minister in the republic era announced impressive promises and pledges and spoke of the need to accelerate the pace of development, but ended the tenure with hardly any tangible outcome. On the contrary, various reasons, such as compulsions of coalition politics, non-cooperation of bureaucracy and inactions were offered as justification for the non-performance. It became a routine practice for the incoming prime minister to issue directives to the government secretaries to show results in good governance, act as citizen responsive, complete development projects in a scheduled time frame and spend at least 80.0 percent of capital expenditure, among other responsibilities. But such directives have yielded little because there was no stringent 'project performance monitoring and control system' that could enhance democratic control of the bureaucracy. All the prime ministers remained practically weak despite their prerogative to rule and take action against the ministers and officials for misuse of authority, squandering of public resources and sluggish implementation of capital projects and poor performance of development plans. Nevertheless, a much higher level of economic performance would have been achieved had the bureaucracy functioned with a commitment to implementing the projects. But in the post-democracy period, the political-bureaucratic paradigm has been one of accusations and counter-accusations between the politicians in power and the bureaucracy; the former accusing the latter of inaction and non-cooperation and the latter accusing the former of politicization of the bureaucracy and partisan management of bureaucracy. In this tussle, the bureaucrats progressively acculturated to party politics and have become factionalized along party lines for the backing of politicians for their promotions, transfer and placements in lucrative offices and other benefits.

1.5 National Pride Projects

The implementation status of 'National Pride Projects' provides one glaring illustration of how the bureaucracy has muddled with the key infrastructure projects that were considered crucial for the country's development. The concept of 'National Pride Projects' was announced in 2012 identifying 17 projects as key to accelerating Nepal's economic growth. Four more projects were added in 2014, making a total of 21 such projects to be implemented with high priority. 'National Pride Projects' are basically infrastructure projects, such as airports, roads, railways, irrigation and hydro-electricity, that are strategically and scientifically defined, are of big size and relatively longer periods of construction, say three to five/six years, and involve huge investment. These projects have significant horizontal and vertical externalities cutting across various subsectors and contributing highly to the development of the country. Despite the high importance accorded to such projects, the progress has been highly disappointing and disgraceful, with most projects lagging far behind the completion deadline and entailing huge cost overruns (Annex 2).

The abysmally slow progress has been persistent over the years despite the periodic discussion on issues, problems and implementation delays in the High-Level National Development Problem Resolution Committee Meeting chaired by the prime minister and attended by ministers, chief secretary and secretaries, vice-chairman and members of the NPC and project chiefs. Such high-level meetings were expected to steer clear all the hurdles and bottlenecks through coordinated action by the concerned line ministries. But these meetings have become only rituals, as everybody talked about the issues, problems and solutions in a very impressive way, but no one seriously attempted to take the needed actions to resolve these issues during his/her tenure in office. This evidence suggests that even in the fundamentally transformed political context, Nepal's bureaucratic system has not changed its tradition-rooted style characterized by rigid adherence to formal rules, sticking to past precedents and clinging to outdated procedures and rent-seeking attitudes.

1.6 Some Explanations of Failure of Planning

Nepal's planning experience has been quite long, perhaps next to India in South Asia, but unlike India, where planning has brought about major structural changes (Chakravarty, 1987), planning in Nepal has been a failure. The Second Five-Year Plan of India (1955–60) developed by P. C. Mahalanobis helped to bring about structural changes in the Indian economy by laying a solid foundation for industrialization and realization of Nehru's vision of a 'socialistic pattern of society' and building a 'self-reliant economy'. Writing about the development in India in 1992, Tayeb stated,

> [S]ome 25 years ago India was perceived as economically backward, with rapid population growth and starvation staring it in the face; it is now the ninth most industrialized country in the world and is self-sufficient in many respects. India, a heavily populated country, has successively utilized its human resource assets in the realm of software development, among other things, and has exploited the niche with increasing success.
>
> (Tayeb, 1992: 159–60)

Britain moved from a state of underdevelopment in roughly 60 years after 1780 (the early years of the Industrial Revolution), the United States in 50 years after 1840, Japan in about 35 years after 1885 and South Korea in 11 years after 1966 (Tayeb, 1992). The East Asian Dragons (Hong Kong, South Korea, Singapore, Indonesia, Thailand and Malaysia) achieved spectacular economic growth during

1960–90 and made inroads in the markets dominated by the Japanese and Western countries.

Nepal spent six decades of planned development, but the economy experienced very little growth in terms of per capita real income and other indicators. A period of six decades is a long period in a nation's history to create production capabilities and raise the well-being of a large majority of people. But planning in Nepal never ever achieved what it proposed to achieve, nor has it brought any structural change in the economy. An economy as small as Nepal could have been managed well and made considerable achievement over a span of six decades of planning, but that opportunity was lost. Nepal also lost the opportunity of benefitting from 'late development syndrome', a term coined by Dore implying learning from the experiences of pioneering countries without having to go through the long-drawn-out process of developing the techniques, practices and technologies by the country itself (Dore, 1973).

Mainstream economists do not hesitate to explain the success of planning in communist countries and failure in Nepal with the argument that communist countries operated under totalitarian political systems and had state ownership of the means of production. But this view is not totally correct. Nepal also had a single-party Panchayat regime during 1960–90 with many features of a communist regime. The king held absolute power in all three organs of the state – namely, executive, judicial and legislative – and things moved on his command. The state had at its command several resources and had the power and authority to direct and regulate the entire economy, including the use of these resources. These included the external economic relation, allocations of scarce capital, monetary and fiscal measures, taxing and spending functions, control over the domain of the market and participation in production. Even in the Indian context, the failure to achieve better performance through planning as in China and Russia is usually justified on the ground that it has been a democratic regime since its emancipation from British rule in 1949 and not the communist regime that prevailed in Russia and China. But these are not, however, plausible explanations. Japan too had a democratic polity during the years of its fastest growth (1954–72) and later, as a democratic country, it emerged as a super economic power with very many excellent indicators of quality of life (Khandwalla, 1999). These cases show that 'regime type' or 'political stability' may be necessary but are not sufficient conditions for higher growth and development. What is also needed is a strong state committed to the growth of the country, visionary leadership, expansion of productive forces and progressive mode of production. However, in present-day underdeveloped countries, irrespective of whether the political regime is democratic, oligarchic or dictatorial, the state is a bourgeois state run by the capitalist, feudal and landlord classes in coalition with the bureaucratic-managerial elites. These classes use the state as a ploy to enlarge their share in output through direct and indirect means by displacing small owners from their means of production, evicting tenants from the land and encroaching state resources, particularly land, forests, rivers and accumulating personal fortunes through tax evasion, wielding subsidies, acquiring lucrative state contracts and embezzling fund which would have gone to the state treasury. Patnaik describes this as

> a process of expropriation, i.e. separation of pre-capitalist producers from their means of production (or directly from their products, which are after all potential means of production), and a process of appropriation, or possession by a few of the things so expropriated.
>
> (Patnaik, 2001: 17)

Way back in 1972, in an article titled 'Why Planning Fails in Nepal?', Wildavsky pointed out five major reasons: (i) insufficient information, (ii) few and poor project proposals, (iii) inability to plan the distribution of foreign aid, (iv) opposition of the Finance Ministry and (v) limited capacity to administer development (Wildavsky, 1972). A period of four-and-a-half decades has passed since then, and some of these problems have been non-existent for many years. Plan formulation in the early period was said to be constrained by a lack of statistical foundation for assessing the problems and insufficient technical manpower. This was true for the first two plans, which had to be prepared without an adequate database of the economy and with limited technical expertise in planning. However, in the later years, these problems have been non-existent, yet planning has failed to deliver the promises made. Nepal's failure to develop through planning raises a number of questions. Is it due to resource constraints? Or is it the lack of trained manpower? Or is it the lack of appropriate design of planning? Or is it the weak implementation mechanism? Or is it the feudal political regime, bourgeoisie bureaucratic system and hierarchical social structure that made planning a failure? We attempt to offer some answers to these questions.

1.6.1 Paucity of Natural Resources

To say that Nepal is a resource-poor country is to gloss over reality. As a matter of fact, Nepal is abundantly supplied with some valuable natural resources that can make her significantly rich. Some of these resources are (i) fertile flat land of the terai with the potential of year-round cultivation of a variety of crops with the provision of modest irrigation facilities, using bountiful groundwater or the innumerable rivers and streams flowing from the high mountains to the Indian plains; (ii) numerous valleys in the mountain regions, which could be cultivated year round with irrigation facilities and the potential of dairy farming in these regions; and (iii) the vast hydropower potential (Shah, 1988). A more realistic assessment of Nepal's natural resources can be made in the framework of six 'Ja' connoting six resources that begins from the Nepali letter 'Ja' – Jal (water), Jamin (land), Jungle (forest), Jadibuti (herbs), Jaibik Bibhidata (biodiversity) and Janasakti (human resources). Each of these 'Ja's' hold a rich potential for the economic transformation of the country from its current low status to one comparable to the developed nations in a couple of decades (Poudel, 2008).

Nepal has vast water resources consisting of 6,000 rivers and streams, numerous lakes and glacial lakes. The three major rivers Gandaki, Koshi and Karnali and other equally significant rivers Bagmati, Mechi, Kankai, Kamala, Tinau, Rapti, Babai and Mahakali hold immense potential for hydropower development and irrigation. Nepal is said to be sitting on a theoretically estimated hydropower potential of 83,500 MW, the largest in South Asia and next to Brazil in the world. Of the estimated power potential, 40,000 MW is economically feasible hydropower potential, but the total installed capacity as of 12 March 2021 was only 3.5 percent (1,386 MW). The history of hydropower production dates back to 1911 when the first power plant, Pharping Hydro-electricity Plant, was started with 500 kW. Since then, more than 11 decades have passed, and hydro-electricity production has increased at a snail's pace. The First Plan had a hydropower production target of 20 MW, but the achievement was a mere 2 MW. During three decades of the Panchayat regime (1960–90), the total generating capacity including hydro and diesel reached 227.08 MW, which served only 8.8 percent of the total population (NPC, 1992). As of 2014/15, hydropower production reached 782.45 MW, which was 40.0 percent deficient of demand estimated at 1,291.1 MW (MOF, 2015). As a consequence, load shedding continued as a recurrent and worsening phenomenon year after year, particularly since 2005/6, and often stretched to the extent of 18 hours a day during dry months, adversely affecting public life as well as growth in the industry and services sectors. There had been high pronouncement by almost every government formed in the post-democracy period to end the energy crisis through short as well as long-run plans, and there were talks about generating 10,000 MW of hydropower in 10 years and 25,000 MW in 20 years but all such pronouncements remained only on paper. Even though power generation did not increase remarkably, better management in the distribution of electricity and control of power leakages contributed to ending the load shedding in the country in 2016. In the past few years, because of the government's drive to expand hydropower generation and increase private-sector hydropower projects, power generation reached 2,205 MW by mid-March 2021, which provided electricity access to 94.0 percent of the total population (MOF, 2021/22), but this is only 5.5 percent of economically feasible potential. This means that Nepal is wasting a substantial amount of perennial white gold because of a lack of appropriate policies and a power export strategy to India.

Nepal's immense water resources offer great potential for extending year-round irrigation to the vast tract of the potential irrigable area estimated to be about 176,600 ha, thereby enhancing agricultural production and ensuring food security for the growing population. According to World Development Indicators 2021, the agricultural irrigated land was only 29.7 percent in 2010. International Water Management Institute (IWMI) reports, 'Nepal has a cultivated area of 2,642,000 ha (18.0 percent of its land area), of which two-thirds (1,766,000 ha) is potentially irrigable. At present, 42.0 percent of the cultivated area has irrigation of some sort, but only 17.0 percent of the cultivated area has year-round irrigation. An estimate shows that less than 8 percent of the country's water potential is used for irrigation' (IWMI, 2021).

Owing to a lack of adequate irrigation facilities, Nepal's agricultural production is subject to the vagaries of monsoon, and this has severely affected attempts in raising productivity by pushing up inputs and credit extension.

Similarly, Nepal is believed to have vast mineral resources hidden in the land as recorded in the historical accounts of ancient foreign missions to Nepal. An Englishman who visited Nepal in the year 1793 with the objective of effecting a negotiation between the Nepalese and the Chinese had mentioned the high quality of Nepalese copper with markets even in European countries and also described the prevalence of gold, silver and iron mines and considerable mass of rock crystal, limestone as well as slate (Kirkpatrick, 2021 [1811]). Various geological surveys made in the past show iron ore deposits in 13 places with estimated reserves of 26.25 million tons in three places, copper deposits in three places, copper cobalt with a proved tonnage of 100,000 tons and possible tonnage of another one million, as well as mica deposits in three places, lead, talc, limestone and gold reserves (Shrestha, 1967). Furthermore, Nepal is also believed to have deposits of gas and petroleum in the Dailekh region, Shiwalik range and some areas of terai, as reported by various foreign exploration companies in the early 1980s, but no serious attention has been paid to explore and exploit such natural resources.

Nepal's rich and varied geographical landscape, biodiversity, flora and fauna present a unique potential for developing tourism, which could both be a large foreign exchange earner and a substantial generator of employment. The prevalence of an appreciable number of high-value herbs and aromatic plants, such as yarsagumba (cordycepssinensis),[5] padmachal (rheumaustrala), chiraito (swertia) and many others, provide immense potential to earn foreign exchange and generate employment opportunities.

Another important resource, mainly seen as a constraint by the rulers of Nepal and the mainstream economists, is the vast human resource, a large proportion of which remains unproductive because of a lack of employment opportunities. The official statistics mask the growing unemployment problem by showing a low and declining unemployment rate between the period 1995/96 and 2010/11 – 4.9 percent in 1995/6, 3.8 percent in 2003/4 and 2.2 percent in 2010/11 (CBS, 2004, 1997, 2011). The problem of unemployment in Nepal cannot be visualized from the conventional definition of not working (as persons not working during the previous seven days of the survey day), as the problem of unemployment is intrinsically related to the problem of disguised unemployment. The Nepal Labour Force Survey of 2008 shows a growing unemployment situation in terms of decline in the employment-to-population ratio in the country (proportion of the population aged 15 and above employed) from 84.3 percent in 1998/9 to 81.7 percent in 2008 (CBS, 2008). The severity of the disguised unemployment is evident from the fact that while 60.4 percent of the economically active population is engaged in agriculture, the share of this sector in GDP has declined over the years and is now marginally over one-fourth.

Nepal also has the advantage of a demographic dividend in terms of the growth of an economically active population defined as the age group of 15–64 years. The population census of 2011 estimated 41.9 percent of the total population (11.1 million out of 26.5 million) as the economically active population, while the census of 2001 estimated 45.7 percent (10.6 million out of 23.2 million) (Suwal and Dahal, 2014). This shows that Nepal's population structure is shifting towards a greater demographic dividend. Such a dividend is, however, dissipated to other countries because of government ineptitude to create employment opportunities in the country. Instead of utilizing the huge young productive force by imparting some technical training and vocational education for nation building, the Nepalese rulers consider it a menace to the bourgeois socio-economic order. The data show that every year, about 600,000 youths migrate to Gulf countries and Malaysia in search of gainful employment, at a heavy social cost involving physical impairment and even loss of life. Youth migration is purposefully encouraged to Korea, Malaysia and Gulf countries through a large number of manpower companies, the introduction of free visas and free tickets to the youths migrating to Malaysia and labour supply agreements with a large number of foreign countries. Thus the demographic dividend of the country is being allowed to be utilized by foreign countries at a very low cost. The Nepalese rulers are not concerned about this, nor are they concerned about the consequences of heavy dependence on workers' remittance as a source of foreign exchange. On the contrary, they seem content on labour migration as a double boon in terms of evasion of the catastrophe of labour unrest due to growth in the 'reserve army of unemployed youths' and easy source of foreign exchange for the state coffers. Workers' remittance has remained one of the major sources of foreign exchange to sustain the growing import volume of the country. As a proportion of GDP, it was 10.3 percent in 2001/2, 29.0 percent in 2014/15 and 22.5 percent in 2020/21. Such high dependence on workers' remittance for the sustenance of the economy has placed the country in a very precarious situation of being called a 'remittance republic' (Poudyal, 2016). Should there be saturation in labour importing countries as a consequence of the end of the construction phase or recession or economic downturn owing to a fall in petroleum prices or the pandemic like COVID-19, the Nepalese economy will face the double effects of huge loss in foreign exchange earnings and adjustment of a large number of returnees, as well as a stream of outward-bound youths.

The country would have been made economically strong, progressive and self-reliant a long time ago were these resources developed and managed synergistically synchronizing the linkages and interrelationships between them. But the rulers of Nepal were never ever concerned with utilizing such wealth of the country.

1.6.2 Internal Conflict and Political Instability

Nepal has remained a highly politically unstable country since the restoration of democracy in 1991. The first democratic general election of 1991 held after the restoration of multiparty democracy placed Nepali Congress in the first position with 110 out of 205 seats. However, the government could not complete the five-year term because of inter-party feuds. The House was dissolved after three-and-a-half years when Prime Minister Girija Prasad Koirala lost a parliamentary vote of confidence due to the abstention of 36 members of his own party. The election of 1994 resulted in a hung parliament; the United Marxist–Leninist (UML) party formed a minority government but was pulled down in nine months. This was followed by frequent making and unmaking of governments and until the third election, prime ministers were changed five times. In the third election held in 1999, the Nepali Congress had a comfortable majority, and during a five-year period, prime ministers were changed three times.

Political instability and frequent change in government have remained more pronounced after Maoists joined mainstream politics. In the last nine years, from 2006 when the country was declared the Democratic Republic of Nepal to 2022, the government was changed 13 times. The failure of the first CA to write a new constitution even in five years and consequently its dissolution in May 2012 made the political environment even more uncertain. It is argued that a country characterized by an unstable political system is prone to low growth because of the reluctance of the private sector to commit to higher investment in an unstable political environment. A study by Asian Development Bank/ Department of International Development, Government/UK/International Labour Organization published in 2009 also identifies insurgency and prolonged political instability as critical constraints of growth in Nepal (ADB/ DFID/ILO, 2009).

The experiences of some countries, however, repudiate the aforementioned argument, showing that growth is possible even under uncertain political environments and conflict situations. The example of Sri Lanka shows that despite domestic conflict for 26 years, it had a higher growth rate than Nepal. It had a growth rate of 6.4 percent in 1990, 6.0 percent in 2000 and 6.8 percent after the restoration of peace in 2010. Afghanistan achieved a 14.3 percent growth rate in 2000 even in a situation of extreme violence and 8.2 percent in 2010. Similarly, Nigeria, despite its decades-long conflict, achieved growth of 8.2 percent in 1990 and 6.7 percent on average in the decade of 2000.

In Nepal conflict has ended and peace has been maintained with the signing of a 12-point agreement between the Maoist and Parliamentary parties in 2005. Despite the political instability and frequent change in government in the last one-and-a-half decade, the economic policy regime remained virtually unchanged. Even when the government was headed by the Maoist Party, hardly any change was made to the previous economic policies and the rules and regulations governing private-sector investment. Property and contractual rights have been kept secured, and no reversal was made of economic liberalization policies and greater reliance on market forces. Hence political instability and frequent changes in government do not provide a much better explanation for the low growth of Nepal.

1.6.3 Planning Machinery and Planning System

The NPC is the apex institution responsible for preparing the periodic national development plans for the all-around development of the country. It is the technical arm of the government and enjoys a certain degree of autonomy from the government. It is concerned with setting the vision, defining objectives, framing strategies, fixing overall as well as sectoral growth targets, determining investment priorities and estimating investment requirements and suggesting sources of financing. The institution of the Planning Commission is as old as the planning system in the country and had undergone several changes in its organizational structure until 1968 when a new planning body, NPC, was formed to take the place of both the National Planning Council and the Planning Ministry formed earlier (Stiller and Yadav, 1979). The prime minister is the chairman of the Commission, and the vice-chairman and the members are appointed by the cabinet, while the chief secretary and the finance secretary are ex-officio members. The prime minister chairs the Commission meetings and gives direction on all major policy issues and suggests the basic approach to be followed when a new plan is being formulated. The members usually are nominated from among the economists, engineers, sociologists, educationists, management experts and retired government secretaries supported by a full-fledged secretariat consisting of one secretary who also serves as the member-secretary of the Commission. Thus the Commission holds the status of mini-cabinet with high authority and institutional significance because it is headed by no less a person other than the prime minister. The line ministries are required to comply with the requisitions of the NPC about the respective ministry's plans, programmes and estimates of current and capital expenditure for the upcoming budget every year. Generally, when a new periodic plan has to be formulated, the Commission is supported by a team of donor-funded, high-paid local and expatriate consultants/advisers.

Despite the high authority and substantial technical backstopping, the outcome of the NPC has been limited to the production of a bigger and bigger volume of plan documents repeating nearly the same picture and same pattern with a ritual compilation of papers prepared by respective line ministries and allocation of resources to them. The process of planning was never made the principal means for removing the fundamental structural constraints on the way to growth, even though planners were never tired of making public speeches about the problems and constraints confronting the economy. Even the UML-affiliated left intellectuals, who assumed the position of vice-chairman and members of the Planning Commission several times after 1994, followed the same stereotype pattern and did not deviate from the bourgeois discourse and the neo-liberal economic paradigm. The same can be said about the Maoist-affiliated intellectuals who had the opportunity to occupy the post of vice-chairman and members a couple of times. They could have made a fundamental departure from the past to set a new course of development to get the country out of the shackles of underdevelopment but did not venture for this. This is probably because of their interest in recognition and saleability in the capitalist market and world institutions which was not possible if they deviated from neo-liberal thinking.

One may identify various deficiencies of the NPC in making planning an effective tool to promote development and change in the country. First, the Nepalese plans suffer from a lack of consistent formulation and effective implementation, which are necessary for attaining the goals and targets set in a plan. Plan formulation in Nepal has never gone beyond a mechanical process of fixing the growth rate for the next planning period on the basis of estimated incremental capital-output ratios in the main sectors of the economy, anticipated investments from the public and private sectors, total investment required and the sources of funds (domestic savings and foreign aid). The NPC is also engaged in the finalization of annual programmes and budgets for the sectoral ministries at the time of government budget preparation by the Ministry of Finance. There has been no change in the nature, role and methodology of planning in the changed political and economic context and no new method of investment planning for the public sector has evolved. No one would disagree that the list of objectives set in the plan documents is indeed very much desired. For example, no one would disagree about the need to attain a higher rate of growth, balanced regional development, reduction in poverty of the people or maximum utilization of labour force, but the question is whether they together made a consistent set of objectives or they were in conflict with one another and pulled each other apart. For example, the objective of higher growth may involve a trade-off with the objective of maximum utilization of the labour force unless it is spelt out that the higher growth rate will lead to the creation of a certain number of additional jobs during the plan period. Likewise, there is also a conflict between growth objectives and reduction in poverty, and the plans never spelt out the balance between the two.

In Western countries, the early plans embodied only a few objectives. In Germany, when planning originated during the First World War and practiced in the 1930s, it was meant for rearming Germany and providing full employment. In Russia, after the October Revolution of 1917, Lenin gave high importance to the electrification of the country as a specific embodiment of the Marxist programme for building socialism, as well as a foundation for long-term development. A long-term plan for electrification worked out in 1920 (GOELRO), aimed at building 30 large electric power stations to provide the energy for the industrial development of all parts of the country and doubling the 1913 output by the end of the decade (Krichenko, 1980). The first post-war French plan also called the Monnet Plan (1947–53), covered only six industries considered most vital for recovery: coal, electricity, cement, steel, agricultural machinery and transport. It included no macroeconomic or social components, which were incorporated in the latter plans. Criticizing the multiple objectives of Indian plans, Desai argues,

> [P]lanning is effective when there is a single objective which overrides all other goals. There is not and cannot be any trade-off. This is why planning was adopted in Germany during the First World War. It is also ideal for a closed economy which was Germany's situation during 1914–18 blockade. But India did not just have one objective for its development path. It wanted industrialization to build a strong basic industry core to ensure some capacity for defence production. It also wanted to tackle poverty and unemployment. It had to feed its population and modernize the countryside.
>
> (Desai, 2005: 192)

As in India, plans in Nepal are made to serve a multitude of objectives. It has been the general characteristic of NPC to formulate the plan guided by the thinking that 'it is important to concentrate on this, but it is also important not to disregard that'. As a consequence, 14 periodic plans passed by without making a discernible impact on any one sector. If one were to choose a single sector in Nepal for the concentration of public resources, it would be the agricultural sector. Nepal's economic prosperity and poverty reduction are inextricably bound up with agriculture, as it is the source of livelihood for about 60.0 percent of the population and holds the key to higher GDP growth rate. It is agriculture which can generate a surplus that can be reinvested for development. Furthermore, agriculture has two-pronged effects on poverty reduction: first increase in agricultural productivity benefits thousands of farmers through higher incomes, and second, there would be a plentiful supply of food items at cheaper prices. An increase in agricultural income stimulates demand for domestically produced goods and services which in turn spurs the growth of industry and services. The experience of countries across the temperate world from England in the mid-18th century to Japan in the late 19th century and in China, India and Vietnam shows that agricultural growth was the precursor to sustained industrial growth. The spectacular development of the British economy for a century after 1750 led by the Industrial Revolution was preceded by nearly a hundred years of an agricultural revolution. Similarly, the rapid and continued expansion of the Japanese agricultural production, following the Meiji Restoration corresponded with a rapid industrialization and all-round economic development in Japan (Ohkawa and Rosovsky, 1960). The Chinese Communist policy concentrated on creating cooperatives and then communes in agriculture for raising surplus by raising productivity. The removal of low productivity constraints in agriculture made the Chinese economy resilient to the Soviet withdrawal of aid to China in 1959 as a result of the Sino-Soviet dispute.

In Nepal, agriculture has been the most neglected sector, not only in terms of resource allocation but also in terms of institutional reform, such as land reform and extension of irrigation facilities. The neglect of the agricultural sector has reversed the food situation of the country from one of surplus to a food deficit country. As documented by Shrestha (1981) from the early issues of the *Indian Trade Journal*, Nepal exported rice and wheat to India (including Tibet, Sikkim and Bhutan) in the Second World War period and the quantum of export of these two food grains during 1942/3 and 1945/6 was 16.2 MT. The quantity exported to India only in 1958/9 and 1959/60 was 22.4 MT (Shrestha, 1981). In 1965, the export of rice from Nepal to India jumped to 348,000 MT, amounting to Rs. 237.8 million, making it the fifth largest rice exporter in the world that year (Gaige, 2009 [1975]: 29). But the situation gradually reversed in the succeeding years, and the country turned into an importer of an increasingly larger volume of rice and various other agricultural products worth millions of Nepalese Rupees every year. Of seven agricultural products imported from India, rice import shows a consistently increasing trend, reflecting a phenomenal jump by 223 times in two decades from Rs. 226.4 million in 2001/2 to Rs. 50,478.2 million in 2020/21 (Table 1.5).

Vegetables constitute the next highest import item with a consistently increasing trend. Even though the government budget of the past few years repeatedly stated to make the country self-reliant in milk, vegetables, rice, egg and poultry meat within two to three years, the dependency on imports from India has enlarged further.

Second, plans are cast in terms of planning for investment expenditure only without being backed up by the material balances plan. Budgetary allocations are made to different sectors without any analysis of overall resource balance, productivity and feasibility studies. Even though the concept of physical planning was introduced in the Sixth Plan, although in partial form, in terms of projections of supply and demand of some development materials, such as cement, iron rod/channel, timber,

Table 1.5 Import of Agricultural Products from India (Rs. in Million)

	2001/2	*2004/5*	*2009/10*	*2014/5*	*2015/6*	*2016/7*	*2017/1*	*2018/19*	*2019/20*	*2020/21*
Rice	226.4	655.0	1,256.5	15,612.6	21,863.2	23,600.9	28,909.9	32,215.0	33,350.5	50,478.2
Vegetables	685.2	899.7	2,079.4	7,988.7	7,725.6	10,645.5	11,038.5	14,609.4	13,582.2	15,277.7
Baby food and milk products	399.2	492.7	708.5	4,659.8	4,685.7	5,904.1	6,711.0	6,675.8	6,069.7	7,094.5
Fruits	216.2	380.0	433.8	3,706.1	5,016.8	4,949.9	5,731.1	10,444.9	8,628.1	10,357.1
Live animals	337.5	346.0	433.3	1,952.4	2,689.7	2,165.3	3,314.9	2,721.4	120.1	122.0
Tobacco	597.2	569.7	1,817.1	2,937.7	2,765.7	2,805.3	2,640.8	2,355.6	2,687.7	2,583.3
Total	2,461.7	3,343.1	6,728.6	36,857.3	447,446.7	50,071.0	58,346.2	69,022.1	64,438.3	85,912.8

Source: Current Macroeconomic and Financial Situation, Various Years Nepal Rastra Bank, Quarterly Economic Bulletin, Mid-April 2015, Nepal Rastra Bank.

chemical fertilizers, mineral oil, petroleum products, explosives, machinery and equipment, this was not continued in the subsequent plans.

Third, the NPC confined itself to plan formulation and shied away from the question of implementation as not falling within its purview. It is engrossed in plan formulation and fixing the annual budget ceiling to the line ministries, while implementation of the plan is left to the line ministries. Even though the NPC has a monitoring and evaluation unit, it has not made any significant inroads in pinpointing the fault lines and suggesting corrective actions to the concerned ministries. In the early years of planning, weak and rudimentary administrative machinery and a shortage of technical manpower were identified as the major constraints in effective implementation. In the last five decades, the NPC has been staffed by highly trained officers with masters/Ph.D. degrees from foreign universities and an expanded institutional set-up. Despite the prime minister heading the Commission to lend it the power and the political backstopping and the chief secretary and finance secretary as ex-officio members to command the inter-ministerial commitments and coordination, the planning exercise was never visionary and never implemented effectively. Although almost all persons who had assumed the position of vice-chairman at different times were prompt in pinpointing poor implementation as the main problem in the non-fulfilment of plan targets, the issue was never taken seriously. Instead of paying attention to the effective implementation of plan projects and programmes falling within their purview, the secretaries often indulge in inter-ministerial accusations and counter-accusations for the non-achievement of targets within a set time.

Fourth, the NPC has been made a political appendage of the ruling parties for appointing party-affiliated persons as vice-chairman and members irrespective of their expertise, capability and commitment. Instead of an ideal five-member commission, the NPC is often crowded with a bunch of members to accommodate the demand of the coalition partners in the government. There was an instance of 12 members, and the NPC secretariat had to ask some incumbents to defer their presence in office by some days for the arrangement of minimum logistics. Even after the formation of a strong left government (coalition of UML and Maoist) following the general election of December 2017, Prime Minister KP Sharma Oli constituted a seven-member commission on 24 April 2018, violating the cabinet decision of 20 March 2018 to limit the number of NPC members to five. When persons guided by diverse political ideologies and different motives are assembled to chart the contours of a country's development, one can hardly expect any innovation in planning methods and commitment to resolving the country's problems. Moreover, the bureaucracy of the NPC is also not enthusiastic to go beyond the routine administrative work, as they think that they are parked there because of partisan transfers.

The aforementioned reasons provide partial explanations for the failure of planning to generate a higher growth rate and alleviate poverty. There is no doubt that there are technical defects and deficiencies in plan formulation, but more fundamentally, they are the clear manifestations of the nature of the Nepalese state, the political and bureaucratic power structure and the interplay of class interest, which we discuss in Chapter 4.

1.7 Indicative Planning

The Eighth Plan stated that planning would be indicative, but there was no discussion on what indicative planning meant and how it was to be different from the previous centralized planning system. According to Devine,

> [T]he theoretical rationale for indicative planning is that by improving the information available to decision-makers, it alters expectations and thereby behaviour. The idea is that the government and the key sectors and enterprises in the economy should get together to discuss their plans for the future. By exchanging information about what they have in mind they make it possible for each of them to modify their intentions in the light of what others are proposing to do.
>
> (Devine, 1988: 40)

However, no exercise was initiated in this direction and no blueprint was prepared on the interface between planning on the one hand and the state, economy and markets on the other. The issues that made planning indicative, such as resolving the problem of imperfect information, early identification of bottlenecks and supply shortages so that investment behaviour could be modified in a timely fashion to reduce the incidence of risk, guiding choices of separate private entities in the market through coordinated information were left unaddressed. Between the period of the Eighth Plan and the until now , several coalition governments of right, left and Madheshi parties were formed, and seven plans (Ninth to Fifteenth) were formulated, but none touched on the issue of indicative planning, as if it was not essential.

The neo-liberal economists in Nepal argue that since Nepal has moved away from a Soviet-style 'command planning strategy' to a private-sector-led and market-guided growth strategy, there is no longer any role for an overarching institution like the NPC. They would even go to the extent of arguing that the existence of NPC is antithetical to the neo-liberal regime and hence the institution should be abolished. It is further argued that as the planning regime during the last 60 years failed to deliver what was expected of it in terms of raising the growth rate and reducing inequalities, it has no relevance in the liberalized environment. Such thinking was a part of the long-driven neo-liberal strategy of the capitalist countries and the global financial institutions to make the nation states weaker in the less developed countries in dealing with the world capitalist system.

The neo-liberal voice was executed by the Sushil Koirala government on 1 September 2014 by announcing the abolishment of the nearly 60-year-old NPC and the creation of a new think-tank institution in its place. The UML, which was a coalition partner in the government, also backed up the decision to scrap the NPC, disregarding whatever was left with its leftist ideology. The decision of Nepal came two weeks after the Indian prime minister Narendra Modi in his 2014 Independence Day address declared the scrapping of the Soviet-style Planning Commission in India and replacing it with a new think-tank body, named the

National Institution for Transforming India. It was a mockery that the Sushil Koirala government then decided to replace the NPC with a government research institute that abolished the 'Institute of Policy Research', the first government think-tank of three members (this author as chairman) established by the preceding Prime Minister Baburam Bhattarai on 11 February 2013. The Institute was abolished without any reason when it was conducting research on three issues of national importance, namely 'double-digit growth', 'financial aspects of federalism' and 'unified security policy'.

The government announcement to demolish the NPC was nowhere questioned and debated, not even by the intellectuals and economists who claimed to be allied with the left camp. On the contrary, rigorous debates had taken place in India on whether it was right to abolish the Planning Commission and what should be the role and functions of the new body (EPW, 2014, 2015). A section of the top economists and intellectuals of both left and right leanings in India strongly criticized the scrapping of the Planning Commission to the extent that the government made deplorable haste in not recognizing the contribution that planning had made to significantly build up the Indian economy, and in the context of market economy, the state had the responsibility of addressing the issues of social concern which could not be entirely left to the private-sector initiatives and interaction of market forces. The left economists further argued that a government pursuing neo-liberal policy and having no intention of taking the country out of the vortex of globalization still needs a national planning body to mould neo-liberalism in its favour (Patnaik, 2014).

The successive governments of Nepal, however, did not carry forward the decision made by the Sushil Koirala government to scrap the NPC but retained it intact as in the past with the same stereotypical role and responsibilities. After a gap of nearly six years, the KP Oli government formed a five-member think-tank on 23 September 2018, but the person picked up for the post of chairman, a retired Tribhuvan University professor, resigned after seven months of tenure for no obvious reason. This throws up the question of whether the government just wants the think-tank to be a showpiece or the person appointed had no belief in himself to drive the institution and produce policy papers of strategic significance.

1.8 Fifteenth Plan

In the context of what was discussed earlier, it would be incomplete without a brief comment on the Fifteenth Plan introduced in 2019, which holds a significance of its own, as it was the first periodic plan brought out by the federal government of the communist party holding an almost two-thirds majority in the parliament and committed to achieving economic prosperity and building socialism in the country. Further, six out of seven federal states also had communist governments with a two-thirds majority. So, the communist government that was in power for three-and-a-half years (2018–21) can be considered the strongest government in two-and-a-half centuries in the history of Nepal to move towards a socialism-oriented development path.

1.8.1 Major Goals and Targets

The broad vision and aspiration of the Fifteenth Plan are echoed in the slogan 'Prosperous Nepal, Happy Nepali', for which a 25-year perspective development plan has been proposed encompassing five successive plans (Fifteenth, Sixteenth, Seventeenth, Eighteenth and Nineteenth Plans). The long-term plan aims at upgrading Nepal from least-developed country status to developing country status by 2022, to upper-middle-income country status by 2030 and to developed country status by 2043/44. The perspective vision proposes to end all types of remnants of discrimination, exclusion and deprivation and build a socialism-oriented prosperous economy. Further, the 25-year planning horizon is delineated into three stages for the realization of 'economic prosperity and happiness':

- i **Generating prosperity and happiness:** the first stage would create the base, particularly physical infrastructure (road, energy, irrigation, National Pride Projects, etc.), information technology and communication and improvement of education and health.
- ii **Accelerating prosperity and happiness:** the second stage (Sixteenth and Seventeenth Plans) would lead to achievement of high indicators of prosperity and happiness along with equitable distribution of benefits of growth. By the end of Seventeenth plan, Nepal would graduate to a middle income country.
- iii **Sustaining prosperity and happiness:** the third stage (Eighteenth and Nineteenth Plans) would achieve balanced and sustainable progress in prosperity and happiness and double-digit growth with social justice and minimum inequality. By the end of this stage, the economy would be self-reliant, free and prosperous and there would be maximum mobilization of available means and resources and the road towards socialism would be strengthened.

The plan proposes to increase per capita income from the existing US$1,047 to US$1,595 by the end of the Fifteenth Plan and to US$12,100 by the end of 2043/44. The average growth rate for the next five years is 9.6 percent, with agricultural sector growth of 5.4 percent, industrial sector growth of 14.6 percent and services sector growth of 9.9 percent per annum (Table 1.6).

The share of agriculture in GDP is targeted to decline from 27.0 percent to 23.0 percent by the end of the Fifteenth Plan and to 9.0 percent by the end of the long-term plan (2043/44), while that of industry is targeted to increase from 15.2 percent to 18.8 percent and to 30.0 percent by 2043/44 and that of services to increase marginally from 57.8 percent to 58.9 percent in the Fifteenth Plan and to 61.0 percent by 2043/44. Population below the poverty line is stipulated to be reduced from 18.7 percent to 9.5 percent by the Fifteenth Plan and to zero by 2043/44.

Table 1.6 Targets of the Fifteenth Plan in Some Major Areas

SN	*Areas*	*Unit*	*2018/19*	*Target (Five years average)*	
				2023/4	*2043/4 (Target)*
1.	**Economic growth[a]**	Percent	6.8	9.6	10.5
1.1	Growth of agriculture	Percent	4.8	5.4	5.9
1.2	Growth of industry	Percent	12.2	14.6	14.9
1.3	Manufacturing	Percent	9.5	12.7	ns
1.4	Services	Percent	7.9	9.9	ns
2.	**Share in GDP (of 2023/4)**				
2.1	Agriculture and forestry	Percent	27.0	22.3	9.0
2.2	Industry	Percent	15.2	18.8	30.0
2.3	Services	Percent	57.8	58.9	61.0
3.	Per capita GNI	US$	1,047	1,595	12,100
4.	Population below poverty line	Percent	18.7	9.5	0
5.	Population in multi-dimensional poverty	Percent	28.6	11.5	3.0
6.	Gini coefficient (wealth)	Coefficient	0.31	0.29	0.25
7.	Human development index	Index	0.579	0.624	0.760
8.	Unemployment rate	Percent	11.4	6.0	3.0
9.	Energy production	MW	1,250	5,000	40,000
10.	Export/GDP ratio	Ratio	8.2	15	ns
11.	Share of agri. products, livestock and food in Total imports	Ratio	14.7	5.0	ns

Source: Fifteenth Plan, NPC, 2019.

a At basic price, ns means not stated.

1.8.2 Flaws of the Fifteenth Plan

The Fifteenth Plan, formulated with the backstopping of a nearly two-thirds majority government of the communist party, was expected to come out as the 'Transformation Plan' aimed at course correction of the Nepalese economy in line with the communist principles, from privatized free-market capitalism to state-supported capitalism, from reliance on foreign aid to self-reliance in economic development, from the concentration of private-sector investment in unproductive areas to productive areas and from inefficient use of resources to efficiency, transparency and accountability in all state activities. But the plan missed this historic opportunity and was confined to jugglery with numbers or as Desai satirically remarks in the context of India a 'make-believe game of new numbers for old' (Desai, 2005: 108), rather than initiating innovative strategy, policies and programmes. Apart from jugglery of numbers, forecasting of GDP growth rate and its components and reduction in poverty rate for a time horizon of 25 year raises a big question of accuracy when estimates of government expenditure and revenue for the upcoming year have never been accurate in Nepal. The economic and social parameters, and many other factors and their behavioural relations on which the projections are founded do not move in a manner presumed by planners and policy makers. Moreover, if we go by the past track of achieving the plan targets, it appears that the Fifteenth Plan as well as its long-term vision and projections would be another disillusionment with planning.

There are various flaws of the Fifteenth Plan, the major ones may be described as follows:

1 **No Departure from Previous Plans**: The Fifteenth Plan has come in the same configuration as the earlier plans. Unlike the previous bodies, the planning body that formulated the Fifteenth Plan had the advantage of not only the stability of members but also members of similar ideological inclinations. But the plan document was a stereotype of the previous plan without any innovative approaches, policies or programmes and without a focus on how the gaps between targets and achievements could be reduced. Because the earlier plans have failed to achieve the stated objectives and targets, there has been a kind of 'plan weariness' and erosion of faith in planning among the intellectuals, academics, media and the general public. This is reflected in the decay of academic debate or discussion for the past several years when a new plan is introduced by the government. The same was apparent in the case of the Fifteenth Plan. The plan came out in the same configuration as in earlier plans, as if no significant political change has occurred in the country.

2 **Achieving Prosperity, Building Socialism and Increasing Happiness**: These words are very catchy as slogans, but the question is: do these together make up a consistent set of objectives, and how are they to be weighted? The prosperity objective conflicts with the socialism objective, as the former would require the concentration of resources in growth-generating sectors, while the latter would require dispersion of resources in pockets of poverty, social security benefits and welfare programmes. As the Soviet experience has shown, building socialism involves fundamental changes in the structure of production, in the system of production relations and the location of productive forces (Krichenko, 1980). To this one can add redistribution of assets, especially of land and income in an equitable manner. The Fifteenth Plan overlooks the need for structural changes in the economy and advocates reforming rather than restructuring the existing systems, institutions and practices to achieve greater economic equality. With regard to increasing happiness, the plan lists six domains: (i) well-being and decent life; (ii) safe, civilized and just society; (iii) healthy and balanced environment; (iv) good governance; (v) comprehensive democracy; and (vi) national unity, security and dignity. There is neither the index of individual domains nor the aggregate index of these to discern the stage of happiness. Though useful in knowing the overall status, the aggregate index does not reveal the vast differences by gender, by age, by caste/ethnics, by regions, by occupation, by education or by income-levels. The plan also has not spelt out specific policies and programmes to (a) increase the percentage of people who are happy and (b) decrease the deficient conditions of people who are not happy.

3 **No Class View**: The Fifteenth Plan, as the earlier plans, is merely an exercise in neo-classical economics. It is all about computation of macro-aggregates of GDP; fixing targets on different lines of production, such as agriculture, industry and services; allocation of resources between agriculture, industry and other sectors; requirement of foreign assistance; etc. The plan - ignores that planning is also an exercise in sociology and politics, and it is the interplay of politics and economics that determines the course of development and sharing of fruits of development between different classes. It is rather strange that a plan prepared by communist government–nominated members under the direction of communist prime minister who chairs the Planning Commission can ignore the politico-economic dynamics of development in plan formulation and view development as a linear progression.

4 **Implementation Capacity**: Planning failed in Nepal because of poor implementation. In the light of past experience, it is questionable whether the government bureaucracy would shed its old shackles and 'reinvent' itself by fundamentally changing its attitude and work style so as to implement the Fifteenth Plan with efficiency and effectiveness. Given the present administrative system and the operating structures, methods and procedures, as well as the mind-set of government bureaucracy at different administrative levels, it is doubtful whether the Fifteenth Plan would be different from the earlier plans in achieving the set targets.

5 **Planning in Federalism**: With the federal structure of the country, there is a need to make a paradigm shift from planning from the top to planning from the bottom, and these need to be synchronized with one another and with the plans of provincial governments. Moreover, the planning machinery developed to suit the unitary political structure of the country may not be appropriate for planning in federalism because of the need for coordination and maintaining a balance between central regulation, direction and control with the autonomy and the policies, rules and system of provincial governments. But the Fifteenth Plan was brought out without much thinking and adequate exercise on the intricacies of planning under federalism.

6 **Minimization of the Role of Agriculture**: Agriculture is the leading sector and foundation of the Nepalese economy by all considerations. But the Fifteenth Plan proposes to downsize its importance in terms of contribution to GDP from 27.6 percent to 23.0 percent by 2023/4 and further to 9.0 percent by 2042/3, while that of the industrial sector is planned to be expanded from 15.2 percent to 18.8 percent by 2023/4 and to 30.0 percent by 2042/3. Agriculture is targeted to grow by 5.4 percent on average, while industry is targeted to grow by 14.6 percent. The plan proposes to promote industrial growth on a weaker base of agricultural growth, which contradicts the history of the Industrial Revolution in England, as analyzed earlier, and is also against Nepal's economic structure. We do not deny the importance of industrial development for economic growth and long-run poverty reduction, but the question is the sustainability of industrialization if not founded on a solid base of agricultural development. Such types of industrialization virtually create dependent industrialization and increase

the vulnerability of the country to outside influences, as experienced during the Panchayat regime in 1992 and also in the democratic era when an undeclared economic blockade was introduced by India in 2015.

1.9 Re-engineering NPC

The expectation that the planning in Nepal would lead to higher overall growth, reduce regional inequality, overcome the impoverishment of the masses and resolve the problems of increasing unemployment, under-employment and disguised unemployment has gone astray. Nepal relied on the neo-classical prescriptions for augmenting growth and reducing inter-regional imbalances and poverty, operating on the terrain of prevalent socio-economic order, responding to its needs and issues and furthering its interests and concerns. This would not lead the nation beyond the present realm of persistence of underdevelopment, poverty and dependency. Therefore, instead of accepting the inherited theoretical postulates uncritically, we need to throw away irrelevant approaches and modify some if they are relevant to our conditions and then construct a new frame offering policies and strategies which lie beyond the existing framework and which lead to self-reliant economic development oriented towards socialism. No institution other than the Planning Commission can be better suited for this exercise.

There are also new issues and problems of greater complexity and sophistication thrown up by the federal structure of the country. There are now 753 local governments, 7 provincial governments and 1 federal government with their own territorial jurisdictions and economic as well as administrative rights and responsibilities. The federal government has the complex responsibility of maintaining harmonious political, economic, financial and administrative relations both horizontally and vertically between and across these territorial jurisdictions. The question is how to move ahead to resolve all such issues in achieving the objectives of economic prosperity and reducing inter-regional imbalance and inequalities. There is no simple answer nor would any answer be acceptable to all. The only institution that can provide an answer would be the NPC. But the NPC in its present structure and working procedures would not do anything more innovative than what it has been doing over many years.

Notes

1 By retarded and underdeveloped, Bagchi means a situation whereby a country has fallen far behind its potential to transform its production capacity into increased production and that its capacity for realizing the potential is constrained by its internal social and political structures and institutions, and by the dependent relations with the advanced capitalist countries (Bagchi, 1982: 20).

2 Nepal's underdevelopment is a manifestation of misguided development of productive forces. The problem lies not in its incapacity to form capital, but in a wrongly structured accumulation that has led to the transformation of a fairly viable, subsistence economy into a defective and crippled peripheral economy with detrimental effects for the majority of the people (Senghaas, 1978).

3 "'Failed development" implies "failure of the country in achieving what it set out to do. It has failed also, and more importantly, because the idea and agents of development themselves may have been corrupted in the process'" (Panday, 1999: x).
4 http://www.answers.com/topic/soviet-economicgrowth
5 A highly potential nature given herb found in the Western Himalayan range of Nepal and considered as herbal Viagra sold at a very high price ranging between Rs. 100,000.0 and Rs.500,000.0 per kg. depending on quality of the herb.

2 Rhetoric of Poverty Alleviation

2.1 Concepts of Poverty

Mainstream economists have initiated substantive discussion and debate on the concept of poverty in the last 30 years, defining, redefining and interpreting the concept and its measures in many different ways. One concept of poverty is absolute poverty, which defines poverty as the lack of income to meet a specified standard of living measured by income or consumption. The other concept of poverty is the relative one, which was developed to address the drawbacks of the concept of absolute poverty, which ignored the depth or degree of poverty of the poor and the distribution of income or inequality among the poor. Corresponding to these concepts of poverty, three distinct measures of poverty have been used by most studies, following the Foster–Greer–Thorbecke poverty measures (Foster et al., 1984). First, the headcount index, which measures the proportion of the population living below a specified threshold income or expenditure called the poverty line. Second, the poverty gap index shows the mean gap between poor people's living standards and the poverty line. Third, the squared poverty gap index, which is the mean of the squared proportionate poverty gaps, reflects the severity of poverty. There is also the concept of 'capability poverty' articulated by Amartya Sen who defines poverty as

> the failure of some basic capabilities to function – a person lacking the opportunity to achieve some minimally acceptable levels of functioning, which can vary from such elementary physical ones as being well nourished, being adequately clothed and sheltered, avoiding preventable morbidity, and so forth, to more complex social achievements such as taking part in the life of the community, being able to appear in public without shame, and so on.
>
> (Sen, 1982: 15)

Sen's concept has been extensively used by the United Nations Development Programme as a broader measure of human development for ranking countries in terms of a composite indicator named Human Development Index, which is computed on the basis of individual country indicators on income, education and health.

DOI: 10.4324/9781003359777-2

2.2 Growth and Poverty Reduction

Much of the mainstream economics literature emphasizes economic growth as the indispensable condition for poverty alleviation. They forward two propositions on the relationship between economic growth and poverty reduction. The first proposition says that economic growth is an essential prerequisite for poverty reduction as growth contributes to poverty reduction through three mechanisms. First, there is the 'income effect' of growth, which means the average income of the poor increases along with growth. Second, economic growth generates employment opportunities so that the poor will have jobs yielding income to sustain their consumption. Third, rapid growth has 'multiplier effects', which raise the return on income-earning assets of the poor and help sustain their consumption. The second proposition says that higher growth may be associated with increases in poverty levels, at least in the short run. In other words, it suggests an aggregate trade-off between growth and equity. Growth requires investment, and this would be possible only if income is concentrated with the capitalist class, which has a higher propensity to save. On the other hand, redistributive measures in the early stages of development would reduce savings and investment, as the poor class has a higher propensity to consume. As per this view, concern for the poor in the early stages of development would adversely affect the rate of growth, without which poverty reduction would not be impossible. The emphasis was on expanding the size of the economic pie because when the pie itself was small, the share of each individual would be small and more so when the population was growing. Thus higher economic growth entailed rising inequality and increasing poverty. This is, however, said to be short-lived as the relationship between inequality and growth was postulated to be an 'inverted U-curve' with inequality increasing in the early phase of economic growth, eventually declining in the later phase. The inverted U-notion was introduced by Kuznets on the basis of the study of change in income distribution in the United States, United Kingdom and two states of Germany (Kuznets, 1955). It is argued that in the early stages of development, increase in income is not accompanied by reduction in inequality, and there may be an increase in the absolute poverty of some groups. However, when the upper limit of the inverted U-curve is reached, growing income would be accompanied by lower inequality and reduced poverty. Three arguments are suggested for this. First, market forces, such as increased demand for labour, higher productivity, higher wages or lower prices would spread the benefits of growth to the lower strata. Second, it was assumed that governments whether democratic or autocratic would take actions to correct the situation of concentration of benefits in order to spread them downward. Third, the building of social overheads, infrastructure and productive capacity was assumed to benefit the poor. This thinking was predominant for a long period of time and the emphasis was laid on the acceleration of the rate of growth with a high faith in the trickle-down mechanism.

Studies undertaken since the 1950s to test the inverted U-curve hypothesis in less developed countries show mixed evidence and at best inconclusive (Kanbur, 2000). The trickle-down hypothesis collapsed in the 1970s, as the development experience of many developing countries during the two decades after the Second World War showed increasing poverty of a large fraction of their population.

Various barriers stemming from the initial skewed income distribution and institutional factors prevented the poor from getting equal access to growth-generated benefits at any level of growth.

2.3 Concern for Poverty Reduction in Nepal

Poverty in Nepal is not the making of the past few decades but is a long-drawn historical process from ancient times. However, poverty became pervasive in the later decades, along with the type of development strategy that Nepal adopted and the absorption of tens of billions of foreign aid in support of that strategy. Information is not available to describe the quantitative status of poverty in the 19th century and the first half of the 20th century,, which marked the end of the 104-year autocratic Rana regime. However, absolute poverty was not much known during the period, as people had no difficulty managing their livelihoods because there was no population pressure on the cultivable land. As Nepal remained a primitive country consisting of mostly agricultural societies, a large majority of people had no high requirements and no expectations. Regmi (1984, 1999) provides a detailed account of the agrarian structure and associated poverty of peasants in early 19th century and 20th century Nepal. Two major factors for the poverty of the lower-rung people during that period were landownership and debt bondage. The privileged aristocrats who owned land granted by the kings and rulers and the landlords of the local agrarian community engaged the poor farmers to cultivate their land on highly unequal sharecropping terms and also forced them to perform other physical works at very low or without wages. The peasants were required not only to pay a multitude of homestead and other taxes but also had to provide unpaid labour services to the state and their landlords. Because of the burden of taxation in money, commodities and labour, an individual peasant cultivating jagir and other lands of taxable categories would tend to be much poorer than an individual owner cultivator with a holding of the same size (Regmi, 1999: 124). In the terai region, a land owner class of 'zamindars' evolved after the introduction of a permanent settlement scheme for hill people and the migratory movement of people from the adjoining areas of northern India to occupy land in terai. The zamindars stood above the peasantry and inhabited tracts of land after driving out the indigenous settlers, while the peasants were left at their mercy and rarely became an object of concern for the government.

Agrarian indebtedness was another factor that drove the peasants into poverty in 19th-century Nepal. Along with the advance of the zamindari system, there was an emergence of another agrarian class, the moneylenders, who supplied credit to the subsistence farmers at an exorbitant rate of interest and in return exploited their labour and appropriated a share in their production. Regmi cites an example of usurious interest in Nuwakot district in 1854: 'We pay Rs. 200 on a loan of Rs. 100, or thirty pathis (108 kg) of salt on a loan of one muri (72 kg) of rice, but the amount of loan always remains the same as before' (Regmi, 1999: 141). In the event of loan default by the farmers and an increase in cumulated loans, the debtor farmers were dispossessed of their land or forced to work as bonded labourers by the moneylenders.

With the end of the Rana regime in 1950 and the opening of the country to the outside world, Nepal stepped on the path of economic development through planning, but poverty was not an issue of concern to the government up until the Sixth Plan (1980–5), which listed 'fulfilment of minimum basic needs of people' as one of its objectives. The earlier plans talked of 'equitable social system' (Second Plan), 'social justice' (Third Plan) 'creation of conditions conducive to the emergence of a society free from exploitation' (Fourth Plan) and increase in the production of daily necessities while increasing national production (Fifth Plan).

For the first time in Nepal's history, the National Planning Commission (NPC) conducted a survey on 'Employment, Income Distribution and Consumption Patterns in Nepal' in 1977 to estimate the magnitude and concentration of poverty. The estimates of poverty were based on a calorie need of 2,256 per person per day and the average minimum level of expenditure for meeting that need was estimated at Rs. 2.0 per day (at 1976/7 prices). In addition, the income measure of poverty defined as Rs. 2.0 per day per person as subsistence income was also used. The proportion of households and population below the poverty line estimated on income measure was higher than that estimated on expenditure measure except for population in the urban area.

The survey revealed that 33.7 percent of the households (31.5 percent of the population) were below the poverty line in terms of consumption measure, while it was 40.3 percent of the households (36.2 percent of the population) in terms of income measure (Table 2.1). The income measure showed higher poverty rates than the consumption measure for both households and population in aggregate as well as in rural and urban areas except for the population in the urban area. Furthermore, the incidence of poverty in rural areas was almost twice as high as in urban areas. The survey also revealed Gini coefficients of 0.60 in rural and 0.55 in urban areas, indicating higher inequality of income distribution in rural than in urban areas. The higher income inequality in rural areas was because of the perpetuation of historically highly unequal distribution of land, which constituted the main source of wealth and income.

The survey also estimated the regional pattern of the incidence of poverty in terms of the percentage of households and population lying below the poverty line by consumption as well as income measure. The regional pattern was presented in terms of four Development Regions (Eastern, Central, Western and Far-Western Development Regions). The Far-Western Region had the highest incidence of income poverty (45.8 percent in aggregate and 47.3 percent in the rural and 35.8 percent in the urban areas), whereas the Western Region had the lowest incidence (29.8 percent in aggregate and 30.0 percent in the rural and 29.8 percent in the urban areas). The Eastern Region and the Central Region were in between

Table 2.1 Households and Population below Poverty Line, 1977

Poverty Measure	*Percentage of Households Below Poverty Line*			*Percentage of Population Below Poverty Line*		
	Rural	*Urban*	*All-Nepal*	*Rural*	*Urban*	*All-Nepal*
Consumption	34.3	19.9	33.7	32.1	20.0	31.5
Income	41.2	22.1	40.3	37.2	17.0	36.2

Source: (NPC, 1978: 117).

with poverty ratios of 35.3 percent (38.6 percent in the rural and 22.0 percent in the urban areas) and 34.6 percent (36.3 percent in the rural and 27.8 percent in the urban areas), respectively.

2.4 Basic Needs Programme

The high poverty and inequality brought out by the 1977 survey alerted the Panchayat rulers, policymakers and planners to the danger to the regime from the poor and deprived people on the backs of outlawed political parties and supporters of democracy. In a move to forestall this danger and woo the poor people, the Sixth Plan (1980–5) listed 'fulfillment of minimum basic needs of people' as one of the objectives of the plan, implying the basic needs approach (BNA) to development for poverty reduction. This, however, was not the ingenuity of Nepalese planners but was simply a copy of what was already in high discourse in the world capitalist institutions like the International Labour Organization, the World Bank and among the western scholars in the mid-1970s. It was the International Labour Organization's World Employment Conference that introduced the BNA in 1976 and was endorsed by major multilateral and bilateral development agencies. This approach was later uncritically adopted as a development strategy for poverty reduction by planners and policymakers in developing countries. India adopted the Minimum Needs Programme – much earlier than Nepal in its Fifth Five-Year Plan in the 1970s. The historical context for this was the 1971 Garibi Hatao (banish poverty) election campaign announced by Prime Minister Indira Gandhi to woo the poor and unprivileged groups of rural India. This slogan was one of the main factors that led Indira and her supporters to triumph in the parliamentary elections. The sceptics argue that the state concern for poverty reduction in India did not come out of humanitarian consideration but out of the fear that social tensions built up in the Indian villages would carry the risk of rebellion against the establishment. As Dube opined, 'The dispossessed and the deprived are no longer compliant and subservient to authority; no more do they accept their fate as inevitable and irreversible. Their simmering discontent has reached a point where frequent convulsions rock the established order. If it is left unattended it would surely lead to anarchy, if not to a revolutionary upsurge. … Anomic tendencies and disturbances generated by the situation are more difficult to handle than organized resistance in which dialogue and compromise are possible' (Dube, 1994: 179). The left Indian intellectuals labelled the government's concern for poverty as arising out of political compulsions of that time to avert the uprisings of the poor. In the words of Joshi,

> [T]he rise of Naxalism and the threat posed by it in the late sixties was one of the main factors responsible for the sense of urgency with which the ruling elite revived the question of land reforms during the close of the sixties and the beginning of the seventies. A report 'Report of the Current Agrarian Tension' released by the Ministry of Home Affairs in December 1969 underlined the unsatisfactory nature of the agrarian structure as the main cause of the agrarian tension and called for urgent attention to land reforms in the interest of rural poor.
>
> (Joshi, 1982: 90)

In essence, the BNA was, however, just another development jargon to mask the failure of capitalist theories in reducing poverty through growth. The bourgeois economists justified the BNA rejecting the need to reduce inequality among nations and within nations, because

> [f]irst, equality, as such, is probably not an objective of great importance to most people other than utilitarian philosophers and ideologues. Second, this lack of concern is justified, because meeting basic needs is morally a more important objective than reducing inequality. Third, reducing inequality is a highly knotty, abstract objective open to many different interpretations and therefore operationally ambiguous.
>
> (Streeten, 1981: 17)

When the Sixth Plan was nearing completion, King Birendra floated the notion of 'Asian Standards' in 1985 to make people dream of a life of Asian Standards in 15 years. He said,

> Let us pledge that we in the remaining years of this century will be able to shake off the poverty imposed on us by our least developed economy and that by the year 2000 AD, we will be able to achieve a standard of living, which is adequate to lead a life with human dignity from Asian Standards.
>
> (NPC, 1987)

This proclamation of the king was highly eulogized by the ministers, palace loyalists and Pancha elites, and frequently uttered in their public speeches. The prime minister and the ministers flew in helicopters to various remote districts to collect poverty data, spending a large amount of government resources. But nothing substantive was done, not even serious thinking on how this challenging issue was to be addressed. No concern was shown to define what was meant by the 'Asian Standards' and how it was going to be achieved. In totality, the programme was too ambitious to achieve given the pace of development and the institutional set up prevalent in the country (Poudyal and Sharma, 1985).

The Sixth Plan ended without any notable achievement in the fulfilment of the minimum basic needs of people. The Seventh Plan (1985–90) document, which devoted 67 pages to reviewing the Sixth Plan's progress, did not touch upon the progress made on fulfilment of the minimum basic needs of people. Moreover, the plan completely disregarded the king's notion of 'Asian Standards' and repeated the Sixth Plan objective of fulfilment of minimum basic needs of people as one of its three objectives along with an increase in production at a higher rate and an increase in productive employment opportunities. It was only two years after the implementation of the Seventh Plan that the NPC brought out a 51-page booklet 'Programme for Fulfilment of Basic Needs' (NPC, 1987). The booklet cited King Birendra's speech on 'Asian Standards' as a prelude but did not even mention it in the text, not to talk of its elaboration and strategy for achieving it. The defiance of even the king's statement by the Panchayat politicians in power, planners and bureaucrats can be interpreted in many ways. It could be that the king was ill-advised to announce the 'Asian Standards', which was later judged to be complicated and unattainable. It could also be that the king was made captive by the advisers and loyalists surrounding him and had limitations to force them to execute his visionary statement.

The document set a duration of 15 years (1985–2000), extending over Seventh, Eighth and Ninth Plans for achieving the targets in basic needs fulfilment. The basic needs were defined in terms of minimum specified quantities of food, clothing, shelter, education, health and security that are necessary to survive and prevent ill-health and illiteracy. These were quantified as 2,250 per capita daily calorie, 11 m of cloth per person per year, floor space of 30 m^2 per household, primary education to all, primary health services to all and psychological security of economic, social and administrative activities to the common people. On the assumption that 65.0 percent of total family budget is spent on food, the basic need income per capita was estimated at Rs. 5.40 per day and Rs. 1,971.0 per annum (NPC, 1987). Fulfilment of basic needs targets required three preconditions simultaneously: supply (production) of listed goods, demand (purchasing power of the target group) and institutional arrangement for linking production with demand. Although the document set the production targets of food grains, clothing textiles, shoes/slippers and expansion of education and health facilities for three successive five-year periods extending up to 2000 to meet the quantified basic needs over a period of 15 years, it did not seriously consider the latter two preconditions. There was no effective programme to make the poor capable of demanding the goods and services. The document laid emphasis on the same conventional schemes of the past, such as Small Farmers' Development Programme, Production Credit for Rural Women, Priority Sector Credit Programme, Intensive Banking Programme, cooperatives and special skill trainings, to provide employment and earning opportunities for the poor. However, these schemes were there for some years and had already failed to benefit the poor people. In fact, the per capita income of Rs. 2,540.0 in 1984/5 was higher than the estimated basic needs income of Rs. 1,971.0. The issue was that of redistribution but remained untouched because it was inimical to the richer sections of the society, which were either in power or aligned to the power circle. So, the state pursued only those development strategies and programmes that did not disturb the existing modes of production and production relations which benefitted the ruling class and the class fractions aligned to it. The consequence was that the privileged groups mostly monopolized the programmes accentuating poverty of the masses and income inequality.

The financial provision was not also matching with the goals. Of the total proposed investment of Rs. 265.2 billion, 12.7 percent was to be generated from revenue surplus, 40.0 percent from foreign aid, 42.3 percent from the private sector and 5 percent was deficit (Table 2.2).

The government was poised to achieve a programme of such ambitious nature with over only about 13 percent of total resources. Moreover, it was planners' myopia to expect that the private sector would expand the production of basic needs items, which generally have a very low margin of profitability. Besides, in an environment characterized by rent seeking, neither the bureaucracy nor the private sector would have any interest in pursuing activities satisfying the basic needs

Table 2.2 Financial Provision of Basic Needs Programme (1985–2000) (at 1984/5 Prices)

Sources	*Total Rs. (Million)*	*Percentage of Total Expenditure*	*Percentage of Public Expenditure*
Revenue surplus	33,590	12.7	21.9
Deficit	13,380	5.0	8.7
Foreign aid	106,130	40.0	69.3
Public expenditure	153,100	57.7	
Private expenditure	112,050	42.3	–
Total expenditure	265,150	100.0	

Source: NPC (1987: 43–44).

Table 2.3 Targets and Achievements of Crop and Livestock Production ('000 metric ton)

SN	*Description*	*Target for 1999/2000*	*Actual Production*	
			1999/2000	*2003/4*
1.	Grains	8,651.0	6,985.0	7,746.0
2.	Pulses	247.0	237.3	265.3
3.	Potatoes	869.0	1,183.0	1,643.0
4.	Vegetables	1,515.0	1,489.7	1,890.1
5.	Fruits	702.0	447.3	511.4
6.	Meat	333.0	189.2	208.4
7.	Milk	1,334.0	1,097.0	1,231.9
8.	Eggs (millions units)	422.0	480.8	575.6
9.	Fish	50.1	31.7	40.0

Source: Ministry of Finance, 2005; NPC (1987: 13).

of the masses. In addition, to expect such a task to be achieved through the initiatives of donors was simply to sidle away from the responsibility.

The Seventh Plan enlarged the basic needs items to include fuel wood, drinking water and minimum rural transportation. Crop and livestock production targets fixed in the plan were not linked up with the targets set for 1999/2000 for fulfilling the basic needs, as enunciated in 1985. Consequently, there was a big shortfall in the actual production of specified crops and livestock products except for potatoes and eggs (Table 2.3).

Production of grains, which was expected to meet 87.3 percent of the calorie needs (2,250 per capita per day) of poor people, was below the target by 19.3 percent. Even in 2003/4, four years after the specified deadline (1999/2000), production of food grains was short of targets by 10.5 percent. Although some increase was witnessed in the production of some items, the poor were not able to benefit because of a lack of income-earning opportunities.

The BNA ended with the end of the Seventh Plan because of the replacement of the Panchayat regime by multiparty democracy in 1991, and there was a shift from basic needs to poverty alleviation in tune with the World Bank strategy.

2.5 Poverty Estimates by Various Institutions

Following the poverty estimation by NPC, various institutions such as Nepal Rastra Bank, the World Bank, Central Bureau of Statistics, Oxford Poverty and Human Development Initiatives and International Centre for Integrated Mountain Development (ICIMOD) have estimated Nepal's poverty for different years.

A multi-purpose household budget survey by Nepal Rastra Bank in 1984/5, eight years after the NPC survey estimated the poverty rate using the basic needs income of Rs. 5.94 for the hills/mountains and Rs. 4.71 for the terai per person per day, was fixed by the NPC (Table 2.4).

The survey estimates revealed that the proportion of the population living below the poverty line in rural areas was 43.1 percent, more than double the 19.2 percent in urban areas. By the ecological belt, the hills had a greater proportion of its population below the poverty line (50.0 percent), as compared to the mountains (44.1 percent) and terai (34.5 percent). The same overall pattern of poverty was observed in terms of percentage of households, but the figures were slightly lower compared to those in terms of population.

The survey also estimated Gini coefficients of 0.57 for all-Nepal and 0.85 and 0.55, respectively, for urban and rural Nepal. A comparison with the NPC estimate of 1977 shows an increase in inequality in urban as compared to rural areas over the last eight years. The increase in income inequality in urban areas was an inevitable consequence of increasing rural-urban migration in search of employment, and the concentration of growth in urban areas was accompanied by unequal distribution of growth benefits among different economic classes. The growing inequality generated a new pattern of economic and social stratification, as well as political inequality, which in turn became self-perpetuating.

In 1991, the World Bank presented three estimates of the population below the poverty line under three sets of assumptions. The first was the poverty line income defined by the NPC but calculated at 1988/9 prices. This showed that 40.0 percent of the population in total and 42.0 percent in rural areas and 15.0 percent in urban areas were below the poverty line (Table 2.5).

The second was the poverty line defined at US$150.0 per capita per annum because the NPC fixed poverty line income was a very conservative definition of poverty. With this poverty line, 71.0 percent of the population fell below absolute poverty. The third was the Lipton criterion which defined poor as those whose

Table 2.4 Incidence of Poverty, 1984/5 (in Percent)

Ecological Region	*Households below Poverty Line*			*Population below Poverty Line*		
	Rural	*Urban*	*All-Nepal*	*Rural*	*Urban*	*All-Nepal*
Terai	34.1	20.2	33.0	35.4	24.1	34.5
Hills	49.8	12.6	47.1	52.7	14.5	50.0
Mountains	36.0	na	36.0	44.0	na	44.1
All-Nepal	40.7	6.1	–	43.1	19.2	–

Source: NRB (1988: 136).

Table 2.5 Incidence of Poverty under Different Poverty Lines (in Percent)

Source	*Definition of Poverty Line*	*Ecological Belt*		*Rural/Urban*		*All-Nepal*
		Hills	*Terai*	*Rural*	*Urban*	
NPC	Rs. 210 person/month in the hills and Rs. 197 person/month in terai	52	28	42	15	40
World Bank	US $150 per capita per annum	75	68	74	42	71
Lipton	Percentage of population which spent 70 .0 percent or more of total expenditure on food	64	68	68	51	66

Source: The World Bank (1991: 8).

food expenditure absorbed 70.0 percent or more of total expenditure. This criterion showed the incidence of poverty to be 66.0 percent.

The World Bank concluded that the incidence of absolute poverty could be in the neighbourhood of 50.0 to 60.0 percent. It further remarked,

> [E]By any reasonable international standard, veryone in Nepal is poor, except for a few professionals, and businessmen, and perhaps some large farmers. The average income in the second decile (i.e. the second richest 10 percent of households) for instance is only about Rs. 500 per capita per month (US $20 per month) – in most countries these families would be among the poorest.
>
> (World Bank, 1991: 8)

2.6 Nepal Living Standards Surveys

The Central Bureau of Statistics (CBS) of the government of Nepal has started estimating the magnitude of poverty by periodically conducting Nepal Living Standards Surveys (NLSS) from 1995/6. The first survey was followed by the second (NLSS II) in 2003/4, eight years after, and the third (NLSS III) was in 2010/11. These surveys provide a wide range of data on demographic and socio-economic characteristics of households, such as family size, housing, education, health, income, employment, consumption, credit, remittances and access to various facilities. The reports also show the proportion of the population below the poverty line defined in terms of consumption expenditure to meet a minimum food (2,220 kcal per day) and non-food requirements to be alive. The 2010/11 NLSS set the per capita annual consumption expenditure of Rs. 19,261.0 (Rs. 11,929.0 for food and Rs. 7,332.0 for non-food) as the poverty line.

2.6.1 Poverty Rate

The results of three rounds of NLSS presented in Table 2.6 show some distinct trends of poverty in Nepal.

Table 2.6 Incidence of Poverty in 1995/6, 2003/4 and 2010/11 (in Percent)

Area/Region	*Incidence of Poverty (Headcount Rate)*		
	NLSS I (1995/6)	*NLSS II (2003/4)*	*NLSS III (2010/11)*
All-Nepal	41.8	30.9	25.2
By urban/rural area			
Urban area	21.6	9.6	15.5
Rural area	43.3	34.6	27.4
By ecological belt			
Mountain	57.0	32.6	42.3
Hill	40.7	34.5	24.3
Terai	40.3	27.6	23.4
By development region			
Eastern	38.9	29.3	21.4
Central	32.5	27.1	21.7
Western	38.6	27.1	22.3
Mid-Western	59.9	44.8	31.7
Far-Western	63.9	41.0	45.6

Source: Poverty in Nepal, CBS, 2004 and 2011.

First, the poverty headcount ratio declined steadily from 41.8 percent in 1995/6 to 30.9 percent in 2003/4 and to 25.2 percent in 2010/11. Second, poverty in rural areas was almost twice as high compared to urban areas, reversing back to the 1995/6 situation, even though there was almost a fourfold difference in poverty rates in 2003/4. Third, by ecological region, the incidence of poverty was highest in the mountains (42.3 percent) and almost the same in the hills (24.3 percent) and the terai (23.4 percent). Fourth, by development region, the Far-Western Region had the highest poverty rate (45.6 percent), followed by the Mid-Western Region (31.7 percent), while the Eastern, Central and Western Regions had almost the same poverty rate ranging between 21.4 percent and 22.3 percent. Fifth, between 2003/4 and 2010/11, the poverty rate increased in urban areas (from 9.6 percent to 15.5 percent), the mountains (from 32.6 percent to 42.3 percent) and the Far-Western Region (from 41.0 percent to 45.6 percent) as against a decline between 1995/6 and 2003/4. The increase in the poverty rate in urban areas in 2010/11 was mainly due to the migration of rural poor to urban areas in search of employment opportunities.

2.6.2 Poverty Differential by Districts

There is a high degree of poverty differential among districts, which has been a continuity of the past several decades. A comparison of poverty rates by districts between 2011 and 2006 (Table 2.7) shows a highly uneven pattern. First, even though the poverty rate declined in the aggregate term, poverty rates across districts vary enormously ranging between the lowest, 4.0 percent in Kaski and the highest, 64.1 percent in Bajura. Second, there is a strong relationship between the geographical remoteness of the district and the poverty rate, as shown by the increase in the poverty rate in 9 out of 16 mountain districts in 2011 as compared

Table 2.7 Change in Poverty Rate by District

SN	*District*	*EB*	*Poverty Rate*		*Change (Percent)*	*SN*	*District*	*EB*	*Poverty Rate*		*Change (Percent)*
			2006	*2011*					*2006*	*2011*	
1	Ilam	H	39.7	7.3	−81.6	39	Surkhet	H	47.0	30.5	−35.1
2	Panchthar	H	52.5	11.4	−78.3	40	Arghakhanchi	H	44.1	28.8	−34.7
3	Syangja	H	35.1	11.8	−66.4	41	Kailali	T	50.4	33.6	−33.3
4	Terhathum	H	42.5	14.6	−65.6	42	Sarlahi	T	26.4	17.7	−33.0
5	Dhankuta	H	46.0	15.9	−65.4	43	Sindhupalchok	M	37.0	25.4	−31.4
6	Kaski	H	11.1	4.0	−64.0	44	Dailekh	H	51.6	35.8	−30.6
7	Parbat	H	34.1	12.7	−62.8	45	Kanchanpur	T	42.4	31.4	−25.9
8	Kavre	H	35.1	13.9	−60.4	46	Chitawan	T	11.9	8.9	−25.2
9	Tanahu	H	34.6	14.8	−57.2	47	Lalitpur	H	10.1	7.6	−24.8
10	Sankhuwasabha	M	48.7	21.0	−56.9	48	Dolakha	M	33.6	26.0	−22.6
11	Dhading	H	43.3	18.8	−56.6	49	Jhapa	T	13.4	10.6	−20.9
12	Rolpa	H	58.7	26.0	−55.7	50	Myagdi	H	34.8	28.6	−17.8
13	Bhojpur	H	52.5	24.4	−53.5	51	Jajarkot	H	44.1	37.7	−14.5
14	Khotang	H	53.5	25.0	−53.3	52	Dhanusa	T	26.9	23.1	−14.1
15	Nawalparasi	T	36.3	17.0	−53.2	53	Kapilbastu	T	40.1	35.5	−11.5
16	Okhaldhunga	H	42.7	20.5	−52.0	54	Achham	H	51.6	47.2	−8.5
17	Palpa	H	42.9	21.6	−49.7	55	Mugu	M	51.0	47.1	−7.6
18	Udayapur	H	50.8	25.9	−49.0	56	Morang	T	17.2	16.5	−4.1
19	Taplejung	M	51.8	27.0	−47.9	57	Kalikot	H	56.8	57.9	1.9
20	Ramechhap	H	48.0	25.6	−46.7	58	Doti	H	46.4	48.9	5.4
21	Lamjung	H	31.5	16.8	−46.7	59	Dadeldhura	H	40.3	43.3	7.4
22	Gorkha	H	38.2	20.4	−46.6	60	Dolpa	M	39.7	42.8	7.8
23	Rukum	H	49.1	26.3	−46.4	61	Rautahat	T	30.2	33.4	10.6
24	Nuwakot	H	37.4	20.3	−45.7	62	Bara	T	26.9	29.9	11.2
25	Solukhumbu	M	46.3	25.7	−44.5	63	Siraha	T	29.0	34.6	19.3
26	Mahottari	T	29.1	16.2	−44.3	64	Bajhang	M	47.3	56.8	20.1
27	Sunsari	T	21.2	12.0	−43.4	65	Baitadi	H	36.8	45.7	24.2

28	Baglung	H	40.2	22.9	−43.0	66	Parsa	T	23.5	29.2	24.3
29	Rupandehi	T	30.0	17.3	−42.3	67	Bajura	M	48.2	64.1	33.0
30	Dang	T	42.9	25.1	−41.5	68	Humla	M	41.5	56.0	34.9
31	Gulmi	H	42.5	25.6	−39.8	69	Darchula	M	37.7	53.0	40.6
32	Rasuwa	M	50.9	31.6	−37.9	70	Saptari	T	28.0	39.5	41.1
33	Pyuthan	H	51.5	32.2	−37.5	71	Jumla	M	34.4	49.0	42.4
34	Salyan	H	45.5	28.8	−36.7	72	Bhaktapur	H	8.7	12.5	43.7
35	Sindhuli	H	60.3	38.3	−36.5	73	Mustang	M	25.8	40.0	55.0
36	Bardiya	T	44.9	28.7	−36.1	74	Kathmandu	H	4.4	7.6	72.7
37	Banke	T	41.2	26.4	−35.9	75	Manang	M	21.2	36.9	74.1
38	Makwanpur	H	43.0	27.9	−35.1						

Source: Small Area Estimation of Poverty …. CBS (2006, 2013).
Note: EB = ecological belt, M = mountain, H = hill, T = terai.

to 2004. For example, Bajura, which is one of the remotest mountain districts, poverty rate had increased to 64.1 percent from 48.2 percent in 2006.

Likewise, all five districts in the Karnali Zone are mountain districts and have high poverty rates: Jumla (49.0 percent), Humla (56.0 percent), Dolpa (42.8 percent) Kalikot 57.9 percent) and Mugu (47.1 percent). With the exception of Mugu, which recorded a decline in poverty rate by 7.6 percentage points in 2011 as compared to 2006, the rest exhibited an increase: Jumla by 42.4 percentage points, Humla by 35.0 percentage points, Dolpa by 7.8 percentage points and Kalikot by 2.0 percentage points. The high poverty rates in the Karnali Zone were a consequence of the feudal nature of the state and politics in Nepal for centuries that discriminated against geographically remote districts in the allocation of resources and delivery of state facilities to the people.

Third, the percentage of poor tends to be lower in urbanized districts; for example, Kaski has the lowest poverty rate (4.0 percent), Illam has 7.3 percent and Kathmandu and Lalitpur have 7.6 percent each, and Bhaktapur has 12.5 percent. The low poverty rate in these districts was the outcome of state reinforcing the inherited advantages of urban districts dominated by the landowning class, upper caste and elite groups that were linked with the top politicians and power circles in the centre and provided the political base for the regime. Even though Kathmandu and Bhaktapur have lower poverty rates, these rates are higher compared to 2006 rates of 4.4 percent and 8.4 percent, respectively. The increase in the percentage of poor in these districts indicates growing urban poverty, which is the result of growing rural-urban migration and state indifference towards effective management of the population pressure on housing as well as basic infrastructure and services. As a consequence, an increasingly larger number of people who migrated to urban areas in search of employment were compelled to join the crowd of urban poor and live as squatters.

2.6.3 Poverty by Caste/Ethnicity

People belonging to minority and ethnic groups are at a great disadvantage to benefit from the facilities and opportunities extended by the government and have limited occupational choices. For instance, poverty is higher among Hill Dalit (43.6 percent), Terai Dalit (38.2 percent), Hill ethnics (28.3 percent, Terai ethnics (25.9 percent) and Terai middle class (28.7 percent) than among Brahmin, Chhetri and Other caste/ethnics (Table 2.8). Men and women from the disadvantaged communities and ethnic tribes are mostly engaged in low-grade, low-paid jobs because of their low or lack of skill and face challenges of job insecurity. Even in same-grade jobs, they are discriminated against at work and in wages. Economic hardships of such families coupled with living in crowded slums often resulted in social quarrels with frequent use of physical violence, child labour, alcoholism, etc., which further aggravated hardships and poverty.

2.7 Multidimensional Poverty

Oxford Poverty and Human Development Initiatives (OPHI) estimated Multidimensional Poverty Index (MPI) for Nepal for 2006 and 2010, incorporating ten indicators across three important dimensions of poverty, such as health,

Table 2.8 Poverty by Caste/Ethnicity

SN	*Caste/Ethnicity*	*Poverty Rate*
1	Hill Brahmin	10.3
2	Hill Chhetri	23.4
3	Terai Brahmin	18.6
4	Terai Middle Caste	28.7
5	Hill Dalit	43.6
6	Terai Dalit	38.2
7	Newar	10.3
8	Hill Ethnics	28.3
9	Terai Ethnics	25.9
10	Muslim	20.2
11	Others	12.3

Source: Poverty in Nepal, CBS (2011).

education and living standard, multiple deprivations that people face at the same time. This Index is broader than income or expenditure measures which do not fully account for other components of human well-being, such as education, health, nutrition, life expectancy and access to clean water and electricity, that are necessary for individuals in order to function effectively in the society. In 2006, the MPI of Nepal was 64.7 percent, while the use of US$1.25 a day per capita as a poverty measure gave a lower figure of 55.0 percent. The poverty level shoots up to 78.0 percent when US$2.0 a day per capita is used as a poverty measure (Sabina and Santos, 2010). All three estimates of poverty made by OPHI are much higher than the government estimate. In 2010, the MPI showed a large reduction compared to 2006 but was still far higher than the NLSS estimate of 25.2 percent.

A study conducted by ICIMOD (2017) in 2011/2 shows wide variation in multidimensional poverty across 23 surveyed districts of Nepal. The report revealed that three (Humla, Bajhang and Mugu) out of nine mountain districts are among the four poorest districts. This indicated that poverty was highly concentrated in the Far-Western and Karnali Regions. On the other hand, two mountain districts in the Eastern Region (Dolakha and Solukhumbu) were among the five districts with the lowest multidimensional poverty rates.

Among the four terai districts surveyed, Saptari had the highest poverty rate (84.9 percent), followed by Siraha (74.1 percent) and Kailali (61.6 percent). Of the ten surveyed hill districts, Jajarkot (79.2 percent), Bhojpur (75.4 percent) and Khotang (73.6 percent) had the highest poverty rates, while two districts (Kavrepalanchok and Terhathum) had the lowest rates (Table 2.9).

2.8 Poverty by Federal Province

The poverty rates by province (Table 2.10) show the highest level of multidimensional poverty rate (51.2 percent) in Karnali Province, which implies that every second person is multidimensionally poor (NPC, 2018). Madesh Province has the second-highest multidimensional poverty rate (47.9 percent), followed by

Table 2.9 MPI Value, Headcount and Intensity by District

SN	*District*	*Index Value*	*Headcount (Percent)*	*Intensity (Percent)*
1	Bajhang	0.45	87.6	51.4
2	Saptari	0.43	84.9	50.4
3	Humla	0.41	90.7	45.7
4	Jajarkot	0.40	79.2	50.1
5	Mugu	0.37	83.9	44.5
6	Khotang	0.35	73.6	47.7
7	Bhojpur	0.35	75.4	46.3
8	Sindhuli	0.35	67.9	51.2
9	Udayapur	0.33	70.1	47.6
10	Taplejung	0.31	68.2	45.6
11	Kailali	0.31	61.6	49.5
12	Siraha	0.30	74.1	40.4
13	Rukum	0.26	58.0	45.0
14	Dailekh	0.26	58.2	44.8
15	Darchula	0.24	54.9	44.2
16	Sunsari	0.21	52.5	40.2
17	Sankhuwasabha	0.20	47.9	41.5
18	Sindhupalchok	0.17	42.2	41.2
19	Gorkha	0.17	41.4	39.8
20	Solukhumbu	0.14	36.1	39.4
21	Terhathum	0.13	29.9	43.1
22	Kavrepalanchok	0.08	20.3	38.6
23	Dolakha	0.04	11.9	37.8

Source: ICIMOD (2017).

Table 2.10 MPI by Province (in Percent)

	Area Share (Percent)	*Population Share (Percent)*	*MPI Value*	*Headcount Ratio (Percent)*	*Intensity (Percent)*
National (total)	147,181 sq. km	26.49 million (2011)	0.127	28.6	44.3
Province 1	17.6	17.1	0.085	19.7	43.2
Madhesh Province	6.6	20.4	0.217	47.9	45.3
Bagmati Province	13.8	20.9	0.051	12.2	41.9
Gandaki Province	15.3	9.1	0.061	14.2	42.9
Lumbini Province	11.8	17.0	0.133	29.9	44.3
Karnali Province	21.6	5.9	0.230	51.2	44.9
Sudurpaschim Province	13.3	9.6	0.146	33.6	43.5

Source: Nepal MPI: Analysis towards Action, 2018, NPC, Government of Nepal.

Sudurpaschim Province (33.6 percent). Bagmati Province has the lowest poverty rate (12.2 percent), while Gandaki Province has the second-lowest rate (14.2 percent).

The highest incidence of poverty in Karnali Province, Madesh Province and Sudurpaschim Province corroborates the earlier findings of concentration of poverty in mountain districts, remote hill districts and backward terai districts. Karnali Province has five mountain districts (Dolpa, Jumla, Kalikot, Mugu and Humla) and five remote hill districts (Rukum, Salyan, Surkhet, Dailekh and Jajarkot). Sudurpaschim Province has three mountain districts (Darchula, Bajhang and Bajura), four remote hill districts (Baitadi, Dadeldhura, Doti and Achham) and one underdeveloped terai district (Kailali), while Madesh Province is a province in the south-eastern region of Nepal bordered by India in the South. It has eight districts which are all in the terai belt (Parsa, Bara, Rauthat, Sarlahi, Mahottari, Dhanusa, Siraha and Saptari). This province hosts the largest proportion of total population (20.4 percent) with the smallest proportion of total area (6.6 percent).

2.9 Nepal's Poverty in SAARC Countries' Context

The SAARC countries (Bangladesh, Bhutan, India, Maldives, Pakistan and Sri Lanka), despite their heterogeneity in terms of geography, population size and level of development, share the common problem of poverty. South Asia had the second-highest concentration of the world's extreme poverty (33.4 percent) in 2013 next to Sub-Saharan Africa, which accounted for the largest share (50.7 percent) of global poor (Deyshappriya, 2018).

Intra-regional comparison of poverty rates across SAARC countries presents considerable challenges because comparable poverty data are not available. However, the World Bank has estimated the poverty rate of individual countries by calculating the proportion of people whose aggregate per capita consumption is lower than US$1.90 a day, the international poverty line (IPL) for low-income countries.

A comparison of poverty rates of SAARC countries in the late 1980s and the late 1990s shows that five countries (Bangladesh, India, Nepal and Sri Lanka experienced a decline and Pakistan an increase in national poverty rate while Sri Lanka had the lowest poverty rate in both decades (Table 2.11)). In the 1980s, Nepal's poverty rate at 42.0 percent was the second highest in the region, next to Bangladesh which had a poverty rate of 58.8 percent. The same pattern prevailed in the 1990s, with Bangladesh reducing poverty by 9.0 percentage points, while the reduction was only 4.0 percentage points in Nepal (ISACPA, 2003). According

Table 2.11 Poverty Rate of SAARC Countries for Different Years (in Percent)

Country	*Late 1980s**	*Late 1990s**	*2012***	*Year****	*at $1.90 a day*
Bangladesh	58.8	49.8	31.5	2016	14.3
Bhutan	–	–	23.2	2017	1.5
India	38.9	26.1	37.2	2011	22.5
Maldives	–	34.0	–	2019	–
Nepal	42.0	38.0	25.2	2010	15.0
Pakistan	26.6	32.2	22.2	2015	4.4
Sri Lanka	25.0	21.0	8.9	2016	0.9
China	–	–	2.8	2019	0.5

Source: * Our Future Our Responsibility: Road Map Towards a Poverty Free South Asia, SAARC, 2003, **The Little Data Book, The World Bank, 2012, *** The World Bank Data.

to World Bank data for 2012, Nepal's national poverty rate at 25.2 percent was the third highest, with India on the top (37.2 percent), followed by Bangladesh (31.5 percent). On the contrary, Pakistan and Bhutan had almost the same national poverty rate (22.2 and 23.2 percent), while Sri Lanka had the lowest rate (0.9 percent).

The World Bank data on the poverty of SAARC countries at $1.90 a day is related to different years and hence not comparable. However, a comparison can be made between Nepal and India as the reference years were almost the same (2010 and 2011, respectively). At $1.90 a day, the poverty rate of Nepal at 15.0 percent was lower than that of India, which had 22.5 percent.

Deyshappriya (2018) estimated the international poverty of SAARC countries at $1.90 a day in 2013 based on the PavcalNet of the World Bank. As shown in Figure 2.1, Nepal has the third highest percentage of population living below the IPL of $1.90 a day, next to India with 21.2 percent and Bangladesh with 18.5 percent. In contrast, Sri Lanka has the lowest headcount index (1.9 percent), while Bhutan reported the second lowest (2.2 percent).

Notably, the international poverty rates of lower-middle-income and low-income countries such as India and Bangladesh are higher than that of the South Asian average and considerably higher than the world average, while that of low-income country Nepal is just the average of South Asian and also higher than the world average. In contrast, Sri Lanka's headcount ratio is the lowest in the region, considerably lower than both South Asian and world averages. Other countries of the region which have lower headcount ratios compared to South Asian and world averages are Bhutan, Maldives and Pakistan. It is worth noting that Nepal's national poverty rate was second highest in the SAARC region in the 1980s and the 1990s and third highest in 2012 as well as at $1.90 a day in 2013.

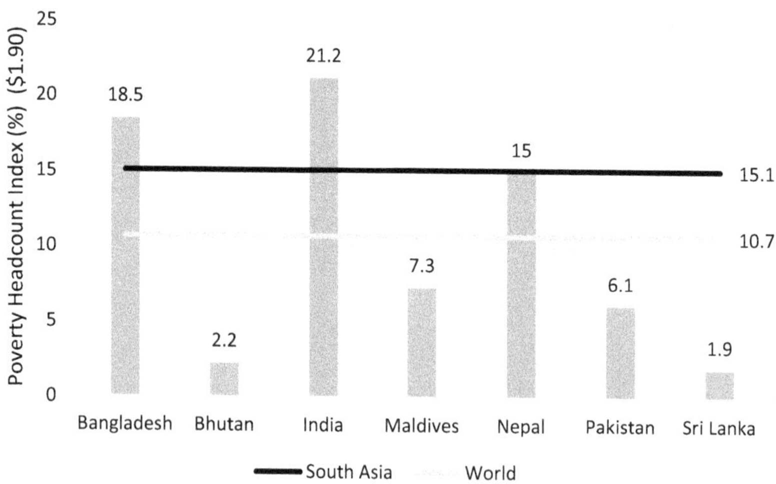

Figure 2.1 Income Poverty of South Asian Countries by 2013.

Source: Deyshappriya (2018).

In contrast, Sri Lanka has been the only country which has consistently exhibited the lowest poverty rate in the region all through the reference years. The comparatively low poverty rate of Sri Lanka is mainly driven by the implementation of policies that boosted poor workers' productivity and provided more effective support to poor households. Productivity was boosted through the right investments in people, like quality education and training, investment in infrastructure in poor areas and reform in the agricultural sector where the majority of the poor are engaged for their livelihoods (Pswarayi-Riddihough, 2016). In addition, state provision of free education and health services, targeted grants, employment creation, land redistribution and employment, social protection programmes and other safety nets, such as *Janasaviya* and *Samurdhi*, have also been significant factors in lowering income poverty.

2.10 Rhetoric of SAARC's Pledges on Regional Poverty Alleviation

SAARC, which is almost dead now mainly because of political feuds between India and Pakistan, had made pledges in its several annual summits to eradicate poverty in the region through joint actions. The SAARC Charter, adopted in December 1985 at the first summit held in Dhaka, mentioned 'enhancing the living standards and improving the welfare of the peoples of South Asia through regional cooperation' as one of the objectives. To this end, the poverty alleviation issue figured as one of the top areas of concern of heads of states of SAARC countries from the sixth summit onwards. The sixth summit that took place in Colombo in 1991 decided to appoint an Independent South Asian Commission on Poverty Alleviation (ISACPA) consisting of eminent persons from member states to conduct an in-depth study and recommend policies to address the pressing poverty issue of the region. The ISACPA brought out a report titled 'Meeting the Challenge' with key recommendations for enhancing regional economic growth and engaging the poor in micro-enterprises and empowering them through social mobilization. The report highlighted various success cases of social mobilization in empowering the poor, such as Bangladesh Rural Advancement Committees, Agha Khan Rural Support Program of Pakistan and SEWA of India. The Seventh SAARC Summit held in Dhaka in 1993 endorsed the ISACPA report and expressed its commitment to eradicate poverty from the region by 2002 through an agenda of action which included a strategy of social mobilization, policy of decentralized agricultural development and small-scale, labour-intensive industrialization and human development, among other activities. However, the commitments remained only on paper, and poverty continued to remain as pressing a problem as in the past with South Asia housing 40.0 percent of the world's poor with historically entrenched deprivation of people across gender, class, caste, religion and locality.

The Eighth SAARC Summit (New Delhi, May 1995) endorsed the recommendations of the finance/planning ministers (Dhaka, July 1994) to establish a three-tier mechanism consisting of (i) a group of secretaries dealing with poverty eradication and social development in member countries as the first tier,

(ii) finance and planning secretaries as the second tier and (iii) finance/planning ministers as the third tier for exchanging information on poverty eradication. There was much fanfare about these tiers in the beginning with meetings in member countries alternatively. The meetings were centred on poverty eradication issues in the region, and each meeting came out with a bunch of recommendations which all appeared as 'old wine in a new bottle'.

In the 11th SAARC summit held in Kathmandu in 2002, heads of state and government expressed serious concern over the extent and depth of poverty in member countries and reiterated the need to reinvigorate regional poverty reduction activities in the context of the UN General Assembly's Millennium Development Goals by 2015, and of other commitments made in the international forums. The summit reconstituted the ISACPA to review the progress of regional cooperation on poverty alleviation and prepare a strategy and a plan of action for a poverty-free South Asia. The ISACPA brought out a report titled 'Our Future Our Responsibility' in 2003 in the same pattern as the first report, documenting the regional best practices and recommending actions for mobilizing the power of the poor, mainstreaming the informal economy, prudent macroeconomics, enhancing gender and other equities and effective, harmonious and all-round cooperation of member states. The report also suggested a target of halving poverty in the region by 2010 through a poverty-reducing growth rate of above 6.0 percent combined with micro- and macro-level policies to address the poor directly.

In the successive summits too, poverty alleviation was declared as the vital objective of SAARC activities. The Islamabad summit (2004), besides declaring poverty alleviation as the priority goal, desired ISACPA to continue working as an advocacy forum and to prepare a set of SAARC Development Goals (SDGs) for future consideration. The Dhaka Summit (2005), declared 2006–15 as the SAARC Decade of Poverty Alleviation and formalized the SAARC Development Fund (SDF). The SDF set up by the 16th SAARC Summit held in Thimphu, Bhutan, in 2010 had the objectives of supporting industrial development, poverty alleviation, protection of environment, institutional/human resource development and promotion of social and infrastructure development projects in the SAARC region. In the 17th summit held in Maldives in 2011, the member countries reiterated the need for deepening regional efforts for poverty alleviation with a commitment to achieve the SDGs soon. The 19th SAARC summit was supposed to be held in Islamabad in November 2016 but was cancelled after India announced its boycott of the summit because of an attack on an Indian army camp in Kashmir (Uri attacks) alleging Pakistan's involvement in the attack. Later, Bangladesh, Afghanistan, Bhutan, Sri Lanka and Maldives also pulled out of the summit. Since then, the SAARC summit has been stalled.

Three decades have gone by since the SAARC was established with regional poverty alleviation as one of the major goals along with the promotion of regional cooperation in agriculture and rural development, industry, trade and finance, environment and energy, science and technology education, security and culture and others. But the achievements have remained abysmal. Commenting on what SAARC has achieved in regional poverty alleviation, Kelegama says,

> Over the last two decades we have seen a plethora of poverty related declarations, high-powered Commissions, Plans of Action on Poverty Alleviation, setting SDGs, promoting regional projects, preparation of SAARC Poverty Profiles, establishing SDF, and so on, to combat poverty in the region. When one looks at SAARC Declarations, it can be seen that there is reference to poverty alleviation in all of them. The intention of SAARC leaders for poverty alleviation needs nothing but praise; however, most of these intentions have far from been achieved. The implementation has been poor and moni toring weak and as a result, none of the set targets on poverty alleviation by SAARC leaders could be achieved.
>
> (Kalegama, 2014)

Some SAARC countries like Sri Lanka achieved some progress in poverty alleviation, but this was mainly due to their own efforts rather than regional initiatives.

2.11 Micro-finance and Poverty Alleviation

Nepal started micro-credit or micro-finance (MF; exclusively women) as a tool for reducing poverty in 1992, replicating the Bangladesh Grameen model of MF delivery. The MF programme is premised on the logic that the poor are constrained by a lack of fund to start self-employment and income-earning activities and providing small amounts of credit would spur them to engage in profitable activities. Traditional commercial banks avoid this population because loans are too small for earning profit and also risky because the borrowers are too poor to offer adequate collateral. This gap was filled by MF banking practices, which are built around providing small loans on a group basis (exclusively women) without collateral and mobilizing tiny savings from group members. The government of Nepal established five Grameen Bikas Banks between 1992 and 1996 (now consolidated into one) as MF banks and also encouraged the private sector to establish MF institutions through an easy licensing policy. As a result, micro-finance institutions (MFIs) proliferated over the years, and their number, as of mid-August 2019, was 90, with 3,667 branches spread in various parts of the country. But this number is reduced in the recent years because of merger as many MFIs were financially unsound, weak in governance and weak in stiff competition, and some were subject to Nepal Rastra Bank's prompt corrective action against capital inadequacy. While there was much fanfare of MF in the beginning, lately its effectiveness in reaching the poor and contributing to lifting them out of poverty has come to be severely questioned. Various studies have shown that with the increase in the number of MFIs, anomalies and distortions have also increased, indicating that MF is not a magic bullet for poverty alleviation (Poudyal, 2007).

First, the MF is a supply-push scheme premised on the classical notion of 'supply creates its own demand', which means that if only credit could be supplied, the poor would automatically demand it to engage in self-employment micro-enterprises and lift themselves out of poverty. This assumes an abundance of investment opportunities in the locality surrounding the poor, and they would be able to engage in profitable activities once the funds were available. This is an erroneous assumption because opportunities may not exist in all places, and even where these exist, the poor may not be knowing and even if they were knowing, managing the activities may not be within their capability. Moreover, starting income-earning activities would require supportive facilities, as well as marketing and physical infrastructure, which may not exist in rural areas. Under such circumstances, expecting the poor to approach the MFIs for credit is to divorce from reality. The outreach of MF has been very low, and even non-eligible borrowers have accessed the facility. A World Bank study in 2002 estimated very low outreach of MF activities with coverage of only 6.5 percent of the total number of poor and observed that 'even after more than a decade of micro-finance in Nepal, most of the poor have not yet even been touched by these activities' (World Bank, 2002: 76). Various evaluation studies of MF activities revealed that the benefits of the schemes did not reach the intended poor, but a sizeable part of the benefits was siphoned off by the relatively better off. Even when the programmes were targeted to the poor, their selection was often biased towards those relatively better off among the poor. A study estimated that 31.4 percent of the clients who benefitted from the MF programme were ineligible borrowers and that the outreach was only 25.2 percent, while another study revealed that 22.5 percent of the beneficiaries of the MF programme were not eligible for the credit (CEPRUD, 2004, 2007). Fundamentally, the MFIs are caught on the horns of a dilemma between the sustainability of the MF programme and providing credit to the poor. Sustainability required a higher interest rate close to the market rate because of high operational costs owing to operation in geographically difficult areas, while reaching the poor with credit required a lower interest rate. The compromise between the two opposing ends has led to the inclusion of even ineligible borrowers in the credit programme. This also explains why the MFIs are unwilling to go to remote and inaccessible parts of hills and mountains where financial services are very few and far between.

Second, many MFIs maintained high recovery rates by binding clients to the repayment of instalments of principal and interest, even before the activities start yielding income. This forced the clients to borrow from another MFI to meet the debt repayment schedule and repetition of this practice over and again. This was made possible by the presence of a multitude of MFIs in the same area, which led to unhealthy competition, such as snatching each other's clients and cross-lending to the same clients. A case study of MF borrowers of the Jhapa and Rupandehi districts of Nepal (Kumar et al., 2019) revealed a number of flaws and mischiefs in the MFIs. First, borrowers actually get far less than the sanctioned credit amount because of the deduction of various charges and fees, such as service charges, loan insurance and livestock insurance, and the first repayment instalment. It was found that on a loan of Rs. 100,000.0, the borrowers got only Rs. 87,266.0. Second, almost all the MF borrowers in the study area had resorted to multiple borrowings due to their failure to repay loans on time. Failure to pay a loan from one MFI pushed them to borrow from the next MFI to repay that loan, and so on, leading to the spiralling of borrowing from several MFIs. Third, borrowers were often mentally tortured by denying them even a few days' extension for repayment of loans by staging sit-ins at their houses, eventually dispossessing them from their small homesteads. Some women farmers burdened under the weight of their MF debts and evictions from their homes had been compelled to commit suicides. These pathetic episodes in the MFI sector raise serious question on governance issues and practices and also the lackadaisical attitude of Nepal Rastra Bank to effectively regulate these financial institutions and control their malpractices.

2.12 Demolition of Squatters' Settlements and Poverty

Squatters' settlements in Kathmandu Valley are mostly located along the river banks and a few other locations. A study shows that there are 40 settlements along the banks of Bagmati, Hanumante, Bishnumati, Dhobikhola and Tukucha rivers and other locations of Kathmandu Valley (Deshar, 2013). On the other hand, Nepal Landless Democratic Union Party estimated 73 squatter settlements in Kathmandu, Lalitpur and Bhaktapur, and stated that out of 29,000 squatter families living in Kathmandu Valley, around 8,000 families lived along the Bagmati river-banks alone (Kathmandu Post, 2017).

The history of squatter settlements on the bank of Bagmati River shows that these were established more than 50 years ago but they were few in comparison to the present. The growth rate was 37.94 percent in 2008, 39.16 percent in 2009, 24.79 percent in 2010 and 15.83 percent in 2011 (Deshar, 2013). According to 'Lumanti Support Group for Shelter', a non-governmental organization (NGO) working in the field of improving shelter conditions of urban poor since 1994, Kathmandu Valley witnessed an increase in the number of squatter settlements from 17 in 1985 to 45 in 2008. On the other hand, the Society for the Preservation of Shelters and Habitation in Nepal estimated that there were approximately four million squatters, living in cities and towns, including 50,000 in Kathmandu in 2007 (Gallagher, 2016).

There is no official data on forced evictions and displacement of squatters' settlements. The eviction of squatters' settlements had already taken place before 2008 in districts, such as Nepalgunj, Dangadhi and other places, but no information is available about these. In the last decade, the largest forceful demolition was that of settlements on the banks of the Bagmati River at Thapathali in Kathmandu. In the past year alone, about a dozen squatters' settlements in different parts of the country were forcefully demolished by local governments. A few cases of demolition presented next broadly indicate the economic hardships and psychological trauma of the evicted settlers.

(i) **Demolition of Settlement at Thapathali**: On 8 May 2012, the government deployed more than 2,000 security personnel to forcefully demolish 260 squatters' huts on the banks of the Bagmati River at Thapathali, rendering them homeless and injuring more than two dozen people. This settlement sprang up around 1968 but surged significantly after 2007 (Kiran and Pahari, 2012). Most of the settlers in the Thapathali settlement area belonged to Janajati (ethnic) groups, of Nepal: the Rais, Limbus, Tamangs, etc., and have migrated from the hilly region and the adjoining districts of Kathmandu Valley, Sindhuli, Kavre and Sindhupalchowk owing to easy accessibility (Kiran and Pahari, 2012). Some of the settlers had spent their hard-earned income and even borrowed money for improvements of dwellings. The huts were bulldozed chaotically amidst cries of women and children, not even allowing time for the community to save whatever precious little belongings, such as utensils, tools, clothes and citizenship and other documents they had. Some saw their income sources, such as a small shop, a vegetable cart and other essential items, destroyed in the demolition. A local school run by an NGO, providing education for some 150 children, was among the first buildings to be destroyed (HIC, 2012).

Government efforts to resettle the displaced settlers in the land of the Himal Cement Factory at Chovar, which has been defunct for over a decade, were protested by local residents. Likewise, the government's plan to settle 58 families in the Sundarighat area of Lalitpur, which was previously acquired for the construction of a sewerage system, was also opposed by the locals on grounds that land earmarked for sewerage construction should not be used for a different purpose and the settlers would spoil the local environment. The plan to resettle the evicted squatters thus went into disarray, and they continued staying there. The latest attempt by Kathmandu metropolitan city to forcefully demolish the settlement on 28 November 2022 was also thwarted by the settlers.

(ii) **Demolition of Settlement at Kusumkhola, Madi**: On 18 July 2020, a joint team of Chitwan National Park officials and the Nepal Army destroyed Chepang (indigenous and vanishing community) settlement at Kusumkhola, Madi, Chitwan, using elephants to pull down the huts and setting fires. According to the 2011 Census, the Chepangs constitute a very small segment of the population, estimated at 68,000, and are categorized as a highly marginalized and vanishing community. The Chepang community had been there from a long time back, probably since 1992, and originated from the hill districts of Gorkha and Makwanpur after being displaced by floods and landslides. It is stated that the Chepang people were allowed by the Madi municipality itself to settle in the Kusum Khola area.

According to the Ward chairman, Sri Hari Subedi,

> The Chepang families have been living in Kusum Khola on government-owned land for almost 30 years now. Apart from not owning their own land, they are deprived of education, jobs, and access to essential services. Thus destroying their homes in such a manner is a condemnable act on the part of park authorities.
>
> (Sakarweb WordPress, 2020)

(iii) **Demolition of Settlements at Hatkohla and Panchamukhi Settlements of Jhapa**: On 9 April 2021, 20 squatters' huts at Hatkhola and Panchamukhi of Damak-7, Jhapa were bulldozed by deploying 100 security forces to construct a shopping complex at a cost of Rs. 40.0

million in the hometown of then prime minister KP Oli. The families had been living there for about four decades. Some settlers, resenting the local government's action of demolition without making alternative housing arrangements, were harassed and even detained in custody. Damak municipality mayor RN Oli, a nephew of KP Oli, defended the demolition, saying that they were not the real landless and had houses elsewhere and were given 15 days' notice for evacuation (Nayapatrika, 2021). The demolition of the settlement was condemned as an act of cruelty to the most vulnerable community by Amnesty International Nepal and the Madi municipality mayor.

(iv) **Demolition of Squatters Settlement at Manohara for Planned Development**: The government started the Manohara Land Pooling Project some 18 years ago to resettle some 742 indigenous and Dalit families in an organized way with infrastructure facilities, such as a road, sewerage, electricity, drinking water, health facility and school, on the basis of the land pooling model. The settlement is stretched along the Hanumante River corridor close to the Tribhuvan International Airport, and squatters have been staying there for the past several years. Under the pretext of developing and modernizing the settlement, squatters were dispersed to different places and even a Korean school was demolished. But the progress remained slow with only 30 percent of the work completed in the last ten years because of reluctance on the part of the government and project authorities to speed up the work. The slow progress of the project has drawn accusations and counter-accusations between the project authorities and the settlers without any outcome. In this tussle, the settlers were to suffer the most.

The forceful demolition of squatters' settlements as those presented earlier and in other places such as Nagarkot, Butwal, Changunarayan and Butwal show a gross violation of the constitution of Nepal which stipulates that every citizen shall have the right to appropriate housing and no citizen shall be evicted from the residence owned by him, nor shall his or her residence be infringed, except in accordance with law (Article 37.1 and 37.2). The evictions in Nagarkot and Butwal reveal government cruelty to human beings, as these demolitions were carried out during the rainy season when people needed their own roofs for protection against rain. Issuing a statement on the Nagarkot incident, the chief of Amnesty International Nepal said, 'I saw people losing their houses and all their belongings overnight in Nagarkot. The local government evicted people from roadsides with the help of police. Such forced eviction is not permitted under international laws to which Nepal is party' and added that government authorities needed to give an alternative to affected people. 'I do not think affected people will reject the local government's offer if they are given a fair deal' (Kamat, 2019).

The issue of landless squatters has been at the centre stage of national politics after the restoration of multiparty democracy following the People's Movement of 1990. The concern by the political parties in power has resulted in the formation of Landless Squatters Problem Resolution Commission to identify and address the problems of landless squatters. In the last 30 years, a total of 15 commissions have been formed, but the landless squatters' problems have remained the same as they were in the beginning. A report by Pokhrel (2018) of the Centre for Investigative Journalism, Nepal reveals a very treacherous picture of misuse of authority by these commissions to register landownership mainly to those persons with political connections, party cadres and kith and kins of commission members despite their possession of land, while leaving out the genuinely landless squatters.

> A total of 15 commissions, including those led by Bal Bahadur Rai and Shailaja Acharya, have been formed in the last 28 years with the same purpose. According to the Ministry of Land Reforms and Management, among these, six commissions distributed 46,694 bighas (11712.6 ha) of land to 154,856 families, so far. However, instead of minimizing the problem, it is getting tricky. If the record of the 14th Commission formed on June 16, 2014 led by Sharada Prasad Subedi is to be considered, there is a staggering figure of 861,000 families, who are landless.
>
> (Pokhrel, 2018)

From 2014 onwards three more commissions were constituted led by Bikram Pandey, Devi Gyanwali and Keshav Niraula, respectively, in 2016, 2019 and 2022. The first two commissions ended not initiating any work and the last (National Land Commission), which is a bigger one, has initiated some work.

Government authorities often justify demolitions on the ground that squatters are illegal occupants of public land and have damaged the aesthetic value of the city. But this is a naive view of the hard reality that lies behind forcing people to live in river corridors and in very unhygienic conditions and heavily polluted environments. The poor people are there not by their desire but by the dire necessity of finding a place for shelter either because they had lost their dwellings due to flood/landslides or because they were made landless by the landed aristocracy and village moneylenders. However, the growth in squatters' settlements cannot be simply taken as the consequences of natural disasters but is linked to the long-drawn historical process of marginalization, deprivation and exclusion of lower caste, aboriginal and ethnic people by the upper caste people and rulers of Nepal in different epochs of time. This is also associated with the rapid rate of urbanization and increasing urban poverty on the one hand and the failure of the government to ensure the protection of the right of people to minimum housing on the other. The search of poor/landless people for settlement space landed them in less valuable lands, such as riverbanks, steep slopes, dumping grounds, abandoned plots, land along roadsides and wasteland. And they are the people who had contributed and are still contributing their labour to build infrastructure, high-rise luxury apartments, office buildings, bungalows and city amenities for the use of the capitalist class and rulers of the country. Moreover, they also work as household maids for the rich and merchant class. Sometimes compulsory eviction of settlements may be necessary to make way for expansion of city area or improvement/expansion of roads or construction of infrastructure projects, but it is inhumane to smash the homes and hard-earned physical property making the settlers worse off than before.

2.13 COVID-19 Pandemic and Poverty

The COVID-19 pandemic 2020–1 severely disrupted the economic activities of the country, with severe impact on the poor. The poor were forced to suffer the most because the measures to slow the spread of the pandemic were more hostile to the poor as compared to the rich. The various ways through which the life was made more difficult to the poor and vulnerable people were:

First, with the onslaught of the pandemic, the government announced a nationwide lockdown suddenly from 24 March 2020 initially for 15 days but extended for two months, imposing a complete ban on the movement of people out of houses and suspension of public transport and other services. Government advised people to stay safe from infection adopting measures, such as physical distancing, washing hands with soap several times a day, using sanitizers frequently, using face masks, eating nutritious food and storing food items for a week. But expecting the poor wage earners and displaced workers who are mostly migrant workers from hills and terai to adopt all such practices was a mockery of reality. They live in crowded conditions with five to ten persons in a small room, which is also used as a makeshift kitchen along with other families in the same building, and share a common toilet and tap or well with limited water supply. As daily wage earners, how could they store food for a week when they did not have money even for one meal a day? They faced a severe food crisis with a greater risk of dying from starvation than from the coronavirus. The government should have arranged free food and water distribution to such people but interfered and banned free food distribution organized by the youths of various volunteer organizations such as 100's Group, Hamro Team Nepal and Hiteri Foundation. About 700 hungry used to come to Khulamanch (Open Theatre) every day, walking for three to five hours, for free meals. This humanitarian work was not tolerable to Kathmandu Metropolis because youths were doing what it should have done during the crisis period. So it harassed and obstructed free food distribution in October 2020, charging the organizations for starting the programme without permission, spreading dirt, polluting the surrounding area and tarnishing the city's beauty.

Second, a large number of migrant workers of Kathmandu and surrounding areas estimated at around 200,000 started their journey back to villages immediately with the announcement of the lockdown to save themselves from further hardships. As public transport was banned, a large number with women and children started walking toward their hometowns with little belongings. But even walking was problematic because they had to escape police vigilance, or else they would be reverted back because of government restrictions on the movement of people. The pathetic condition of such people was narrated as: 'When spotted on the highway on Tuesday, some ten persons, (all wage earners) had been on the road for straight three days from Kathmandu to walk 200 km to their villages in Rautahat district. They said that they slept where they could, ate what they could find along the way, the lucky ones could hitch a ride part of the way, and all along they had to dodge police check points. We thought it is better to go back to our villages rather than stay hungry five people to a room in Kathmandu' (Mishra, 2020). Another media reported, '[S]ome people walked 400–500 km to their home situated in Far-West Nepal and a group of 17 labourers walked from Kathmandu to Rajapur, Bardiya in Western Nepal covering a distance of 575 km for a week' (PTI/Kathmandu, 2020).

Third, production halt in the informal sector, particularly non-agriculture, which encompasses trade, craft, transport, hotels, restaurants, etc., that are mainly labour intensive in nature laid off millions of workers at one shot. According to Nepal Labour Force Survey (NLF) 2017/18, of the total labour force of 7.09 million, 4.41 million (62.2 percent) were engaged in the informal sector, and of those employed in the informal sector, 2.9 million (65.9 percent) were engaged in the non-agricultural sector, and of those employed in the informal sector, 23.4 percent were in elementary occupations, followed by craft workers with 21.6 percent and service and sales workers with 21.4 percent. The survey further indicated that 90.9 percent of informal sector and 81.8 percent of formal sector workers were from rural areas (CBS, 2017/18). Almost all such workers in the informal sector and those working on a daily (41.5 percent of total) and weekly wage basis were out of a job and faced survival crises.

Fourth, poor wage earners and those displaced from their jobs died for want of food and medical treatment, while some committed suicide due to psychological stress emanating from financial stress. Complete information about such deaths is not available because all deaths do not get reported in the national media. However, a few cases, such as the pathetic deaths of Surya Bahadur Tamang (hill ethnic) and Malar Sada (terai ethnic low-caste untouchable Mushar) due to starvation reveal the tear-jerking condition of the poor during the lockdown. Tamang, a porter in Kathmandu city for several decades, was found dead on the sidewalks of Kirtipur on 23 May, exactly two months after the lockdown started. When found dead, he was still clutching the woven jute strap he used to carry loads on his back (Joshi, 2020). Sada, working in Biratnagar as a wage labourer, walked 120 km to his village Pathari in Saptari (terai) in mid-April, a month after the nationwide lockdown, without any money because the contractor had refused to pay, citing the lockdown. Sada's three sons were stuck in Gujrat (India) where they had gone to work and had no money to send home. After a month of homecoming, Sada set out one evening with a spade and umbrella with the hope of finding some underground foodstuff for the family, but the next morning, he was found lying in the field. He succumbed to death the next day because of acute hunger, as the family had nothing to eat for the past five days. Families of several other Mushar youths, who were stuck in Gujarat and other Indian cities for want of money, faced severe food crisis and most of the children suffered from being underweight (Timilsena et al., 2020).

Owing to unbearable hardships and starvation caused by the lockdown, a large number of poor ended their lives by committing suicide. A study revealed that in the first month of the nationwide lockdown, a total of 487 people committed suicide, which was 20 percent more compared with mid-February to mid-March when the number stood at 410 (Neupane, 2020). The data compiled by Nepal Police showed that during the first 74 days of lockdown, a total of 1,227 suicide (16.5 a day) cases were filed, which was considerably higher than that of the previous year which had 5,785 cases of suicide (15.8 a day) during the whole year

(Poudel, 2020). Based on police data and projections, the World Health Organization had put Nepal as a country with the seventh highest suicide rate (24.9 per 100,000) in the world (Pun and Devkota, 2021). There were also several cases of suicide attempts by school-going children because of psychological stress due to their confinement to homes for a prolonged period and lack of entertainment facilities.

Fifth, COVID-19 increased poverty by affecting foreign employment, which has been the major source of foreign currency for the country and has played a significant role in improving the livelihood conditions of many poor households. It is estimated that remittances sent by foreign workers constituted about two-thirds of their family income and contributed to the education of children and access to health services. The effect on poverty has occurred in two ways. First, workers who were about to depart for foreign employment were held back because of suspension of international flights. The government also suspended the issuance of labour permits for those seeking to go for foreign employment from 23 February 2020. Second, the return of a large number of Nepalese migrant workers from the Gulf and other key destinations owing to the loss of jobs had a severe impact on the living condition of their families. A report prepared by Foreign Employment Board estimated 127,000 migrant workers would return back due to job loss and an additional 400,000 would come back in the mid-term due to the expiration of visas and non-renewal of contracts (FEB, 2021). In addition, thousands of Nepalese migrants working in India rushed back to Nepal, walking long distances after losing their jobs through various points of the 1,170 km long open border.

The attitude shown by the government towards poor workers during the COVID-19 pandemic presents a very inhumane picture. When the pandemic spread in the country, the communist party government failed to keep the promises that the party would safeguard the rights of the working class and lower class people to basic needs; work for their well-being and safety of their health was seen nowhere when they really needed it. The government neither provided free food nor cash transfers to these people for easing their food crisis nor supported them with funds for medical expenses. Rather, it interfered with free food distribution to the jobless workers by some voluntary organizations, harassed outgoing workers, instead of facilitating their home return, and slipped in providing extensive testing and prompt procurement and administration of anti-COVID vaccines. As we will explain later, the penchant of some ministers for commission delayed the procurement of test kits, resulting in sub-standard imports.

2.14 Illusion of Poverty Reduction

The poverty scenario of the country as depicted by government data gives the impression of high success in poverty reduction over the last two decades. But as discussed earlier, this is illusionary compared to poverty estimates made by NGOs and international organizations.. Therefore, it would be worthwhile to examine why this has been so.

2.14.1 *Fallacy of Aggregate Figures*

The government data show considerable progress in poverty alleviation since 1995/6. The proportion of the population living below the poverty line was 41.8 percent in 1995/6, but it came down to 18.7 percent in 2017/18. Likewise, a report by NPC also proclaims substantial and ground-breaking progress in reducing multidimensional poverty over the years. According to this report, Nepal halved its MPI between 2006 and 2014 from 59.0 percent in 2006 to 39.0 percent in 2011 and 29.0 percent in 2014 (NPC, 2018).

But the aggregate figure could be deceptive for poor individuals because the issue of poverty is conceptualized as income poverty and is interpreted as mainly resulting from sluggish economic growth, which in turn is attributed to low investment. This is an oversimplified view of the mechanics of poverty and does not help much in understanding how poverty is generated, continued and perpetuated. And the policies and programmes upcoming from such neo-liberal discourse are too broad and mostly aimed at reducing aggregate poverty. This discourse fails to visualize that not all individuals escape from poverty simultaneously, while some may escape from it, others may slip into it.

2.14.2 *Myth of Poverty Reduction*

Between NLSS I and II (1995/6 and 2003/4), poverty declined by 26.1 percentage points or 3.7 percentage points per year on average. This was claimed as a product of 11 years of democratic rule and the product of the Nepali Congress government, which ruled the country most of the years (Mahat, 2005). The democracy-poverty link is questionable because along with democracy, the Nepali Congress government also initiated economic liberalization strategy and reliance on operation of market forces, which were followed in tandem by successive governments. The economic liberalization strategy is anchored in the private ownership of property which is treated as a basic right not to be violated. With initial unequal wealth distribution remaining intact, economic liberalization and greater reliance on market forces tend to disproportionately favour the rich and the capitalist class rather than helping to reduce poverty.

The democratic period in Nepal was characterized by low growth with no progressive asset redistribution schemes and no substantive poverty reduction measures that could have a discernible impact on poverty reduction. Furthermore, from 1995/6 to 2005/6, the entire state machinery, along with a large proportion of government resources, was concentrated on crushing the Maoist armed rebellion. It was, in fact, the Maoist insurgency rather than the government efforts that led to a decline in the poverty rate in two ways. First, owing to the conflict situation in the country, a large number of youths from rural areas went to Malaysia and Gulf countries for gainful employment, and this contributed to increasing income and subsequently higher consumption of their families staying in the villages. The NLSS data show that the proportion of households receiving remittance income increased from 23.4 percent in 1995/6 to 31.9 percent in 2003/4 and to 55.8

percent in 2010/11. The average amount of remittance per recipient household increased from Rs. 15,160.0 per household in 1995/6 to Rs. 34,698.0 per household in 2003/4 and to Rs. 80,436.0 in 2010/11 (CBS, 2011, V2: 80). Second, the exodus of youths from the country created labour shortages in the agricultural as well as non-agricultural (urban/semi-urban) sectors, which pushed up wage rates, which meant a higher income for wage earners and subsequently higher consumption levels and reduction in poverty situations.

2.14.3 Unrealistic Poverty Line

The NLSS of 2010/11 used the poverty line consumption of Rs. 19,261.0 per capita per year to estimate the poverty rate. The US dollar equivalent of this amount at the prevailing exchange rate ($1 = Rs. 72.27) turns out to be $267.00 or $22.25 per month, which comes to less than one-fourth of a dollar per day. This means that the poverty line set by Nepal was abysmally lower than the IPL set by the World Bank at $1.90 per day. It is argued that even the $1.90 per day poverty line is not a realistic measure of poverty as 'anyone living in the US knows that living on $2/day is inadequate to even afford breakfast, let alone adequate nutrition, shelter, or clothing' (Karma, 2019). This means that the consumption standard set by Nepal does not give a realistic estimate of the poverty rate in the country. If we set $1.90/day as the poverty line, the poverty rate would shoot up to more than twice higher than the NLSS (III) estimate of 25.2 percent.

2.14.4 Neglect of Mountain and Remote Hill Districts

The mountain districts in Far-and Mid-Western Regions and some districts of terai where of poverty was widespread and severe, were neglected in the Panchayat regime, they remained neglected in democracy era and continue to be neglected even in the republic era. The NPC study of 1977 revealed highest poverty rate in Far-Western Region (45.8 percent) which included 8 remote mountain districts (Dolpa, Jumla, Mugu, Humla, Kalikot, Bajura, Bajhang and Darchula), 11 hill districts (Rukum, Rolpa, Pyuthan, Salyan, Jajarkot, Dailekh, Surkhet, Achham, Doti, Baitadi, and Dadeldhura) and 5 terai districts (Dangdeukhuri, Banke, Berdiya, Kailali and Kanchanpur). The NPC study findings were corroborated by the NRB study undertaken in 1984/5, which revealed that half of the population of hills and 44.1 percent of mountains were below the poverty line.

The high incidence of poverty in the Far-Western Development Region unfolded by the NPC survey was not heeded by the Panchayat rulers, nor were the findings of the NRB survey taken seriously. Even though the regime divided the country into five regions for balanced development, the remote and backward regions were left in an ambience of hopelessness and continued deprivation. This was in part a result of a feudal political regime that prevailed for 30 years from 1961 to 1991 but also reflects the concentration of development activities in accessible districts and districts which served the self-enriching interests of feudal politicians and elites belonging to higher-income-earning groups.

The era of democratic government that lasted for about 17 years (1991–2008) also failed to improve the poverty situation in the Mid-Western and Far-Western Development Regions. The NLSS I (1995/6) revealed that poverty was twice as high in rural than in urban areas, and more than half of the population in the mountains, 41.0 percent in the hills and 40.0 percent in the terai were below the poverty line. In the NLSS II (2003/4), the incidence of poverty declined by varying rates, but poverty in rural areas was almost four times higher than in urban areas, and the highest incidence of poverty was recorded in the Mid-Western Region (45.0 percent), followed by the Far-Western Region (41.0 percent). The NLSS I and II were conducted in the democratic era and improvement in the poverty situation in NLSS II was not due to government efforts, rather this was due to exogenous factors. Nepal was declared a republic in 2008, and the NLSS conducted three years later showed the poverty rate in rural areas as almost two times higher than in urban areas, with the highest poverty rate (45.6 percent) in the Far-Western Region. The mountain districts Bajura and Bajhang of the Far-Western Region had the highest and third highest poverty rates (64.1 and 56.8 percent respectively) in the country. Likewise, the mountain districts Kalikot and Humla had the second-highest (57.9 percent) and fourth-highest (56.0 percent) poverty rates. The study conducted by ICIMOD in 2017 also revealed the highest poverty rate (90.7 percent) in Humla (Mid-Western Mountain), while Bajhang (Far-Western Mountain) had the second-highest poverty rate (87.6 percent) and Saptari (Eastern Terai) had the third highest poverty rate (84.9 percent).

2.14.5 Worsening Income Inequality

Income inequality has worsened over the years, with a tiny part of the population pre-empting the benefits of whatever little growth had taken place, leaving the vast majority below the subsistence level. As early as 1994, Macfarlane observed,

> Thus on the one hand we have the national statistics of growing literacy, improved health, water, roads, trade, while on the other, the majority of population are, year by year, growing poorer and worse fed and the environment is rapidly deteriorating. This is a strange contradiction. Furthermore, the contrast between a small affluent minority in Kathmandu and other towns who enjoy almost first world standards and the 95 percent who live in poverty is growing ever sharper.
>
> (Macfarlane, 1994: 108–9)

This observation of Macfarlane was reinforced by the results of three rounds of NLSS, which show increasing inequality in income distribution between the rich and the poor over the period 1995/6–2010/11 (Table 2.12).

The distribution of income by decile groups of the population shows that the bottom 80.0 percent shared less than half of total income and their share has continuously declined from 49.8 percent in 1996/7 to 46.6 percent in 2003/4 and further to 43.8 percent in 2010/11. The distribution of consumption also shows the same pattern, but the share of the bottom 80.0 percent increased slightly from

Table 2.12 Distribution of Income and Consumption (in Percent)

Decile of Population	*Income*			*Consumption*	
	1995/6	*2003/4*	*2010/11*	*2003/4*	*2010/11*
Lowest	1.7	2.1	1.5	2.6	3.2
Second	3.6	3.2	2.6	3.6	4.4
Third	4.5	4.0	3.4	4.3	5.1
Fourth	5.5	4.9	4.4	5.0	6.0
Fifth	6.4	5.8	5.4	5.8	7.0
Sixth	7.6	7.0	6.7	6.9	8.1
Seventh	9.1	8.6	8.5	8.3	9.5
Eighth	11.3	11.0	11.2	10.2	11.7
Ninth	15.3	15.7	16.7	14.2	15.6
Tenth	34.9	37.7	39.5	39.1	29.6
Average (Rs.)	7,690	15,162	41,659	15,848	34,829

Source: Nepal Living Standards Survey Report, 1996, 2004 and 2011, CBS, Government of Nepal.

46.7 percent in 2003/4 to 54.8 percent in 2010/11. It is quite clear that the distribution of income is somewhat less unequal and widening further than that of expenditure. From the distributional point of view, both income and consumption expenditure have certain weaknesses as a proxy for 'permanent income'. As Bardhan argues,

> Since current income is often subject to more transient factors, consumption expenditure is sometimes regarded as a better proxy for the distribution of 'permanent income'. Of course, the problem of transient elements may be partially taken care of by pooling and averaging the income data for quite a few years. Again consumption expenditure does not fully reflect the accretion to economic power which income may represent better, even though the way in which income is usually estimated leaves out many important elements of this accretion to economic power (e.g., unrealized capital gains). In any case, consideration of the distribution of current magnitudes like income or consumption independently of asset distribution and organizational structure of the economy gives us only a partial picture of the distribution of economic power.
>
> (Bardhan, 2017: 83)

The Gini coefficient was of the order of 0.43 in 1995/6 but increased to 0.46 in 2003/4 and further to 0.49 in 2010/11. The secular increase in the Gini coefficient over the last 15 years firmly establishes growing income inequality among individuals. This means that the largest gains of development accrued to a small group of the dominant class consisting of landlords and rich farmers, the big industrialists, higher-level bureaucrats and elites as well as professionals estimated to be about 2 to 3 percent of the total population, while the mass of the population consisting of the working class, unemployed or underemployed workers and the poor peasants had only a nominal share in the benefits of development.

Poverty and income inequality in Nepal have been the correlates of inequality in assets, particularly land, which constitutes the main asset in an agrarian country like Nepal. It is the ownership of land that determines the social, political and economic power, as well as access to facilities and opportunities opened up by the government. Land in Nepal has been historically unevenly distributed to maintain the feudal system and exploit the poor and disadvantaged people.

The historically instituted unequal access to land remained unchanged over the years, resulting in growing inequality between a small group of landlords and the mass of peasants. A Farm Management Study carried out by the Ministry of Food and Agriculture in 1961 showed that 46.0 percent of the farm households owned land ranging between 0.15 ha to 0.50 ha accounting for only 10.0 percent of the total cultivated area, while 25 percent of the households held 1.0 ha to above 3.0 ha, controlling as much as 75.0 percent of the total cultivated area (MFA, 1971). In the Panchayat regime, King Mahendra introduced the Land Reform Act in 1964, which for the first time fixed the ceiling on land holdings and the rent on land, but the measures were largely ineffective because the way these were introduced favoured the landlords and rich farmers. The Act was replete with purposively designed loopholes and was implemented in stages throughout the country to safeguard the interest of the privileged classes and big landlords and enable them to make redistribution of land in excess of prescribed ceilings to their heirs in anticipation of land reform (Poudyal, 1983).

A study made in 1972 showed no progress in the highly skewed distribution of agricultural land holding even after the implementation of the Land Act. The study revealed that 53.5 percent of the households had less than 1.0 ha and accounted for only 10.5 percent of the total cultivated area, 36.6 percent of the households had 1 to 5 ha, and they controlled 30.0 percent of the total cultivated area, while 9.9 percent of the households had 15 ha and above size holdings accounted for as much as 59.0 percent of the total land (Zaman, 1973). A survey conducted by the NPC in 1977 showed that marginal and small farmers constituting 57.0 percent of the households cultivated less than 2 ha in the terai and 0.5 ha in the hills (NPC, 1978). The three rounds of the NLSS conducted in 1995/6, 2003/4 and 2010/11 also show the persistence of unequal distribution of land till now (Table 2.13).

Table 2.13 Distribution of Agricultural Land (in Percent)

Farm Size	*1995/6*		*2003/4*		*2010/11*	
	HHs	*Area*	*HHs*	*Area*	*HHs*	*Area*
Up to 0.5 ha	39.9	8.6	44.8	13.2	52.7	18.5
0.5 ha to 2.0 ha	47.2	43.5	47,2	55.4	42.9	53.4
Above 2.0 ha	12.9	47.8	8.0	31.3	4.4	22.2

Source: NLSS Report, 1997, 2004 and 2011, CBS, Government of Nepal.
Note: HHs means agricultural households and Area means area of agricultural land.

Table 2.13 reveals a high level of inequality in land distribution between smallholder peasants and large landholders. In 1995/6, the smallholder peasants (possessing up to 0.5 ha) constituted 39.9 percent, which increased to 44.8 percent in 2003/4 and further to 52.7 percent in 2010/11. They accounted for only 8.6 percent, 13.2 percent and 18.5 percent of total agricultural land in the respective years. On the other hand, the large landholders (possessing above 2.0 ha) constituted a small proportion of total agricultural households – 12.9 percent in 1995/6, 8.0 percent in 2003/4 and 4.4 percent in 2010/11 but possessed disproportionately large land area, –47.8 percent, 31.3 percent and 22.2 percent, respectively. Peasants falling in the middle range (0.5 ha to 2.0 ha) appear to have more or less a balance between the proportion of households and share in total land area.

2.15 Explanations of Poverty in Nepal

2.15.1 Neo-liberal Explanation

The neo-liberal thinking on poverty is premised on the notion of free-market ideology, self-interest and private property. Their explanations of poverty and remedies for poverty alleviation suffer from various weaknesses, which are briefly evaluated in the following sections.

First, the neo-liberal economists of Nepal, both in academic and policymaking institutions like the NPC, in consonance with the World Bank, view Nepal's pervasive poverty as stemming from a limited resource base, location between two large countries, landlocked geography, rapid population growth and poor economic performance (Dahal, 2004; World Bank, 1991). Emphasizing population factors as the main hindrance in poverty alleviation and suggesting cosmetic measures, a World Bank report says,

> The basic cause of poverty in Nepal is excessive population pressure on an insufficient resource base rather than inegalitarian distribution of available wealth. The weakness of the base stems from natural disadvantages which hinder modern sector growth (e.g., a difficult topography and location), manifested in an unskilled work force and weak managerial capacity…redistributive land reform does not to currently be a prospect in Nepal.
>
> (World Bank, 1990: 22, 36)

In a similar vein, a report prepared by NPC with the financial support of the World Bank and UK's Department of International Development and foreign experts states, 'The major contributing indicators to overall poverty in Nepal and in rural Nepal are malnutrition and insufficient years of schooling' (NPC, 2018: viii). These indicators are virtually the symptoms of poverty and not the factors causing poverty. Such neo-liberal explanations of poverty provided a firm basis for the planners and policymakers of Nepal not to even talk of the need for redistribution of assets or other out-of-mainstream measures for poverty reduction, but plead for raising growth and improving health and education facilities, presuming that the poor would also equally benefit.

Second, neo-liberal economists plead for equipping the poor with skills rather than providing food which satisfies their hunger of the day. They go by an old development dictum that 'if you give a man a fish, you feed him for a day; if you teach him to fish, you feed him for a lifetime'. This seems fine, but the sceptics within the neo-liberal circle argue that without the right to fish, the teaching of fishing skills would not be enough for enabling a man to fish. Amartya Sen, a doyen of neo-liberal thinkers, goes a step further and adds that rights alone are not sufficient and individuals need capabilities to exercise the rights. In all these discourses they overlook an important point that when many other people compete to fish in the same pond or river, fish stocks will soon be depleted. So what is also equally necessary and even more important is that the man has ownership of a fish pond so that he can replenish the pond with fresh fishlings as fish stocks drop. This directly raises the issue of asset/income redistribution, but neo-liberals argue that attempts to redistribute assets/income from the rich to the poor would distort market processes and lead to lower efficiency.

Third, neo-liberal economists argue that developing the free-market system may be the best solution for reducing poverty. It is advocated that free markets open up trade opportunities, increase competition, boost productivity and enhance prosperity and as a result decrease poverty. They cite the examples of capitalist countries' success in reducing inequality and poverty as evidence of the effectiveness of the free-market system in poverty reduction. But in underdeveloped countries, the free-market system has brought more misery to the poor rather than helping them to get out of poverty. Markets always exclude the poor because as buyers, they have no means to purchase, and as sellers, they have nothing to sell. Even if markets may create equal opportunities for all because of initial inequality in income and wealth, a significant proportion of the poor remains precluded from participation in the markets. As Nayak says,

> If the initial distribution of resources is iniquitous, in terms of certain ethical criteria, there is no presumption that operation of the market system left to itself may bring about equity. Indeed, in a system with unequal bargaining power amongst agents, the market system may bring about accentuation of inequity.
>
> (Nayak, 1996: 18)

Another effect of economic liberalization policies has been the cut in subsidies on food, fertilizer prices and interest on agricultural loans to the farmers. There is no denying the fact that even when the subsidy programme was under operation, it suffered from various loopholes and the feudal social structure made the rural bourgeoisie siphon benefits away from the target groups. The IMF and the World Bank advise the less developed countries to undertake projects justified on cost-effectiveness and financial sustainability, but projects required to benefit the poor do not usually meet these criteria. This means poor tend to be bypassed from the benefits of projects undertaken under the neo-liberal prescriptions.

Fourth, neo-liberal economists emphasize the primacy of growth for poverty reduction. They argue that growth or prosperity benefits all, even though some groups benefit more than other groups. However, the development experience of several low-income countries brought the percept of neo-liberal economists that growth would suffice to reduce poverty into serious question. It was then advocated that the objective of reducing poverty and unemployment would require a high growth rate of 8.0 to 10.0 percent or more because it is only in a situation of high growth that the trickle-down theory will work.. As Krishna says,

> Policy is formulated with the faith that since growth can hardly be bad, it must therefore be good for the poor. It is proposed, further, that poverty will be fixed if growth is high enough, and statisticians calculate rate of growth "required" to reduce poverty. But poverty is hardly such a malleable variable, which will decline in predictable ways in response to economic growth.
>
> (Krishna, 2014: 111)

And, contrary to neoclassical argument of trickle-down, most of the growth trickled-up to the rich and almost nothing trickled down to the poor. Moreover, in a situation of existing high inequality that exists in Nepal, the trickle-down impact of growth is retarded and forces that perpetuate inequality are reinforced, further widening the gulf between the rich and the poor. In recent years, a new metaphor of development economics connoted by the phrase 'inclusive growth' is being articulated to camouflage the failure of poverty reduction through a 'growth first' or 'growth with equity' strategy in underdeveloped countries. However, the sceptics of liberal economic growth say that poverty is harder to address through broad-based economic growth policies now than some three decades ago (Blank, 1997). The success of inclusive growth would require, as the experience of East Asia shows, early land redistribution and then the systematic pursuit of labour-intensive manufactured exports (Kohli, 2012). But the South Asian countries, including Nepal, deliberately avoided this path because it was inimical to the interest of the dominant classes which represented the government all through the history of the country. Nepal had the opportunity to pursue this path because the country had a communist government a couple of times in the past and uninterruptedly for more than three years between 2018 and 2021, but it did not endeavour to displease the dominant classes for financial pursuits and electoral politics. Even though land reforms were introduced at times, redistribution of land hardly reached the poor tillers.

Fifth, neo-liberals believe that individuals are guided by their self-interest, and so they would always try to maximize personal benefits by utilizing the existing or exploring potential opportunities. And if some do not react to a change in opportunity and avoid effort and seek pleasure, they are not rational individuals and are themselves to be blamed for what they are. Based on this premise, various types of government programmes for rural development were introduced in Nepal expecting that the poor will self-target and benefit themselves. But what the planners and policymakers abstracted perhaps purposively was that in a state of high initial socio-economic differentiation, the poor lag behind, and the rich garner most of the benefits from such programmes. Even the programmes designed exclusively for the poor failed to benefit them, as these were introduced on the basis of what the government and the NGOs thought were good for the poor rather than the needs and preferences of the poor.

2.15.2 Social Explanation

The mainstream intellects of Nepal consider poverty as a given characteristic feature of Nepalese society through the ages. According to this view, poverty is an inescapable phenomenon and an outcome of an individual's failure to struggle in the society. As such, studies on poverty and articles related to poverty issues have focussed on identifying the poor, describing various characteristics of the poor and suggesting what ought to be done to lift them out of poverty, but not on why they are poor and why poverty is reproduced and perpetuated. For many years, the rulers of Nepal indoctrinated people with the Hindu philosophy that considers poverty as a condition ordained by God, and hence not reversible, deserving only compassion to the poor. People were indoctrinated to believe that their hardships and sufferings were due to their misdeeds in their previous lives and can only be salvaged by performing certain religious acts in the present life for a better-quality re-birth in the future. Furthermore, the society was divided into four classes, Brahmin, Kshatriya, Vaishya and Shudra, on a hierarchical basis for the preservation of the exploitative economic and social system. The Brahmins were on the top to work as priests and advisors to the kings; the Chhetris were on the second to be the rulers and warriors; the Vaisyas were on the third to be engaged in commercial and trading activities; the Sudras were on the bottom to perform blacksmithing (Kami), tailoring (damai), shoemaking (cobbler) gold ornament making (goldsmith), toilet cleaning (chhame, pode) and butchering (kasain). The Sudras were also tagged as untouchables. The relationship between the upper caste and the lower caste was postulated to be a dominant-dependent relation. The upper castes by the strength of their land holdings, wealth, education and higher-level position in the state machinery wielded the power and social control and thus were in a position to dominate and expropriate the lower castes, ethnic groups and tenants in various forms. The Hindu religion and its prescriptions were reinforced time and again over the course of history, such as the declaration of Nepal as the only 'Hindu kingdom' in the world and the king as the only 'Hindu king' for unhindered exploitation and subjugation of the poor and lower caste people by the upper caste (Brahmin/Chhetri) people. The lower caste people, particularly the untouchables, were denied participation in all activities that involved physical touch with the upper castes. They were restricted entry to upper caste house and Hindu temples, and not allowed to touch cooked food and water meant for the upper caste people. They were even denied participation in social gatherings, community meetings and ceremonies, and even if allowed to participate, they had to maintain a certain distance from the upper caste people. Such socially generated beliefs, values and taboos had a far-reaching influence on the children to absorb such practices. The caste and class differentiation continued to be reinforced in the course of state activities and conduit of development policies and programmes, mostly benefitting the feudal groups, which wielded the power or were aligned to the power circle, subjugating the poor to the status of mere objects of their favour and kindness.

There are two other social factors that are both a cause and consequence of poverty and that drive the poor and above-poverty-line households into further destitution. First, incidences of critical illness, such as cancer or kidney failure, have high health-care costs, and poor households are often forced to sell off whatever meagre assets they have or borrow from private moneylenders at exorbitant interest. The effect of grave illness in driving families into poverty now as compared to the past is very touchingly described by an elderly villager in Rajasthan, India:

> In the old days, the aged people fall sick and they would die. Their survivors would grieve and be unhappy, but they would pick up their lives eventually and carry on much as before. Now the old people fall sick, and their children run up huge debts caring for them. The old people die, nevertheless, and they leave behind ruined families.
>
> (Krishna, 2014: 120)

Although a health insurance scheme of limited scale has been recently introduced in Nepal to get poor households out of 'the medical poverty trap', it has no meaning for those who have no money to pay the premium or if the treatment requires a huge amount of money.

Second, disability also keeps poor households locked into poverty. In Nepal, as in any other underdeveloped country, individuals with disabilities are disproportionately among the poorest of the poor. The National Census 2011 shows that approximately 2.0 percent of Nepalese live with a disability. But this figure is questioned as not reflecting the actual situation. For a long period of time, disability was not a state concern and people with disabilities had great difficulty in access to health, education, rehabilitation, support, etc., and were considered not worthy of any job. The constitution of Nepal 2015 talks of the right to education of physically and visually impaired persons and persons with hearing and speech impairment and guarantees inclusion of people with disabilities in the federal as well as state legislatures. There also exist various types of support, such as free education and certain educational allowances, social welfare allowance of Rs. 2,000.0 per month and reservation of 5.0 percent of all jobs in the civil service to persons with disability. Government financial support to persons with disability is minuscule compared to the cost of living and health-care expenses. The right to education carries no meaning for disabled persons if not supported with an adequate monthly allowance and friendly social and infrastructural facilities.

2.15.3 Political Explanation

During the rule of kings and Ranas for nearly two-and-a-half decades, the poor, ethnic community and disadvantaged people were kept politically in abeyance and were treated as subjects to be ruled. For 30 years, the Panchayat regime prohibited alternative political thoughts and forced the common people to accept the system as the best for Nepal. This was a part of the strategy for appropriating a disproportionate share of national wealth for strengthening the regime and benefitting the bourgeoisie class supportive of the regime.

The restoration of multiparty democracy in 1991 brought freedom to the people, such as free speech, free press, freedom to write, freedom to choose jobs, freedom to conduct public meetings, freedom to participate in politics and freedom to elect the leaders, but all such freedoms were beneficial to politicians, business groups, well-to-do persons and educated people but had no meaning to the lower caste, ethnic groups, marginalized people and toiling masses, as they did not possess the necessary capabilities to benefit from these freedoms. Democracy also brought freedom to trade, invest and innovate, but this was also of no value to the poor, as they had no objects to trade and no resources to invest. The only thing they could trade was the labour embodied in their bodies, but they were not in a position to sell this in the country, as there were no employment opportunities for the unskilled and low-educated labour force. The unemployed youths could not politically react to their unemployment and distress but rather sought foreign employment in Gulf countries, Malaysia and other destinations with the hope of a better future and improvement in the living standard of the family. However, not all those who go abroad for employment return back home alive and or in good physical and mental condition. Many youths have lost their lives while at work and their dead bodies are returned home in coffins. Such incidents have increased each year, along with the increase in the number of youths going abroad for employment. On 24 July 2021, Nepal Airlines brought 24 dead bodies and the mortal remains of three persons from Malaysia, while 10 dead bodies were still lying in South Asian countries awaiting airlift. According to Ministry of Finance data, a total of 6,236 persons died while in foreign employment during the period 2013/4 and mid-March 2020 (MOF, 2020/1). A newspaper report states that in 2020/1 alone, 1,073 Nepalese workers lost their lives in Malaysia and over the last 14 years, 9,237 dead bodies were brought back to Nepal in coffins (Nayapatrika, 2021). The actual number may be far higher because the deaths against which no compensation is paid are unrecorded. Families of the deceased workers who had gone to foreign employment with the dream of earning money to repay the debt and improving family well-being have fallen into a debt trap and slipped into acute poverty. The government gets away from the responsibility of preventing the families of the deceased or injured person from descending into poverty by paying compensation of only seven hundred thousand rupees.

For a long period of time, the poor and marginalized people did not have the opportunity to participate in the national legislature and high-level bodies that formulated plans and policies. Even during the democratic period between 1990 and 2006, there was very poor representation of poor and lower caste people in the House of Representatives. On the other hand, the rich and middle class, mainly belonging to the higher caste (Brahmin/Chhetri), wielded political and bureaucratic power, but they had no interest in introducing far-reaching poverty reduction programmes. With the emergence of the Maoist party as a major political force in 2006 and transformation of the country into a federal democratic republic and inclusive politics with proportional election system, ethnic minorities, Dalits and women are now also represented in the parliament and the cabinet. The 2015 constitution of Nepal mandates each party to ensure that women make up one-third of the total number of representatives in both the House of Representatives and the Province Assemblies. Furthermore, the Province Assembly Election Act has made it mandatory for each party to incorporate six 'inclusion' groups in the 'proportional representation' (PR) list in specified proportion – 31.2 percent Khas Arya, 28.7 percent Adivasi Janajati (aborigines), 15.3 percent Dalit, 6.6 percent Tharu and 4.4 percent Muslim. Besides, the House of Representatives and Province Assembly Election Acts state that within each inclusion group 50 percent of the elected representatives/candidates must be women. As the percentage of women elected under 'first-past-the-post' principle (candidate with highest number of votes is the winner of parliamentary seat) in the 2017 general election was only 3.7 percent (6 persons only), a larger chunk of PR seats was filled by women to satisfy the constitutional provision. Despite this, neither the House of Representatives nor the Province Assemblies are engaged in meaningful debate and discussion on the dynamics and forces which have generated and perpetuated poverty and inequality between classes and between the voiceless and the articulate. The members in both the federal (House of Representatives and National Assembly) and provincial parliaments have simply continued 'business as usual', not reflecting the spirit that was expected of communist lawmakers.

In an agrarian country, land reform is potentially the most significant programme of asset redistribution in favour of poor farmers and landless people. But this has become a highly loaded political issue in Nepal. Nepal's political scene until 2007 was dominated by two major political parties, the Nepali Congress (NC) and the Unified Marxist-Leninist Party (UML) and each projected itself as a party that would steer Nepal out of backwardness and mass poverty. The NC desired this to be achieved through the philosophy of 'democratic socialism', propounded by BP Koirala, who was the first elected prime minister of Nepal in 1959. Democratic socialism was defined as liberal democracy with social justice. BP Koirala had a concern for the poor, and this was expressed as 'each Nepali household with a home, small tract of land and one pair of oxen'. After the restoration of democracy in 1991, the NC formed the first majority government in 1992 and remained in power for three years and also headed coalition governments later, but failed to introduce measures to translate its ideology of democratic socialism and BP Koirala's vision into reality. It was only in 2001 when Sher Bahadur Deuba was prime minister that a land reform programme was announced for the first time by reducing the land ceiling fixed in 1964, but it was not executed.

The UML embraced the ideology of 'People's Multiparty Democracy' propounded by the late Madan Bhandari in 1993 and advocated 'land to the tillers'. When in power for the first time as the minority government for nine months in 1994/5, the UML formed a high-level Land Reform Commission known as Badal Commission to recommend land reform measures. The Commission identified problems and recommended a ceiling on land holding for a family by ecological belts, estimated the amount of land in excess of the ceiling and distribution of excess land to landless and poor households (HLLRC, 2000). But the government did not show concern with implementing the recommendations of the Commission, not even later when the party was in government several times. Even the Maoist party which was more radical than UML ignored the slogan of 'scientific land reform', which was stressed as one of its avowed objectives. Despite their Marxist ideology, the UML and the Maoist, while in government as leaders or coalition partners, operated on the terrain of bourgeois politics and along the neo-liberal economic paradigm initiated in the early 1990s by the NC government under the dictates of IMF and the World Bank.

2.16 Knowledge Gap in Poverty Analysis

Numerous studies of poverty in Nepal have been done in the last two decades, but they have mostly focussed on estimating the poverty rate and correlating poverty with various socio-economic factors. Furthermore, no differentiation is made between escape from and descent into poverty for gaining policy-relevant knowledge. As different reasons are associated with escaping poverty and falling into poverty, which also vary by local context, two separate anti-poverty policies are required as suggested by Krishna (Krishna, 2014): One set to help promote escape from poverty and a different set to help control descent into poverty. Krishna identifies ill-health and high health-care expenses, customary expenses on marriage and death feasts, high-interest loans and irrigation failures as the major reasons associated with descent. On the other hand, escape from poverty would require employment, diversification of income sources mainly through the informal sector, industrial growth and irrigation (Krishna, 2014).

Other major factors that push people into poverty and make the poor 'poorest' in Nepal are the natural disasters, such as earthquakes, floods, landslides and droughts, fire and infectious diseases. Nepal is among the 11th most earthquake-prone countries in the world (NPC, 2015) and hence it is always in constant risk of earthquakes. A great earthquake hit Nepal on 25 April 2015 that pushed many people into poverty and exacerbated the poverty of those already living precarious lives. The NPC (2015) estimated that the earthquake pushed around 700,000 additional people (2.5 to 3.5 percent of the total population) into poverty.

Similarly, the country is highly vulnerable to floods and landslides because the major rivers of Nepal originate from the higher Himalayas, Mahabharat Hills and Siwalik and Churia Hills and flow down to the hills and then to the flat land of terai and finally join the Ganges (Ganga) of India in Bihar. The poorest people live on steep slopes in the mountains and hills and in flood-prone areas or embankments of rivers in the terai and depend upon marginal land or daily wage for livelihood. So they are the ones to be hardest hit by landslides and floods. When such disasters occur, these people are left homeless, injured and bereaved and stripped of the small plots of low-grade land on which they survive. As a consequence, they descend into poverty or extreme poverty and deprivation.

The government as well as donor agencies involved in Nepal's development process boast of a decrease in the poverty rate, which is portrayed as the success of their efforts and resources over the years. This may be so in aggregate terms, but the aggregate figure masks the reality of stark poverty that prevails at the local level, in a specific context and in a specific source of living. Moreover, poverty and economic inequality cannot simply be economic phenomena, these are outcomes of the politico-historical process and an inevitable consequence of a semi-feudalistic society. This thinking has to be in the mind-set of authorities and policymakers in power while designing poverty reduction and redistributive measures. But it is doubtful whether this would be possible, as the major political parties, planners and policymakers of Nepal, whatever genre they belong to, thrive on accepting what is percolated down from the orbit of the neo-liberal capitalist world.

3 Dependency on Foreign Aid

3.1 Critics of Aid

Aid is criticized not only by neo-Marxists but also by some Western neo-liberal economists, even though there are a large number of intellectuals who blindly support aid as an indispensable factor for the development of poor countries. The neo-Marxists criticize foreign aid as a mechanism of neo-colonial political control over poor countries to keep them always under their subjugation. For them, foreign aid, in short, is a form of imperialism. Those who support aid are mostly from the aid industry which has pressure to expand aid for its business and those who are diehard neo-classical. The neo-liberal economists argue that growth in developing countries is constrained either by a shortage of domestic savings (the savings gap) or by a shortage of export earnings (the trade gap). According to them, aid promotes growth through two mechanisms: (i) aid supplements domestic savings, thus increasing the amount of investment, and (ii) aid increases domestic capacity to import capital goods and technology (Chenery and Strout, 1966). But this contention rests on two assumptions: (i) the relationship between investment and growth is stable in the short to medium terms, and (ii) foreign aid is entirely used for investment and not for consumption. These assumptions do not generally hold in reality and hence the contention that aid promotes growth cannot be accepted as true. A number of empirical studies conducted in the last 40 years to investigate the relationship between aid and growth do not also provide any conclusive evidence. A large number of these studies are based on cross-sectional data and hence their findings cannot be taken for granted for any individual country because of country-specific variations in geopolitical and socio-economic factors, administrative efficiency and governance indicators. Even individual country studies do not provide logical insight for another individual country because each country is a specific case.

Among the neo-liberal economists, Peter Bauer was one of the earliest to criticize aid as neither necessary nor sufficient for development. According to him, aid increases the power of government, leads to corruption, misallocates resources and erodes civil society. Therefore, he argues that economic achievement does not depend on aid but depends on personal, cultural, social and political factors, that is, people's own faculties, motivations and mores, their institutions and policies of

DOI: 10.4324/9781003359777-3

the rulers (Bauer, 1972). Graham Hancock, a British writer and journalist, attacks foreign aid with numerous examples from developing countries of Asia, Africa and Latin America of inappropriateness, inefficiencies and corruption of aid projects. He argues that foreign aid is typically irrelevant, as it enriches only development professionals, Western contractors and third-world bureaucrats, and it enables exploitative regimes to continue following misguided and wasteful policies. In conclusion, Hancock dismisses the argument that foreign aid must be continued because 'the poor can't survive without it'. Rather,

> when the middle men of the aid industry have been shut out, it will become possible for people to rediscover ways to 'help' one another directly according to their needs and aspirations as they themselves define them, in line with priorities they themselves have set, and guided by their own agendas.
>
> (Hancock, 1989: 193)

Bill Easterly, a former World Bank economist, provides numerous case studies on the failure of aid in reversing or halting the slide in growth of income per capita toward zero (Easterly, 2006: 25). The dependency theorists assert that aid is actually provided in order to exploit the recipient countries and keep them perpetually dependent on their mercy (Seligson and Passe-Smith, 2004). Dambisa Moyo writing in the context of Africa argues that aid has made African countries poorer and growth slower, fostered dependency, encouraged corruption and ultimately perpetuated poor governance (Moyo, 2009). Foreign aid is also criticized on the ground that it may induce an appreciation of the real exchange rate leading to lower exports and higher imports, a situation depicted as the 'Dutch disease'. Besides aid is fungible, which implies that aid given for one purpose allows the government to shift its own resources to less important activities which would not have been undertaken otherwise.

3.2 Aid Flow to Nepal

Nepal's history of foreign aid starts in 1951 following the overthrow of the 104-year Rana regime (1847–1951). During the Rana regime, except alliance with Britain, Nepal remained virtually a closed country to the outside world. The relation with Britain was also solely for seeking British support by the Rana rulers for which they even allowed free recruitment of Gurkha soldiers in the British army. With the opening of the country to the external world, the United States ushered in as the first donor country with the aid of US$2,000.00 or Rs. 15,360.00 (US$1 = Rs. 7.68) in January 1951, just a month before the ousting of Rana regime. Although the US aid amount was minuscule, it dragged Nepal into the vortex of Cold War politics, and, consequently, larger and larger amounts of aid started flowing into Nepal from both the capitalist block led by the United States and the socialist block led by the former Soviet Union in a competitive way. The United States and India were the major donors in the early years, while other

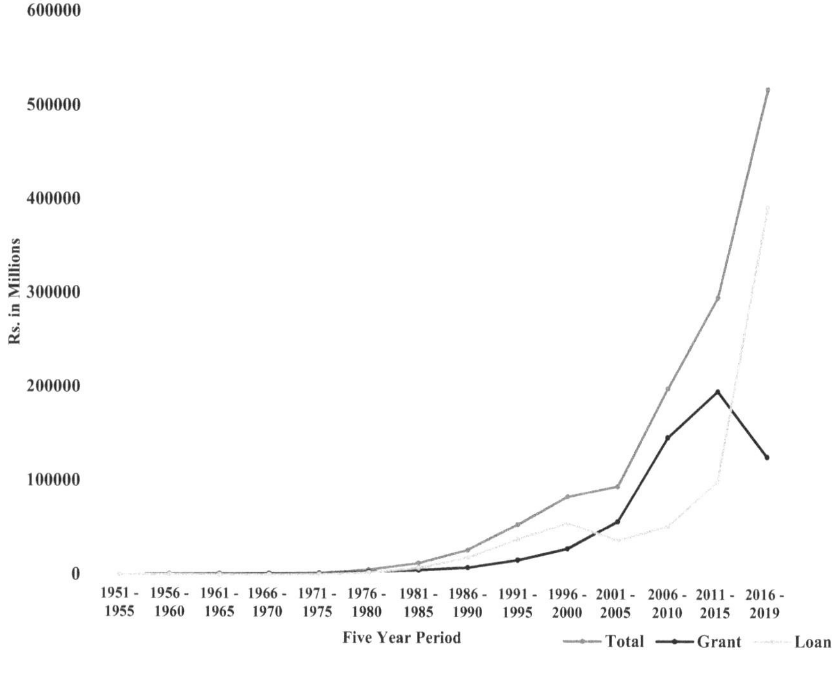

Figure 3.1 Trend of Aid and Its Composition.

nations made their incursion after Nepal initiated a planned process of development in 1956. This shows that aid started pouring into Nepal before it could set the direction of development, and this ensued a process of donor influence in Nepal's development discourse and policy orientation.

In the early four years between 1951/2 and 1955/6, foreign aid inflow to Nepal was only Rs. 95.0 million. Thereafter, the amount of aid inflow started to increase every year with the exception decline in some years (Figure 3.1). There was a sixfold increase in total aid from Rs. 5,749.8 million in the '70s to Rs. 34,563.4 million in the 1980s. The decline in foreign aid in 1962/3 and 1966/7 compared to the previous year was, respectively, due to the Indo-Chinese armed conflict of 1962 and the Indo-Pakistan War of 1965. The reasons for the decline in aid inflow in the later years are not known, but one possible reason could be donors' perception of Nepal as a poor performer in the use of aid. The marked increase in aid inflow in 1991/2 can be explained by donors' eagerness to maintain their stake in the changed political scenario of Nepal and to have an influence on the political parties that were to be seated in the government. The increase in aid flow in the years following the restoration of democracy in 1990 was due to the growth of aid culture and the self-rating of success by then-finance ministers of Nepal in terms of the amount of aid they could muster during their tenure in the Ministry of Finance.

3.3 Changing Composition and Source of Aid

3.3.1 Grants and Loans

Aid flow to Nepal has changed significantly during the last four decades, both in terms of composition and source. In the first decade of aid receipts, the entire aid was in grant form. From 1961/2, share of grants started to decline but still remained predominant up to 1976/7. Loans started to flow from 1961/2 with a minuscule amount (Rs. 1.0 million or 0.5 percent) and accounted for over 60 percent of aid between 1983/4 and 2000/1. The picture reversed between 2002/3 and 2013/14 with grants accounting for over 60 percent of total aid, but loans accounted for the largest share in the last three years.

In the early years (between 1951/2 and 1979/80), India, the United States and China were the major providers of grants. Of the total bilateral grants of Rs. 5239.3 million during the period, India shared 38.3 percent followed by the United States with 23.2 percent, China 14.3 percent, and United Kingdom 9.8 percent (Poudyal, 1982). From the mid-'70s, other countries like Canada, Japan, Switzerland, the Federal Republic of Germany and some other donors also started providing a modest amount of grants. The major providers of Rs. 518.9 million multilateral grants during the period between 1971/72 and 1979/80 were, the UN Development Programme (UNDP) accounting for the largest share (40.5 percent), followed by World Food Programme (21.3 percent) and UNICEF (13.8 percent) (Poudyal, 1982).

3.3.2 Bilateral and Multilateral Aid

Up to 1974/5, all aid to Nepal was entirely from bilateral sources, while aid from multilateral sources started to flow from the mid-'70s (with Rs. 174.9 million in 1975/6) but increased steadily in the successive years, accounting for an increasingly larger proportion of total aid. The multilateral aid mostly consists of loans, excepting a modest proportion of grants in the form of technical assistance (TA). The main sources of multilateral aid are the World Bank and the Asian Development Bank, which mainly provide assistance from their concessional windows; the International Development Association; and the Asian Development Fund. Inflow of aid from multilateral sources surpassed that of bilateral sources from 1982/83 and was over 70.0 percent in 2016/17 and 2017/18 and 80.0 percent in 2019/20.

3.3.3 Government Preference

The government has a preference for grants over loans because these are free of obligation to repay. But the intrinsic purpose is the opportunity for misappropriation of funds meant for project implementation in a variety of ways. Moreover, grants ease the resource constraint of development projects and allow the government to relax tax efforts to gain political popularity. This implies that the government is irrational in the sense that it does not make the best use of resources if received free of cost. On the other hand, a rational government would use resources irrespective of whether free or not with equal concern for deriving maximum

Table 3.1 Composition of Aid (Rs. in Million)

FY	*Total*	*Grant*	*Loan*	*% Grant*	*% Loan*	*FY*	*Total*	*Grant*	*Loan*	*% Grant*	*% Loan*
1951/2–1955/6	95	95	0	100.0	0.0	1988/9	5,666.9	1,478.2	4,188.7	26.1	73.9
1956/7	27.3	27.3	0	100.0	0.0	1989/90	6,427.1	1,798.8	4,628.3	28.0	72.0
1957/8	58.1	58.1	0	100.0	0.0	1990/1	5,990	1,630	4,360	27.2	72.8
1958/9	35.1	35.1	0	100.0	0.0	1991/2	7,800.4	1,531	6,269.4	19.6	80.4
1959/60	125.3	125.3	0	100.0	0.0	1992/3	9,235.6	3,273.9	5,961.7	35.4	64.6
1960/1	125.1	125.1	0	100.0	0.0	1993/4	11,557.2	2,393.6	9,163.6	20.7	79.3
1961/2	182.6	181.6	1	99.5	0.5	1194/5	11,249.4	3,937.1	7,312.3	35.0	65.0
1962/3	88.1	76.5	11.6	86.8	13.2	1995/6	14,289	4,825.1	9,463.9	33.8	66.2
1963/4	177.3	165.9	11.4	93.6	6.4	1996/7	15,031.9	5,988.3	9,043.6	39.8	60.2
1964/5	146.9	141	5.9	96.0	4.0	1997/8	16,457.1	5,402.6	11,054.5	32.8	67.2
1965/6	178.6	175.3	3.3	98.2	1.8	1998/9	16,189	4,336.6	11,852.4	26.8	73.2
1966/7	145.9	142.2	3.7	97.5	2.5	1999/2000	17,523.9	5,711.7	11,812.2	32.6	67.4
1967/8	158.1	158.1	0	100.0	0.0	2000/1	18,797.4	6,753.4	12,044	35.9	64.1
1968/9	185.9	185.9	0	100.0	0.0	2001/2	14,384.8	6,686.2	7,698.6	46.5	53.5
1969/70	251.3	243.7	7.6	97.0	3.0	2002/3	15,885.5	11,339.1	4,546.4	71.4	28.6
1970/1	303.2	270.7	32.5	89.3	10.7	2003/4	18,912.4	11,283.4	7,629	59.7	40.3
1971/2	281	241.1	39.9	85.8	14.2	2004/5	23,657.3	14,391.2	9,266.1	60.8	39.2
1972/3	227.6	180.2	47.4	79.2	20.8	2005/6	22,041.8	13,827.5	8,214.3	62.7	37.3
1973/4	310.5	222.6	87.9	71.7	28.3	2006/7	25,854.4	15,800.9	10,053.5	61.1	38.9
1974/5	386.7	282.8	103.9	73.1	26.9	2007/8	29,300.6	20,320.7	8,979.9	69.4	30.6
1975/6	505.6	359.7	145.9	71.1	28.9	2008/9	36,351.7	26,382.8	9,968.9	72.6	27.4
1976/7	556.9	392.5	164.4	70.5	29.5	2009/10	49,769.4	38,546	11,223.4	77.4	22.6
1977/8	848.4	466.6	381.8	55.0	45.0	2010/1	57,997.8	45,922.1	12,075.7	79.2	20.8
1978/9	989.4	599.3	390.1	60.6	39.4	2011/2	51,893.4	40,810.3	11,083.1	78.6	21.4
1979/80	13,40.5	805.6	534.9	60.1	39.9	2012/3	47,199.2	35,229.8	11,969.4	74.6	25.4

1980/1	1,562.2	808.9	753.3	51.8	48.2	2013/4	60,204.6	42,205.8	17,998.8	70.1	29.9
1981/2	1,723.2	992.5	730.7	57.6	42.4	2014/5	63,901.6	38,285.8	25,615.8	59.9	40.1
1982/3	2,075.9	1,090.1	985.8	52.5	47.5	2015/6	72,772.3	39,544	33,228.3	54.3	45.7
1983/4	2,547.5	876.6	1,670.9	34.4	65.6	2016/7	99,841.5	40,819.3	59,022.2	40.9	59.1
1984/5	2,676.4	923.4	1,753	34.5	65.5	2017/8	131,551.4	39,318.7	92,232.7	29.9	70.1
1985/6	3,491.5	1,120.6	2,370.9	32.1	67.9	2018/9	147,271.2	22,898.7	124,372.5	15.5	84.5
1986/7	3,314.4	1,078.3	2,236.1	32.5	67.5	2019/20	139,704.4	23,215.7	116,488.7	16.6	83.4
1987/8	5,078.5	1,984.2	3,094.3	39.1	60.9	Total	1,294,910.2	590,520.1	704,390.1	45.6	54.4

Source: S. R. Poudyal, Foreign Aid in Nepal, 1982, Economic Survey, Various Years, Ministry of Finance.

benefit. In addition to irrational use, grants carry a cost of the moral hazard of yielding to the strategic, political and commercial interests of donors because grants are not free gifts, as these apparently seem to be. This is proved by the recent controversy over the US grant of $500 million under the Millennium Challenge Corporation (MCC) and various grants provided by India and China to Nepal on different occasions.

With regard to source, multilateral aid is preferred over bilateral aid, as the latter is provided to promote donors' geo-strategic, political and economic interests with little regard to the recipient country's needs and concerns. On the other hand, multilateral aid is considered to be less politically biased, free from donors' geo-strategic interests and more likely to be to serve the recipients' needs. Furthermore, multilateral aid is believed to be cheaper, to disperse accountability as well as to be more politically neutral and needs-driven (Apodaca, 2017).

With the end of the Cold War, the ideological confrontation between the United States and the Soviet Union which dominated the world political scenario for 45 years from 1945 to 1990 also faded away, and the bilateral aid started to be increasingly routed through multilateral financial institutions, such as the International Monetary Fund, the World Bank, the Asian Development Bank and the United Nations Development Programme. However, this was an indirect way of fulfilling the political, ideological and strategic motives of bilateral donors, as the ownership structure of IMF and the World Bank is concentrated in a few major developed countries. Furthermore, channelling foreign aid to underdeveloped countries through multilateral financial institutions provided an effective mechanism to impose neo-liberal policy reforms and conditionality upon the recipient countries, as desired by the major shareholders of these institutions.

3.3.4 Commitment vs. Disbursement

Aid received by Nepal lags behind the amount committed by donors. The aid disbursement-commitment ratio of the last 45 years shows an erratic trend with an appallingly low ratio in some years and an exceptionally high ratio in three years. The average annual growth rate of commitment is 28.1 percent while that of disbursement is 15.1 percent (Annex 3). The average commitment-disbursement ratio over a 45-year period is 53.2 percent. This shows that during the last 45 years only half of the committed amount was disbursed.

Donors repeatedly point out lack of improvement in absorptive capacity for low disbursement as compared to commitment. But this is a one-sided view and conceals the failure of donor agencies to keep up their promises and also justifies parallel or vertical funding. Nepal country reports on 'Monitoring the Paris Declaration' prepared by the Ministry of Finance (MOF) report donor-related factors for the low utilization of aid in Nepal. These are the unwillingness of donors to release the committed amount of aid, fulfilment of conditions for the release of aid instalment, delays in disbursing the amount spent by Nepal in advance and release of aid only if it matches with donors' priorities and interests, and donors' often complicated reporting requirements and disbursement processes. Sometimes donors refrain from releasing committed funds on the pretext of weak governance, unsatisfactory democratic practices, violation of human rights and public security. These reports also point out implementation problems on Nepal's side, but the repeated assertion of absorptive capacity constraint as recorded in the annual portfolio meeting reports of the MOF is an escape way to fulfil the self-interest of donor agencies. On the pretext of low absorptive capacity, donors earmark a large chunk of aid to enhance Nepal's ability through TA. A former secretary with several years' working experience in the Foreign Aid Division of the MOF observes that almost 76.0 percent of total aid is siphoned off by the donors to their own countries in the form of consultancy fees, technology charges, remuneration to expatriate advisors, experts and technicians (Naya Patrika, 2021 September).

3.3.5 Disbursement by Sector

Aid has covered almost all sectors and activities in Nepal. The government's inability to prepare concrete project/programme proposals allowed donors to have an upper hand in the selection of projects and activities of their interest. The infrastructure sector (transport, communication and power) received the largest chunk of aid (58.7 percent) in the five-year period of 1975/6 and 1979/80 and continued to account for the largest share until 2000/1 and 2004/5. As will be discussed in the next section, there was a congruence of interest between Nepal and its northern and southern neighbours in building major roads in the 1960s and 1970s. But the expansion of road connectivity did not lead to increased production because the flow of aid to agriculture, the largest production sector of Nepal, was low, and aid flow to industry, another commodity production sector was the lowest. This reflects that donors' do not want Nepal to progress towards a self-reliant economy. Nor is the government of Nepal interested in developing a production sector out of its own resources because of its obsession with foreign aid. It appears that the Nepal government would not be able to carry out many of its usual functions, such as the delivery of health services, drinking water and educational facilities, without aid. The government has developed a mentality of accepting even minuscule amounts of aid for activities that could have been managed by itself. For example, the MOF accepted Rs. 100,000.0 from NTPF of Finland and Rs. 400,000 from Save the Children (Naya Patrika, 2021 September). The ruling elites and mainstream economists of Nepal prop up the rulers by advocating the need for more foreign aid to escape the low growth trap and persistent poverty on the grounds of a low aid gross domestic product (GDP) ratio and low per capita aid.

3.4 Motives of Aid to Nepal

Foreign aid donors to Nepal have their own political, strategic and economic interests but all these are masked by saying that aid is meant for Nepal's development. The first major US aid initiative itself, which was centred on Europe, was motivated by political and commercial considerations. This aid initiative, popularly known as the 'Marshall Plan', as it was proposed by Secretary of State George Marshall and also termed the 'European Recovery Plan', was meant to reconstruct Europe and its economy severely ravaged by World War II. The US channelled

US$13.3 billion to 16 European countries over four years, as it anticipated that reconstruction of European economy would increase American exports and trade revenue that would strengthen its position as a global economic power. The American aid programme was made an integral part of its foreign policy with the announcement of Point Four Program by the 33rd US President Harry S. Truman in his 1949 inaugural address. The fourth point of the Point Four Program was related to availing US TA to underdeveloped areas for development based on the concepts of democratic fair-dealing.[1]

> The Truman Doctrine, when considered alongside the Marshall Plan and US cold war policy documents, it becomes apparent that primary aim of US aid was prevention of the global spread of communist influence, particularly the Soviet expansion, while improvement of lives internationally was secondary.
>
> (Winterhalt, 2018: 1–2)

Tarnoff and Lawson (2016) report that US leaders and policymakers view foreign assistance as an 'essential instrument of U.S. foreign policy' which has 'increasingly been associated with national security policy'. Foreign aid is used as one of a number of tools to further donors' foreign policy goals. Foreign aid also allows the donor state access and influence in the domestic and foreign affairs of other states (Apodaca, 2017).

Aid flow to Nepal started with two major motives of donors. First, when Nepal became free from the shackles of the Rana regime, the country was at the bottom of the development ladder by many standards. The country had very low per capita income, low skills, limited financial resources and poor economic and social infrastructure (roads, schools, hospitals, drinking water), which were considered indispensable for development. An early study shows that in 1956/7, the country had only 3,097 MT of food grain production, 2,000 MT of sugar production, 660 km of road, 5 telephone lines, 6,000 kW of electricity, 1,500 primary and secondary schools, 649 hospital beds and 4.0 percent literacy rate (Pradhan, 1976). People had high expectations that the miserable condition in which they were forced to live by the Rana rulers would improve with the change in political power from Rana to Shah kings. This expectation was presumed as a 'revolution of rising expectations' by the Americans, and they held that, if not satisfied, it would drive frustrated millions to seek radical political solutions, which could only mean communism (Mihaly, 2002 [1965]). So the United States initiated the lead in assisting Nepal, and India followed too, haunted by the same spectre, and by the 1960s, Nepal became the focus of orchestrated worldwide pity from a variety of countries and world organizations for a variety of activities to prevent the growth of communism. As a matter of fact, there was a kind of competition among diverse donors with divergent ideologies to make an imprint of their own in the just opened-up virgin land through aid.

Second, apart from the 'revolution of rising expectation' that was suspected to trigger communism from internal discontent, the Americans and the Indians believed that Nepal was also externally vulnerable to communist influence from China, which bordered Nepal on the northern side. So the US and Indian motives for aid to Nepal had the common goal of insulating Nepal from Chinese influence.

However, they adopted different strategies to achieve this goal. The Americans believed that it was the agricultural sector which was most vulnerable to communism because a large majority of people lived in agriculture with primitive and stagnant economic life. So the early American aid focussed on agricultural projects, and in 1987, a mega project, the Rapti Valley Development Project, was launched with the objective of increasing household income and well-being by strengthening village and district economic capabilities and expanding resources, infrastructure and social services. The project area included five districts (Dang, Rolpa, Pyuthan, Salyan and Rukum), which were some of the poorest and remotest districts of the country. But the project outcomes were miserable. The project was a great opportunity lost, as land distribution was by no means equal; too many large landholdings were sold to politicians in Kathmandu, who were interested in a quick return; farmers got into debt and were forced to sell the land at a low price; and by 1963, the vast majority of farmers in the valley were farming with the archaic farm techniques that their ancestors used. Furthermore, there was no evidence of productivity increase, but the US projects expanded the government's recurrent costs for salaries and service programmes, making Nepal dependent on external financing to meet this enlarged budget (Mihaly, 2002 [1965]). A study conducted by the US Agency for International Development (USAID) concluded, 'It did open 11,500 hectares of terai land for cultivation, but for a $2.0 million effort it proved disappointing' (Skerry et al., 1991). What the American aid did was destroy the environment, eliminate the indigenous tribal people and enrich more of the majority of relatively better among the poor migrants than before the intervention.

India, on the other hand, held that communism as represented by China could be best excluded by maintaining a 'special relationship' with Nepal and by keeping Nepal subservient to the Indian economy. So the Indians designed their early aid programmes through which Nepal could be subjected to its control. We can illustrate this with two early projects both started in 1953 with Indian aid. First, the reconstruction of Gaucharan airport of Kathmandu (renamed Tribhuvan International Airport in 1964), was designed for only small aircraft. It did not permit bigger planes crossing the Himalayas just to debar the entry of Chinese planes into Kathmandu. For a long period of time, the switchboard of the airport was under the control of the Indian Embassy in Kathmandu. Second, the construction of the 125-km-long Tribhuvan Rajpath that linked Kathmandu with Raxaul, a border town of Bihar in India was meant to serve Indian security and commercial interest. The highway, built by Indian army engineers with little Nepalese participation and designed unnecessarily long with several zigzags through mountainous terrain, suited India's security and commerce interests rather than helping Nepal's development. Moreover, India retained the administration and maintenance of the highway until August 1965 (Malla, 2012). This highway not only eased the entry of Indian security forces in case of Chinese aggression over Nepal and therefrom to India but also opened the Nepalese market for cheap Indian goods. The influx of cheap Indian manufactured goods in Nepal from the early years ensued a process that was further reinforced by the clause of preferential treatment to each other's goods in the trade treaties between the two countries virtually slammed the growth of national industries in Nepal.

The American and Indian aid could not, however, debar the entry of Chinese aid to Nepal. China entered Nepal in 1956 with grant assistance of $12.6 million (cash and commodities). This was followed by aid for the construction of the 115 km Kodari road linking Kathmandu to Khasa border of the Tibet Autonomous Region of China in 1963 as a counter to the Indian domination over Nepal. China also supported the establishment of a number of import substituting industries that would help Nepal to reduce its dependence on India. The Chinese entry into Nepal spurred both India and the United States to raise their respective assistance to Nepal. Soviet Russia started its aid programme in 1959, and like China, the Russian aid also focussed on the construction of roads and establishment of a few import substituting industries. With the end of the Cold War, US-Soviet competition in aid flow to Nepal ended. However, a new kind of aid cold war between China and the United States has ensued to hold Nepal under each country's power and influence. China wants Nepal's support on the Tibetan issue, particularly its commitment to the 'One China policy'; control of anti-China political activities by Tibetan refugees staying in Nepal, estimated to be around 20,000; and stringent restriction on cross-border movements. On the other hand, the United States wants Nepal's cooperation in providing support to the Tibetan refugees through the USAID, respect of refugees' human rights, religious freedoms and cultural identities and the rights to peaceful protest. Apart from this, it is understood that a major reason behind the United States pushing a US $500 million grant to Nepal under the MCC was to counter Nepal's signing of an Memorandum of Understanding with China for bilateral cooperation under the Chinese Belt and Road Initiative (BRI) on 12 May 2017. It was just four months later that the MCC was signed between Nepal and the MCC chief on 14 September 2017. The United States also wanted Nepal to be a part of the State Partnership Programme (SPP) for American support to Nepal's military for training, education and related activities in 2019, but after it became a hotly debated political issue, Nepal's cabinet decided not to move ahead on the SPP on 20 June 2022. All these suggest that America is quite apprehensive of BRI posing a significant challenge to its strategic interests in Nepal and a threat to its dominant world role.

3.5 The American MCC Grant Controversy

In seven decades of aid history in Nepal, no other foreign grant came under more intense public furor and political controversy than the MCC grant of US$500.0 million or NRs 55.0 billion approximately. The MCC was founded in 2004 by the then-president of the United States George Bush with ratification from Congress to provide aid to poor and middle-income countries. MCC signs either a compact or a Threshold Agreement with a partner country. The compact is a large five-year programme to fund specific projects meant for stimulating growth and reducing poverty, whereas the Threshold Programme is smaller and intended for policy and institutional reforms.

The compact was signed by then-finance minister of Nepal Gyanendra Bahadur Karki under the government of Nepali Congress (NC) president Sher Bahadur Deuba and chief executive officer of MCC, Jonathan G. Nash, on 14 September 2017.

The major projects to be financed by the compact grant are (a) set up a 400 kV transmission line running 300 km on the Lapsiphedi–Galchhi–Damauli–Sunawal power corridor which will connect Indian and Nepali power markets and (b) maintenance of around 300 km of roads on the East-West Highway. Nepal signed the compact, which states the goal 'to reduce poverty through economic growth and also strengthen good governance, economic freedom, and investments in the people of Nepal'. Nepal started the process for the MCC grant in 2012, and all successive governments carried this forward; eventually, the office of the Millennium Challenge Account-Nepal was established in 2015 under the Development Board Act with approval from the cabinet (MOF, 2020).

The MCC grant flared up into an intense political debate when the compact was registered in the parliament on 15 July 2019 for endorsement when KP Oli of the Nepal Communist Party (NCP) was prime minister. The debate first sparked off within the ruling NCP (a party formed through unification UML led by chairman KP Oli and Maoists Party led by chairman Prachanda) with Prime Minister KP Oli and Foreign Minister Pradeep Gyanwali wanting the compact to be endorsed by the parliament, while other influential party leaders, including Bhim Rawal of UML and some Maoist lawmakers, criticized the compact, arguing that some clauses of the agreement undermined Nepal's sovereignty and contained US strategic interests. Other smaller left parties also voiced criticisms against MCC on its intention of countering China's BRI and bringing Nepal under the American security fold. The statement of David J. Ranz, assistant secretary for South Asia at the US State Department, during his Nepal visit in May 2019, that MCC was an important part of the Indo-Pacific Strategy further flared up anti-compact campaign, demonstrations and public speeches. Prime Minister KP Oli held Central Committee meetings to sort out the issue but without any outcome, and eventually, the party secretariat formed a three-member task force under the leadership of senior party leader and former prime minister Jhala Nath Khanal with Foreign Minister Pradeep Gyanwali and Bhim Rawal as members to study and recommend the way forward. The committee suggested amendments to some articles and sub-articles of the agreement prior to ratification through the parliament, but this was not heeded by KP Oli government.

The major issues of controversy and debate on the MCC Compact grant may be described as follows:

(a) **Ratification of MCC Compact by the Parliament**: The MCC Compact does not explicitly state that it needs to be ratified by Nepal's parliament. However, Article 7 of the agreement says, 'The parties understand that this compact, upon entry into force, will prevail over the domestic laws of Nepal'. Implementation of this clause necessitates ratification of the compact by parliament, as provisioned in the Nepal Treaty Act, 1990 (2047 BS). The MCC lobbyists argue that as the provisions in the compact are ratified by US Congress, it is necessary that Nepal desiring the grant should ratify it from parliament. They further argue that because MCC is a huge grant, the US government desires uninterrupted completion of the project irrespective of changes in government, and this would be possible only if it is ratified by parliament. It is also argued that ratification by parliament would keep the project out of the influence of the unstable politics of Nepal and give it continuity in execution.

(b) **Connection with Indo-Pacific Strategy**: One of the major criticisms against the MCC is that it is related to the Indo-Pacific Strategy (IPS), which is a US military and security programme directed against countering the influence of China, North Korea and Russia over smaller and developing countries in the Indo-Pacific region. The IPS is specifically aimed at controlling the Chinese expansion towards becoming the world's largest economic power. Even though the agreement does not show any indication of the MCC grant as being related to US security strategy, a study of various US national security strategies and IPS papers reveals that this is not so. It would, therefore, be worthwhile to examine the link between MCC and IPS and US security strategy.

i The forty-third US president George W. Bush's first National Security Strategy (NSS) report released on 20 September 2002 outlines the American grand strategy of 'distinctly American internationalism' to further US interests through economic assistance to nations, decisive security actions, cooperative stability and economic progress. The report mentions the Millennium Challenge Account as a scheme for extending development assistance to countries that follow American values and principles. It says, 'The United States will deliver greater development assistance through the New Millennium Challenge Account to nations that govern justly, invest in their people, and encourage economic freedom' (USA, 2002). The strategy further says,

> We propose a 50 percent increase in the core development assistance given by the United States. While continuing our present programs, including humanitarian assistance based on need alone, these billions of new dollars will form a new Millennium Challenge Account for projects in countries whose governments rule justly, invest in obligation to measure the success of our development assistance by whether it is delivering results. For this reason, we will continue to demand that our own development assistance as well as assistance from the multilateral development banks has measurable goals and concrete benchmarks for achieving those goals.
>
> (USA, 2002: 21–2)

ii The IPS was announced by President Donald Trump in November 2017 with the objective of deepening and expanding US strategic partnerships with countries of the Indo-Pacific region that span the Pacific Ocean to the Indian subcontinent so as to contain China's rise as a world power. In June 2019, the US Department of Defense issued a major new policy document, the *Indo-Pacific Strategy Report*, which stated, 'Inter-state strategic competition, defined by geopolitical rivalry between free and repressive world order visions, is the primary concern for U.S. national security'. In December 2017, President Trump issued the US NSS, of which the Fourth Pillar 'Advance American Influence' shows concern over the expansion of Chinese and Russian investments in the developing world to expand influence and gain competitive advantages against the United States. 'China is investing billions of dollars in infrastructure across the globe. Russia, too, projects its influence economically, through the control of key energy and other infrastructure throughout parts of Europe and Central Asia' (USA, 2017: 38). What is hinted with regard to Chinese infrastructure project is the 'Belt and Road Initiative' which was launched in 2013 by President Xi Jinping aimed at creating a vast network of railways, energy pipelines, and highways through the mountainous former Soviet republics to Pakistan, India, and the rest of Southeast Asia. As a counter to this massive Chinese investment project, the United States has advanced the MCC to expand its influence in the world. A paragraph of the NSS states, 'The United States will use diplomacy and assistance to encourage states to make choices that improve governance, rule of law, and sustainable development. We already do this through the Millennium Challenge Corporation, which selects countries that are committed to reform and monitors and evaluates their projects' (USA, 2017: 39).

iii The IPS paper released by the US Department of Defense on 1 June 2019 lists Nepal as one of the countries in the Indian Ocean Region along with India, Sri Lanka, the Maldives and Bangladesh for expanding American partnerships to respond to shared regional challenges. The paragraph on Nepal says,

> The United States seeks to expand our defense relationship with Nepal, focused on HA/DR (humanitarian assistance and disaster relief), peacekeeping operations, defense professionalization, ground force capacity and counter terrorism. Our growing defense partnership can be seen in the establishment of US Army Pacific-led Land Forces Talks in June 2018, our senior-most military dialogue in Nepal.
>
> (USA, 2019a: 36)

(c) The US Department of State document *A Free and Open Indo-Pacific: Advancing a Shared Vision* released on 4 November 2019 mentions MCC as an economic pillar of IPS.

> To date, support has included $2.9 billion through the Department of State and USAID for the economic pillar of the Indo-Pacific Strategy since the beginning of the Trump Administration, and hundreds of millions more through other agencies, including the U.S. Millennium Challenge Corporation (MCC) and the Overseas Private Investment Corporation (OPIC).
>
> (USA, 2019b: 13)

(d) **USA Has Upper Hand in the Audit of MCC Expenses**: Section 3.7(c) clause of the MCC Agreement binds the government of Nepal to permit authorized representatives of MCC, the Inspector General of MCC, the US Government Accountability Office, any auditor responsible for an audit contemplated in the agreement. It is not only that the MCC has the authority to audit MCC funding but also that it has the right to audit the government's use of MCC funding (Section 3.8(d)).

(e) **Power Export to India**: The proponents of MCC argue that the cross-border transmission line connecting Butwal in Nepal with Gorakhpur in India would enable the export of Nepal's surplus power to India. But it could also be that it would be India to export power to Nepal because of cheaper Indian production. Hence it is contentious to argue that Nepal would attract investment in large hydropower plants to generate thousands of megawatts to export to India. It could be just that Nepal would be confined to small power plants mostly for localized domestic consumption.

The MCC grant controversy in Nepal unnecessarily dragged China and the United States into accusations and counter-accusations with each other. When the BRI was announced by China, the United States initiated the IPS in 2017 to counter China's economic and strategic influence in the region. On the MCC issue, the statement of a senior US State Department official, Alice G Wells, 'The Government of Nepal is sovereign, that it does not take dictation from China, and that it will do what is in the best interests of its country to advance the economic welfare of its people' sparked off Chinese comment that 'Beijing welcomed any international assistance to Nepal, if it is for economic cooperation' (Chinese Ambassador to Nepal Hou Yanqi).

The MCC issue was side-lined for some time in the fierce political battle between KP Oli on the one hand and Maoist and Jhala Nath Khanal–Madhav Nepal group within the NCP on the other after KP Oli dissolved the House on 20 December 2020. The MCC issue was again raised after Sher Bahadur Deuba of NC became prime minister on 13 July 2021, following the disunification of NCP as United Marxist–Leninist (UML) and Maoists as in their pre-merger status and formation of a separate party by Jhala Nath Khanal–Madhav Nepal faction of UML. After some weeks into Deuba's appointment as prime minister, Fatema Z. Sumar and Zonathan Brooks, vice president and deputy vice president at the Compact Operations, visited Nepal on 9 September 2021 to assess what the coalition parties in the new government and the main opposition party (UML) thought about MCC. In early February 2022, US Assistant Secretary of State Donald Lu warned that the United States would review its relations with Nepal if the MCC Compact was not ratified by parliament by the 28 February deadline.

Prior to that, the government had asked for clarification from the MCC on 11 major questions and supplementary concerns. The questions included whether MCC was a part of the IPS or not, whether the MCC grant would bring Nepal within the American security alliance, whether the MCC Compact was above Nepal's constitution, whether the compact impinged on Nepal's sovereignty and national interests and so on. The MCC quickly replied to all questions without giving any benefit of the doubt to Nepal in a manner that anyone could expect from a donor agency given the nature of the questions. Even after all this, there was no consensus in the government because the major coalition parties (Maoist and Unified Socialist) in the government were opposed to ratification of the compact without some amendments in the agreement, while the opposition party, UML made endorsement conditional upon fulfilment of its political demand. As the deadline approached, Prime Minister Deuba was on the horns of a dilemma: if he sought the support of UML in rectifying the MCC, he would have to break the coalition which the UML wanted, but if he broke the coalition, it would be unethical because the coalition was the foundation upon which he was made prime minister. Deuba also feared that breaking the coalition would bring together Maoist, UML and Unified Socialist into an election alliance in the May local elections and also in the federal and provincial elections, which would be a setback to the NC. On the other hand, the UML had been obstructing the proceedings of the House since August 2021, demanding the resignation of Speaker of the House Agni Prasad Sapkota on the charge of refusing its request to take action against 14 of its lawmakers for defecting party to form a new party (Unified Socialist) led by Madhav Nepal. The UML also used the endorsement of MCC as a political bargaining card to come back to the government by dismantling the coalition. The coalition parties, Maoists and unified Socialist also wanted to avoid the breakdown but were hesitant to rectify MCC in its present form because of the risk of pro-American tag by the party cadres and left intellectuals. Ultimately, a middle course was worked out in the form of an 'interpretative declaration' to be attached to MCC which provided face-saving to the Maoist, and the MCC was ratified through the parliament on 27 February, one day prior to the deadline, amid uproars by the UML.

Whatever may be the benefits and associated price of the MCC grant, this has exposed how superpowers use development aid as an instrument for pursuing their geopolitical and strategic interest in developing nations like Nepal. Through MCC, the United States wants to incorporate Nepal into its IPS and intensify Washington and New Delhi's anti-China coalition to contain China's hegemony in the region through Nepal and counter the BRI aimed at connecting countries in Central, South and Southeast Asia with China. The United States is also apprehensive of the Chinese economic and strategic potential to replace it as the world's sole superpower. Owing to its geo-strategic location, Nepal is in the vortex of a cold tussle between the United States and China, with India having the same interest as the United States, and this has posed challenges to Nepal in maintaining its 'equidistant diplomacy' with all three countries. Nepal is in a thorny trilemma in its economic, political and diplomatic relations with China, India and the United States, not only because China and India are two big powers with large territories bordering Nepal, while the United States is still the world's only superpower and strategic player of global order, but also because all three are the largest providers of foreign assistance to Nepal.

3.6 Has Aid Helped?

The first critic of aid to Nepal was an American economist, E. B. Mihaly, who after studying the first 12 years (1951–62) of aid business in Nepal, observed that the foreign aid programme was politically motivated and failed to work because of faulty assumptions. Mihaly concluded, '[B]ecause of the shape and direction they gave to the aid programmes, aid not only failed to give a significant boost to Nepal's economy, but it may even have made growth more difficult to achieve' and made a gloomy remark, 'Nepal's increased reliance on foreign support could, in the long run, jeopardize its independence and distort its foreign policy' (Mihaly, 2002 [1965]: 209, 216).

Another early study made in 1972 covering the period 1964/5–1967/8 concluded, 'Aid substituted for domestic savings in capital formation and as a consequence has actually reduced the need to mobilize national savings' (Rana, 1972: 4–5). The study, however, noted that during the decade of 1960, almost all the expansion of roads and a large part of the changes in health and education were made possible by foreign aid. Describing the role of foreign aid during the Panchayat regime, Gaige derived the conclusion that foreign aid assisted the monarchy in creating a better-equipped and better-trained army, strengthening the 'status quo' and evading and avoiding institutional and political reforms by absorbing the educated middle class who were seen as the potentially restive force for change in the administrative payrolls (Gaige, 2009 [1975]).

A research study evaluating the utility of foreign aid received by Nepal during the period 1950–80 observed that foreign aid had a variety of adverse repercussions and undesired consequences. These were identified as (i) development of prestige projects, i. e., airports, hotels, communication, water sewerage, etc., that served the interest of privileged class and metropolis; (ii) foreign experts who came as a part of assistance received sky-high salaries and perks, which demoralized the Nepalese counterparts of equal status; (iii) foreign advisers received twice the salary they would receive in America, which motivated even incompetent and inefficient persons to join the advisory set, and high salaries made the advisers prolong their stay and recommend more advisors for further carrying out the work; (iv) foreign experts worked from the lens of the personal and political interest of the countries they represented and what they learnt from the books and experience of other countries than by the ground realities of Nepal; and (v) fostering of complacent attitudes in government machinery in exploring domestic revenue resources and developing correct institutions and policies for self-sustained progress (Poudyal, 1982).

An early work which used savings as a dependent variable and GDP and foreign aid both current and lagged as independent variables for the period between 1964/5 and 1981/2 showed (a) coefficient of GDP with a positive sign and significant while that of foreign aid negative, but not significant; (b) coefficient of GDP with positive sign and significant while that of foreign aid lagged negative and significant at 5 percent level; and (c) coefficient of GDP lagged with positive sign and significant while that of foreign aid lagged negative and significant at 10 percent (Poudyal, 1986). These findings broadly suggest that savings are negatively affected by foreign aid.

A seminar by the Integrated Development System (IDS) of Nepal in 1983 (October 5) concluded (IDS, 1984): (i) Foreign aid did not help to change the social structure, nor did it help to narrow down the gap between the upper class and the lower class and between the rural and the urban areas. On the contrary, what it did was speed up the monetization of the rural economy, contributing to the penetration of the Indian market within Nepal and transfer of capital from rural to urban areas, benefitting those classes which determined the content and channels of foreign aid inflow into Nepal. (ii) Foreign aid made no perceptible impact on the general levels of poverty and the conditions of poorer and disadvantaged people. The Integrated Rural Development Programmes (IRDPs) did not benefit the poor but became the tools for the bureaucracy, politicians and local elites to mould the benefits in their favour in the name of the poor. (iii) Foreign aid did not benefit women, as various development activities, including the foreign-funded IRDPs and other rural projects, such as the Rural Save Grain Project and Vegetable Seed Production Project, and the components covered by these (increasing production, employment, forestry, soil and water management, animal husbandry, etc.) took for granted male and female farmers as 'rural farmers'. This conception overlooked the fact that in the rural socio-economic milieu, it is the males who represent the farm family in the society and outside activities, receive the benefits of development projects supplied by the government as well as non-government agencies and participate in them. (iv) Foreign aid in the agricultural sector had the objective of increasing production by supporting the development of irrigation and other infrastructure, supply of inputs, machinery and equipment, research, training and strengthening of institutions. But all these had very little impact on raising agricultural production, with the average growth rate being 0.7 percent per annum during the period 1970/1 and 1982/3. Food production increased only by a little over 1.0 percent per annum, which was also due to an increase in the area under food crops, and the performance in the livestock sector was equally disappointing. (v) Foreign aid made the entry of a large number of expatriate advisors and provided opportunities for training and higher education to a larger number of civil service staff abroad, but all these had no perceptible impact on raising the work proficiency of the bureaucracy. (vi) Foreign aid led to a situation where Nepal did not have its own strategy of development, other than the dutiful recital of development themes that were fashionable at a particular point in time; development strategy tended to follow aid rather than vice versa.

The assessment made in 2002 also corroborates that foreign aid has not helped to reduce poverty in Nepal. The report says,

> Despite a heavy donor presence and sustained high levels of aid to Nepal (with foreign agencies contributing some 60% of Nepal's development budget) and the existence of a wide variety of development programmes, the number of people falling below the poverty line has not decreased over the last twenty years.
> (Seddon and Hussein, 2002: 2)

One particular sector in which the impact of foreign aid can be observed is the road network. For instance, in 1960/1, the length of road was only 701 km, which increased to 8,025 km in 1991/2 (MEP, 1965; MOF, 1992/3). This has been made possible due to foreign aid, as the largest proportion of aid up to 2004/5 was channelled into transport and communication. The real question to ask is, has the expansion of the road network contributed to enlarging the production base of the economy? The answer to this is largely no – if the roads had impacted on enlarging the production base, the situation of ever-growing imports of rice, vegetables and fruits to meet the domestic demand would not have occurred. The roads were meant only for internal security so that troops could be transported swiftly to put down armed insurrections within the country, as they were in 1974/5 during the 'troubles' in the far north with the *khampas* (Blaikie et al., 1980). The roads not only failed to enhance the productive capacity of the economy but also tarnished rural artisan production, such as shoemaking, tailoring and making of metal utensils associated respectively with the occupational groups, Sarki, Damai, and Kami owing to an influx of cheaper ready-made substitutes from neighbouring countries due to road connectivity (Blaikie et al., 1980).

Furthermore, the roads were built without many geological and environmental assessments, and this has caused severe environmental degradation and ecological crisis. An American sociologist visiting Nepal way back in 1974 narrated a bleak picture of environmental degradation due to forest clearance for road construction. The alarming picture was reflected by the surfacing of an immense new island of 40,000 square miles of Himalayan silts in the Bay of Bengal spotted by an Earth Resources Technology Satellite. Part of it started down from the headwaters of the Brahmaputra River in Tibet and the rest had travelled 1,500 miles or so down the Ganges from Nepal. Ironically, this has happened with a standing army of foreign advisers in the country and directing operations for a quarter of a century, during which Nepalese have cut down three-quarters of their trees (American Sociologist, 1974). The East-West Highway built by the Chinese, Russians, Indians, Americans, British, the World Bank and others, each claiming a section, and many other roads constructed crisscrossing the forbidding terrain and hills have significantly eased the movement of people and goods, but the impact has been more environmental harm than good. There has been a strong tendency among people to go where the road goes along 3 to 4 km, build shops and lodges, clearing trees and vegetation while damaging the geological, hydrological and agricultural environments and leaving the old patterns of settlement to ruin. The shrinking food supplies from the surrounding areas because of a lack of farmworkers owing to migration within and outside the country has rendered such roadside businesses a fledging commercial activity mainly fed by imported goods and materials.

A regression analysis was carried out to test the relationship between GDP and foreign aid with Nepal's data spanning over a period of 45 years (1974/5–2018/9) with GDP as the dependent variable and investment, population and foreign aid as independent variables. The regression results were as follows:

$$\begin{aligned} \ln \mathrm{GDP}_t &= 0.66 + 0.77 \ \ln \mathrm{INV}_t + 1.38 \ \ln \mathrm{POP}_t - 0.11 \ \ln \mathrm{F}_t \\ &\quad (1.62)\ (19.41) \qquad (5.86) \qquad (-2.07) \\ \mathrm{R}^{-2} &= 0.99,\ \mathrm{F} = 7024.0,\ \mathrm{DW} = 1.69 \end{aligned}$$

Note: Figures in parentheses are t values. The coefficients are all significant at the 5.0 percent level.

All variables are in current prices. The population is used as a proxy for the labour force. The coefficients of investment and population are positive and statistically significant, while foreign aid has a significant negative coefficient which implies that the elasticity of GDP with respect to foreign aid is negative. The overall fit is exceptionally high as shown by very high value of R^{-2}, and there is no autocorrelation. One has, therefore, reason to infer that increases in foreign aid lead to reduction in GDP.

3.7 Utility of TA

Every foreign aid flow to Nepal has invariably a component of TA, which is justified on the grounds of the flow of new ideas, transfer of knowledge, skills and technologies from the developed to the underdeveloped countries to enhance absorptive capacity and lead to more effective use of aid. TA comes in four different forms, such as (a) policy development, (b) institutional development, (c) capacity building and (d) project or programme support. Whatever may be the form of TA, it involves sending short-or long-term foreign experts or consultants in diverse areas of specialization; providing scholarships, training, study tours or seminars to the Nepalese nationals in developed countries; and funding short-term and long-term training and workshops in the country.

Foreign experts started advising Nepal during the Rana regime but became more pronounced and pervasive in the later years with Nepal's adoption of development planning and flow of aid from different countries and international aid agencies. A comparison of data on TA received by Nepal form 2014/5 to 2018/9 shows that the total number of projects exceeded 300 each year except in 2015/6, and the amount of TA was nearly Rs. 50.0 billion in the last two years (Table 3.2).

There have been no serious evaluation studies on the contribution of TA to building institutions and fostering the processes needed for Nepal's development. Evaluation reports of the World Bank and other agencies' TA in various countries, as documented by Chakravarti reveals,

> (a) a 1982 World Bank evaluation of 95 completed projects found that only 36.0 percent of the projects had achieved substantial progress and around 50.0 percent had been partially successful; (b) another evaluation of World Bank's technical assistance activities worldwide in 1990 showed that over 40.0 percent had a negligible institutional impact; (c) the 1991 World Bank Technical Assistance Task Force report found that of 50 technical assistance loans to support structural adjustment lending in the 1980s, only less than one-third of cases had substantial success; (d) in Sub-Saharan Africa, of 1689 World Bank projects with institutional development objectives approved between 1971 and 1991, only 29.0 percent had a substantial impact, while the impact on the rest was either modest or negligible; (e) a review of 300 US Agency for International Development (USAID) projects containing an institution-building component found that only about half had achieved their immediate objectives;

Table 3.2 TA from Donors and INGOs (Rs. in Billion)

FY	*From Donors*				*From INGOs*			*Overall Total*	
	Bilateral	*Multilateral*	*Total No. of Projects*	*Amount*	*No. of INGOs*	*No. of Projects*	*Amount*	*No. of Projects*	*Amount*
2014/5	48	105	153	20.7	124	159	9.2	312	29.9
2015/6	44	89	133	19.6	106	150	9.8	283	29.4
2016/7	56	78	134	22.5	135	179	15.8	313	38.3
2017/8	50	91	141	25.1	139	194	22.8	335	47.9
2018/9	57	78	135	24.7	148	204	25.0	339	49.7

Source: Computation based on 'Statement of Technical and Other Assistance', Annual Issues, MOF, Government of Nepal.

> (f) A UN Development Programme/Food and Agricultural Organization (UNDP/FAO) evaluation of support to 33 research institutions found that one-third of the institutions had closed down after four years, and, more generally, the condition in many had deteriorated, while others were failing to become self-reliant; (g) a review of technical assistance activities of several Nordic countries found that, of the 324 expatriate positions considered, 80 percent could be classified as administrators, while only 20 percent could be considered as institution builders; and (h) the Berg report (1993) commissioned by the UNDP found that technical cooperation did not work well, was costly, ineffective and had little lasting impact and providing employment to the donor organizations' nationals and business to their INGOs and other institutions.
>
> (Chakravarti, 2005: 56–9)

Similarly, Morgan observes that in many instances, TA has led to a sense of dependence and crowding out national initiatives; it has led to encouraging countries to put in place the wrong policies, organizations and institutions and eroded the ownership, commitment and independent action of national actors (Morgan, 2002). These findings and observations made with regard to TA in different contexts equally hold true for any individual country like Nepal. In the specific context of Nepal, the major reasons for the low usefulness of TA are as follows:

First, as in most other countries, TA is used wastefully in Nepal because it is viewed as a 'free good' and is mostly donor-driven, rather than arising from the clearly identified, prioritized and calibrated needs of the Nepalese economy. Because TA is grant-financed, there is a general tendency of officials of Nepal to readily accept it not because the country really needs the project but because of their desire for equipment, goods and foreign travel for no cost and even lucrative jobs after retirement from government office. As one top bureaucrat of Nepal, based on his own working experience in coordinating foreign aid resources of the country for a long period of time, observes,

> One cannot say that senior civil servants or other senior public officials and dignitaries work for donors in a visible way, while they are sitting. However, when they get retired, they immediately join donors' offices – some of them the very next day. Their joining to donors' offices, be it as staff members or as advisers, experts or consultants, create a gap of skills and experiences, within the recipient, at the same time help donors to design and implement parallel projects and creating parallel units.
>
> (Ghimire, 2019: 161–2)

Some officials even resort to the unbelievable practice of pleasing donor agencies for squandering aid money for personal benefit.

> Some years ago, a Project Chief concerned with women's development in Nepal used the project's funds to publish a calendar which showed a flower

> pot being watered by different jugs, each representing a specific donor by name. The plant itself (representing the project) comprised a number of branches, each one a district in which the project had a tiny activity or two. The image carried no development message and solely as a means to gratify donor officials for the Project Officer's personal gain.
>
> (Shrestha, 1992: 11)

Second, donors tend to act as principal authorities, whether in terms of agenda setting, resource control or decision-making, to achieve their interests. There are several instances of donors' unpleasing attitudes or pungent remarks or even threats when Nepalese officials try to interrogate certain provisions of TA funding or the contents of the country report proposed by them. In some cases, the concerned government office for which the TA is meant is kept in dark because of donor intention to spend money on activities of their choice and interest. The report by Dhakal (2019) lists some instances: (a) The UNDP, under the 'Parliament Support Project', was to spend Rs. 600.0 million in the next five years for the training of federal and provincial parliamentarians. But the Speaker of the House was unaware of the agreement made on 23 April 2018 in the parliament secretariat until a question was raised by a Member of Parliament. (b) The National Human Rights Commission was kept in abeyance of the Rs. 3.0 billion agreement made by the MOF with Denmark for a 'Peace, Human Rights and Governance Improvement Project' for three years. The agreement was made in 2014, and the Commission came to know about this only at the end of 2017. (c) When the government barred foreigners from observing the local elections of 2017, the American Embassy sent a note to the Ministry of Foreign Affairs on 5 May 2017 alleging it as a bad practice that would jeopardize American assistance in the future, stating, 'American taxpayers' money is spent on Nepal's democracy, peace process, political parties and election candidates'. (d) The Indian assistance agreement made in 2009 for the construction of a police training centre remains stagnant owing to the then Indian Ambassador Rakesh Sood's demand of employing his nominee as chief of the centre for a tenure of five years and Nepal's stand to reduce the tenure to one year. (e) The report of 'Nepal Peace Trust Fund Project' funded by Denmark and other donors to be published under the banner of the National Planning Commission (NPC) was not published due to two objectionable statements: (a) nearly 0.40 million Nepalese have not received citizenship, and (b) all Nepalese cannot vote. Objections over these statements by a senior official of the NPC was backfired when the Danish representative questioned the authority of the official. (f) The tussle on selecting a team to visit India for the study of a social service system between the donor representative and director general of the Prison Management Department, Yuba Raj Pandey, led to the withdrawal of UK government DFID funded project called the 'Open Prison and Community Service System'. These are only some representative examples of the large number of cases of donors' high-handedness in the management of TA given to Nepal.

Third, a large chunk of TA is spent on staff salaries, consultancy services and vehicles procured from the donor country or agency. Information on the cost structure of TA projects in Nepal is not readily available, but a TA project implemented by the United Nations (UN) or another donor agency shows

> (a) 50–60 percent of the value is accounted for by expatriate costs, consultancies, staff travels and benefits; (b) 20–30 percent are allocated to training, seminars, workshops and travel abroad mainly for government officials; (c) about 10 percent of the funds go towards the provision of computers, vehicles and other equipment; and (d) 10 percent is meant for administrative overheads.
>
> (Chakravarti, 2005: 54)

Research published by the UK-based organization Action Aid in 2006 found that TA increases the cost of aid by at least 25.0 percent and states, 'The official figures probably underestimate the amount being spent in this area, since most project and programme allocations hide significant spending on TA' (Action Aid, 2005: 22).

Fourth, the expatriate consultants in Nepal have produced piles of reports with wide-ranging titles, but the question is whether these have been of some value to Nepal for improving the administrative system or macroeconomic management. Most of the reports produced by these consultants are non-existent and some lie piled up with dust in various government offices. An early study on the role of foreign experts in the administration of Nepal drew the following major conclusions:

> Foreign advisors are more or less guided by the personal and political interest of the country they represent; they seem to have no confidence in themselves and in the success of their mission, and they have a tendency to analyze Nepal's problems from the experience of other countries; they tend to make recommendations for more advisors on the same issues, who would also do the same job.
>
> (Gongol, 1973)

The inflow of expatriate experts by thousands since Nepal started receiving aid prompted an American professor to say that Nepal was 'under-nourished and over-advised' (Shrestha, 1992).

3.8 Aid Financing of Government Expenditure

Nepal's fiscal performance is characterized by weak revenue mobilization and excessive growth of government expenditure, resulting in an ever-widening budgetary deficit. As a proportion of GDP, internal revenue has ranged between 7.0 percent and 21.8 percent, while expenditure has ranged between 11.8 percent and 26.4 percent on average in each five-year period starting from 1974/5 to 2018/19 (Table 3.3). The emergence and expansion of growing government expenditure and consequently budget deficit cannot be explained only in terms of economic or financial reasons. It has much to do with the mutual self-interest of politicians in power, bureaucrats and the emerging neo-feudal class. As a consequence, the

Table 3.3 Aid Financing of Government Expenditure (in Percent)

Period[a]	*Foreign Aid/ GDP*	*Per Capita Foreign Aid (Rs.)*	*Rev/ GDP*	*Exp/ GDP*	*Revenue Sur/Capital Expenditure*	*Foreign Aid/Capital Expenditure*
1974/5–1978/9	3.4	49.9	7.0	11.8	38.4	43.9
1979/80–1983/4	6.0	123.5	8.6	17.9	25.4	48.9
1984/5–1988/9	6.1	242.6	9.0	18.6	21.8	49.5
1989/90–1993/4	5.5	452.5	9.2	13.2	23.5	47.6
1994/5–1998/9	5.3	723.5	11.0	18.1	23.1	56.8
1999/2000–2003/4	3.7	756.5	11.3	17.3	19.4	61.5
2004/5–2008/9	3.6	1,122.8	12.7	19.3	25.2	61.4
2009/10–2013/4	3.4	2,042.7	16.4	19.2	38.0	86.1
2014/15–2018/9	3.8	3,675.8	21.8	26.4	33.5	55.2

Source: Budget Speech Various Years, MOF; Population Censuses, Central Bureau of Statistics, Economic Survey, Various Years, MOF, Government of Nepal.

a Average of five years.

budget deficit has been a permanent feature of Nepal's budget ever since the budgetary exercise was started in 1952, and it has become structural in nature.

On the revenue side, the politicians of the ruling party always tend to avoid tax measures and hikes in tax rates that displeased the capitalist class, industrialists and rich farmers for securing the vote bank and for mustering election finance. Revenue is also reduced through tax rebates and concessions, tax evasion and lower valuation of taxable income, leading to an increase in the government's budget deficit. In addition, the availability of foreign aid has also propelled the government to relax revenue collection efforts and increase expenditure. The theory suggests that aid and tax are alternative sources of revenue and when aid is available, the government may relax its efforts to raise tax revenue or improve tax administration and compliance. In order to assess whether foreign aid reduced tax revenue in Nepal, a regression equation of tax revenue with GDP and foreign aid lag as independent variables was estimated for the period 1974/5–2018/9. The justification for the use of foreign aid lag is that the current-year tax revenue decision is based on the amount of foreign aid received the previous year. The estimation gave the following result:

$$\ln TR_t = -5.24 + 1.31 \;\ln GDP_t - 0.113 \;\ln F(t-1)$$
$$(-16.05) \quad (12.94) \quad (-1.05)$$
$$R^{-2} = 0.99,\; F = 2{,}898.15,\; DW = 0.27$$

Note: Figures in parentheses are t values.

The coefficient of GDP has the correct sign, suggesting that tax revenue has an elasticity of 1.3 percent with respect to GDP, while foreign aid lag has negative elasticity, which is not significant. The overall goodness of fit as indicated by the high value of R^{-2} is very satisfactory, but there is the presence of autocorrelation. An alternative equation with both GDP and foreign aid lagged was also estimated, and the result shows that the coefficient of GDP is positive and statistically significant, while that of foreign aid lagged, though positive, is not significant. The value of R^{-2} shows a very good fit, but autocorrelation is a problem. The estimated equation was:

$$\ln TR_t = -4.83 + 1.03\ \ln GDP(t-1) + 0.002\ \ln F(t-1)$$
$$(-14.89) \quad (11.87) \quad (0.02)$$
$$R^{-2} = 0.99,\ F = 2{,}527.5,\ DW = 0.43$$

The negative sign of the coefficient of foreign aid in this and earlier equation gives some ground to reason that foreign aid has a negative effect on tax revenue.

On the expenditure side, the availability of foreign aid has prompted the government to squander resources for unnecessary expenditure and allocate funds to satisfy the politicians' demand for projects in their constituencies. In order to obscure low revenue mobilization performance, as well as the size of the budget deficit, the income side of the budget is presented under the heading 'receipts' in which foreign grants are added to the revenue. The inclusion of foreign grants on the receipts side would obviously make the size of the budget deficit smaller than it would have been otherwise. The consequence of lagging revenue and expanding expenditure has resulted in a small revenue surplus (revenue-current expenditure) for financing capital expenditure. As can be seen in Table 3.3, revenue surplus has met capital expenditure only to the extent of 19.4 percent to 38.4 percent during the period 1974/5–2018/9. The high dependence on foreign aid for fiscal expansion and execution of development projects would not have been a cause for serious concern had there been higher economic growth, improvement in productivity and reduction in poverty. But the analysis of the growth scenario in Chapter 1 and poverty in Chapter 2 reveals that there has been neither a growth turnaround in the economy, except a random fluke in one or two years, nor has there been an overall improvement in the living standards of the vast majority of poor people.

3.9 Aid Financing of Development Plans

The contribution of foreign aid to financing public-sector/capital expenditure of Nepal's periodic development plans has remained quite high throughout the plans. In the First Plan, the amount of foreign aid exceeded the total expenditure, but thereafter, the proportion of foreign aid financing declined in the three subsequent plans and remained 45.0 percent in the Fourth and Fifth Plans. In the Sixth Plan, foreign aid financing shot up to 63.7 percent and remained quite high in the successive plans (between 58.9 percent and 78.6 percent) with the exception of the Fourteenth Plan in which aid financing of public-sector outlay was 33.9 percent. In the Fifteenth Plan aid, financing of capital expenditure increased to 42.7 percent.

One of the consequences of high reliance on aid for financing capital expenditure and public-sector expenditure of plans has been donor influence or direction in national as well as sectoral policymaking processes. They have made aid conditional on the fulfilment of certain conditionalities by Nepal. These conditionalities were pushed by the IMF and the World Bank on their loan facilities which meant policy reforms in the direction of neo-liberalism that consisted of deregulation,

Table 3.4 Aid Financing of Public-Sector Expenditure in Plans (Rs. in Millions)

Plan	*Total Outlay*	*Foreign Aid*	*Foreign Aid/ Public-Sector/Capital Expenditure (%)*
First	330.0	370.9	112.4
Public sector			
Second[a]	600.0	500.0	83.4
Public sector			
Third	2,500.0	1,050	60.4
Public sector	1,740.0		
Fourth	3,540.0	1,490.0	58.5
Public sector	2,550		
Fifth (min)	9,170.0	2,776.5	45.0
Public sector	6,170.0	3,395.0	45.0
(max)	11,404.0		
Public sector	7,545.0		
Sixth	33,940.0	13,050.0	63.7
Public sector	20,490.0		
Seventh	50,410.0	19,662.9	72.9
Public sector	27,000.0		
Eighth	113,479.0	74,355.0	65.5
Total development outlay			
Ninth	189,580.0	111,546.0	58.9
Capital exp.			
Tenth (6.2% growth rate)	505,200.0	134,620.0	57.5
Total exp.	234,030.0		
Development exp.			
Interim[a]	511,378.0	140,660.0	78.6
Capital exp.	178,990.0		
Twelfth[a]	565,140.0	249,280.0	68.5
Capital exp.	364,340.0		
Thirteenth[a]	1,471,568.0	341,590.0	73.7
Public sector	464,010.0		
Fourteenth[a]	2,424,960.0	323,240.0	33.9
Public sector	954,420.0		
Fifteenth	9,958,330.0	1,714,560.0	42.7
Capital exp.	4,015,520.0		

Source: Plan Documents, National Planning Commission, Kathmandu.

a Indicates three-year duration.

privatization, free markets and individuation, which are also named 'Washington Consensus'. In this context, Berg says, with aid 'budget constraints are softened: aid inflows permit hesitant governments to put off hard decisions. Local policy initiatives tend to disappear; officials know that what counts is what donors think and want, so technocrats become passive and politicians deresponsibilized' (Berg, 1993: 298). The Nepalese situation is described as follows: 'This has given rise to a kind of contemporary dependency which has robbed the government of its autonomy as well as the will to pursue the country's development, administrative or other policies independently' (Pandey, 1989). Even the Foreign Aid Policy, which should have been purely an internal initiative, is finalized after consultation with the donors. A report from the MOF says, 'The Ministry of Finance is revising the Foreign Aid Policy, 2002. A preliminary revision was presented and discussed with stakeholders at a pre-consultation session of the Nepal Donors' Consultative Meeting in February 2008. Based on the comments and suggestions received, the Ministry of Finance is working on a new draft' (MOF, 2008a: 35).

A case study of the influence of foreign aid in the policy process in forestry and local governance reveals donors' mediation since 1952 for a range of activities, such as the formulation of a new forest policy, conception of community forestry and the development of a Master Plan and its implementation, local governance, etc. The assistance was augmented after the political change in 1990, concentrating directly on developing and implementing decentralization policies and legislation. However, the aid-supported reforms in policies in these two sectors failed to deliver the desired outcome, as the changes were more aligned with the priorities of donors and their functionaries rather than the changing context of Nepal (Gautam and Pokharel, 2011).

Another consequence of prolonged reliance on aid has made Nepal a virgin ground for testing a number of different approaches and schemes developed by Western donors and multilateral lending agencies. Because the projects/programmes were aid supported, the government exercised nominal control in designing them, selecting consultants for the feasibility surveys and the implementation and evaluation of the projects/programmes. But most of these approaches did not turn out to be relevant to the country and failed to sustain after the end of aid money, disrupting the prevailing system. As an example, the New Education System Plan, 1971, implemented with the assistance of the World Bank, was meant for improving Nepal's education system by introducing the semester system. But after some years, it was abandoned because of various operational modalities that were beyond the capacity of Nepal. Evaluation studies of some foreign projects/programmes reveal that projects/activities continued operation so long as extra funds were provisioned by the donors, as there was no plan for sustainability beyond the termination of aid support. Once the aid stopped, the programmes stopped functioning and reverted to the initial position, leaving behind abandoned staff and equipment, such as computers, laptops and motorcycles, and a great deal of public discontent and frustration.

3.10 Foreign Debt and Debt Servicing

Debt service ratios (expressed as the ratio of principal and interest payments on foreign debt to the earnings from export of goods and services) are used as indicators of the sustainability of a country's debt service obligations, but there are no standard rules to determine what values are within a reasonable limit. It depends upon a country's rate of growth, export earnings and foreign exchange receipts from other sources. Generally, this ratio is expected to be between 0 and 20.0 percent. However, if the debt service ratios are high, much of a country's export earnings will be depleted in servicing its debt and payment of debt service obligations, posing a severe balance of payments problem, particularly when export earnings fall unexpectedly.

Nepal has witnessed a significant increase in foreign indebtedness in the past four-and-a-half decades. Nepal's cumulative debt outstanding had a staggering increase in volume in each consecutive five years starting from 1974/5 to 1999/2000. Thereafter, the increase in volume was lower but still high. The total stock of external debt which was a mere Rs. 0.35 billion in 1974/5 more than doubled in 1979/80. It shot up to Rs. 36.80 billion in 1989/90 and further to Rs. 594.93 billion in 2019/20. Starting at a relatively modest 2.1 percent of GDP four-and-a-half decades ago, the outstanding debt was 50.0 percent of GDP in 1994/5 and 1999/2000 (Table 3.5). Even though this ratio has steadily declined in recent years, it may shoot up again, creating a situation of debt overhang, which means a debt burden so large that the country cannot take on additional debt to finance future projects.

As a consequence of increasing foreign indebtedness, the amount of debt service rose from a meagre Rs. 11.2 million in 1974/5 to Rs. 2.98 billion in 1994/5 and to Rs. 28.80 billion in 2019/20. The debt service ratio increased from 1.3 percent in 1974/5 to 21.8 percent in 1989/90 and to 35.5 percent in 2016/7. However, it decreased in the two subsequent years (27.6 percent and 25.3 percent, respectively) but increased to 29.3 percent in 2019/20 (Table 3.5). Nepal spends more on debt service than it does on education and health care, which are crucial elements for a country's growth and development. For instance, the budget for 2020/1 has earmarked Rs. 17.21 billion for education and Rs. 11.51 billion for health, while the debt service was Rs. 24.54 billion in 2018/9 and Rs. 22.45 billion the year before.

If we look at the debt service to fresh borrowing ratio, the situation was worst in 2004/05 and 2009/10 when debt service outpaced fresh borrowing by 4.6 and 82.0 percent, respectively. Except for the last three years, debt service took away a large proportion of fresh borrowing. When a large proportion of fresh borrowing is required to service debt, relatively fewer funds will be available for investment projects, which drives growth and development, and a foreign loan may become a serious burden to the economy. Given the sluggish economic growth, precarious resource base, lack of structural transformation and unproductive use of foreign aid, Nepal's increasing dependence on external borrowing for budgetary and other purposes in the absence of expansion of productive sectors of the economy and meagre increase in foreign exchange earnings may have serious internal as well as external financial distress on the economy.

3.11 Debt Service Ratio of Nepal and SAARC Countries

A comparison of Nepal's debt service ratio computed from the government data (Table 3.5) with Asian Development Bank (ADB) data shows a big difference – ADB data is two to four times lower. Comparison with SAARC countries for the last eight years shows that Nepal had the highest ratio in 2012, 2015 and 2016 and the second-highest ratio in the other five years. Maldives had the lowest ratio all through the years ranging from 2.1 percent to 3.1 percent except in 2012 and 2019, while Bangladesh had the second lowest ratio, almost the same as Maldives. India had the third-lowest ratio that ranged from 5.8 percent to 8.8 percent (Table 3.6).

Table 3.5 Foreign Debt and Debt Servicing (Rs. in Millions)

FY	*Net Outstanding Debt*	*Borrowing*	*Debt Service*	*Exports*	*Debt Servicing/ Export (%)*	*Debt Servicing/ Borrowing (%)*	*Outstanding Debt/GDP (%)*
1974/5	346.1	96.5	11.2	889.6	1.3	11.6	2.1
1979/80	1,807.3	530.8	23.0	1,150.5	2.0	4.3	7.7
1984/5	9,203.2	1,753.1	189.5	2,740.6	6.9	10.8	19.8
1989/90	36,800.9	5,959.6	1,121.9	5,156.2	21.8	18.8	35.6
1994/5	113,001.0	7,312.2	2,984.7	17,639.2	16.9	40.8	51.6
1999/2000	190,691.0	12,362.4	5,321.4	49,822.7	10.7	43.0	50.2
2004/5	219,642.0	7,743.7	8,101.3	58,705.7	13.8	104.6	41.2
2009/10	256,243.0	7,254.0	13,201.1	60,824.0	21.7	182.0	21.5
2014/5	343,261.8	29,264.2	20,077.9	85,319.0	23.5	68.6	16.1
2015/6	388,762.8	43,774.0	21,106.0	70,117.0	30.1	48.2	17.3
2016/7	413,978.8	58,012.5	25,966.7	73,049.0	35.5	44.8	15.5
2017/8	526,154.1	98,904.6	22,449.6	81,360.0	27.6	22.7	17.3
2018/9	594,926.2	94,400.8	24,544.0	97,110.0	25.3	26.0	17.2
2019/20	819,667.1	173,023.2	28,798.1	97,709.0	29.5	17.6	

Source: Economic Survey, Various Years, MOF, Government of Nepal and Computation.

Table 3.6 Debt Service Ratio of Nepal and SAARC Countries (Percent)

Country	*2012*	*2013*	*2014*	*2015*	*2016*	*2017*	*2018*	*2019*
Bangladesh	2.4	2.5	2.7	3.2	2.8	3.0	3.5	3.4
Bhutan	12.9	17.5	27.1	19.8	14.5	24.8	23.4	15.8
India	5.9	5.9	7.6	8.8	8.3	7.5	6.4	5.8
Maldives	2.9	2.1	2.3	2.3	2.6	2.7	3.1	6.0
Nepal	10.6	9.5	8.9	8.1	9.9	10.8	8.3	8.2
Nepal[a]	22.4	21.8	23.5	30.1	35.5	27.6	25.3	29.3
Pakistan	15.2	19.0	21.6	18.0	19.4	29.6	24.9	39.3
Sri Lanka	19.7	26.8	20.8	28.2	25.6	23.9	28.9	29.7[b]

Sources: Asian Development Bank Data Library: Debt Service Ratio in Asia and the Pacific, Asian Development Outlook (https://data.adb.org/dataset/debt-service-ratio-asia-and-pacific-asian-development-outlook).

a Economic Survey, Various Issues, Ministry Finance, Government of Nepal.
b Central Bank of Sri Lanka, Annual Report, 2020.

3.12 Aid Fragmentation

A serious problem of foreign aid in Nepal is the proliferation of aid in almost every activity that one can think of and for even a very small amount. This has resulted in aid fragmentation in terms of both donor and government line-ministry. According to the MOF, Nepal receives foreign assistance from over 40 donors, and there are 34 resident development partners and six non-resident partners extending assistance to Nepal and their aid is scattered over diverse projects/programmes (MOF, 2012). This has posed severe challenges in aid management because of the requirement to comply with so many kinds of guidelines and procedures in implementing and monitoring projects. Besides, there are severe problems of coordination, inefficiency, high transaction and management costs, duplications and rivalries among donors resulting in lower effectiveness.

A report by the MOF states,

> OECD analysis of aid fragmentation in Nepal over the period 2005–2009 shows that for almost all sectors and donors the increase in the volume of aid over this period has been marked with an increase in fragmentation (number of donors per sector) and proliferation (number of sectors per donor).
>
> (MOF, 2011: 4)

The TA also remains fragmented with many TA projects or components being implemented by donors directly over which government has less control. A comparison of aid fragmentation index computed by the MOF by using Herfindhal Index (ranges between 0 and 1 indicating respectively entirely fragmented and a perfectly un-fragmented portfolio) shows that each donor in 2010/11 was engaged in nine different sectors on average, while the engagement of each donor in 2018/19 was eight different line ministries, on average, with some engaged with up to 25 ministries (MOF, 2012, 2019a). Donors with a very large volume of aid scattered in many projects have low fragmentation scores, while donors with a small amount of aid and involvement in one or a few projects have high scores. In 2018/19, by donor, the UN had the highest fragmentation (0.08) with 163 projects spread over 25 ministries. Next to it was Switzerland with a score of 0.09 with 31 projects spread over 12 ministries. The Asian Development Bank and the United Kingdom had the same score (0.11) with 76 and 34 projects spread over 14 and 18 ministries, respectively. The lowest concentration (1.0) was observed in the Nordic Development Fund and Saudi Arabia with one project and one ministry each. The MOF assesses the situation in 2018/19 as high aid fragmentation (MOF, 2019a).

Analysis of aid fragmentation from the perspective of line ministries in 2010/11 shows very high levels of fragmentation in some ministries, such as the Ministry of Local Development (0.11) with 18 donors involved in 46 projects. The Ministry of Peace and Reconstruction and the Ministry of Agriculture and Cooperation had the same score as that of the Ministry of Local Development, with 31 and 33 projects and the involvement of 16 and 14 donors, respectively. The Ministry of Health and Population had the second-highest level of aid fragmentation (score 0.12) with the highest number of projects (81) and also the highest number of donors (21). On the other hand, the Ministry of Land Reforms and Management and the Ministry of Law and Justice had no aid fragmentation (score 1.0) because these had one and four projects with the involvement of one and four donors, respectively. The situation in 2018/9 does not appear better than in 2011/12. While aid was less fragmented in the case of some ministries, some ministries had a high level of fragmentation.

The issue of aid fragmentation was first raised internationally in the first high-level international forum (HLF) on 'aid effectiveness' held in Rome in 2003 and was reiterated in the second HLF held in Paris in 2005. But this is not heeded by the donors.

3.13 Aid and Proliferation of NGOs

Nepal witnessed the massive proliferation of non-governmental and international non-governmental organizations (NGOs/INGOs), particularly after the 1990 political change and adoption of neo-liberal economic policy by the successive rightist, centrist and leftist governments. Prior to 1990, there were only a couple of NGOs with nationwide spread, such as the Family Planning Association of Nepal established in 1959, working in the field of family planning and reproductive health services and advocacy, and Nepal Red Cross Society established in 1963, working in the field of humanitarian and disaster relief activities. The scenario has changed drastically over the last three decades. With the increase in the number of donors as well as the increasing inflow of aid, there has been substantial growth in the number of NGOs and INGOs. Although correct figures for NGOs and INGOs working in Nepal are not readily available, the records of the Nepal Social Welfare Council (SWC), where the NGOs/ INGOs are legally required to register, show that as of 18 June 2019, some 50,393 NGOs and 230 INGOs are registered with the SWC (SWC, 2020) but not all of them are active, about which no information is available. As most NGOs are sustained with donor or INGO money, those failing to receive money constantly have disappeared and new ones have emerged with the receipt of external or internal funds. It is estimated that about 80.0 percent of NGOs' work is funded by INGOs and donor agencies. As in the case of NGOs, the number of INGOs has grown substantially after the political change in 1990. From 15 before 1990, the present estimate, according to SWC, is 230. The Association of International NGOs has 140 INGOs registered with it. The INGOs, also known as 'briefcase NGOs', receive funds from global organizations/communities and their respective countries.

The growth of NGOs/INGOs in underdeveloped countries like Nepal is an outcome of a conscious neo-liberal strategy of Western capitalist countries and multilateral financial organizations to weaken the role of the state. The state is projected to be inferior to INGOs/NGOs in terms of governance, flexibility, innovativeness, responsiveness, leadership quality, efficiency and decision-making. Such an argument provided justification for the promotion of INGOs/NGOs in underdeveloped countries, pouring money on them to carry out some of the aid-funded projects/programmes with the intrinsic objective of downsizing the state. As direct pouring of money was not possible, donors started the practice of off-budget disbursement and partially succeeded in doing so because of government officials' attitude of 'not to displease the donors' to be in their good book for personal benefits out of aid money spent this way. The MOF data shows that a sizeable portion of Official Development Assistance (ODA) bypasses Nepal's public financial management system. This was 32.0 percent in 2008 MOF (2008b), and after declining somewhat in the subsequent two years, it increased to 35.0 percent and 37.0 percent in 2014/15 and 2015/16, respectively. In the 2018 and 2019, the off-budget disbursement was 27 percent and 22.0 percent (2018, 2019/20a). The spending of a large proportion of ODA out of the government budgetary process has a number of implications for the country. First, there has been wasteful use of funds, as no one is responsible for ensuring results for money spent. Second, aid channelled through the INGOs bypassing the national budgetary system has reduced government control over both the resources and development activities. When there is no government control over the resources, it may not have interest and ownership of the activities. As a consequence, NGO activities get confined to short-term goals and die out with the end of INGO funding. The physical structures created for the projects/programmes, machine/equipment purchased and the staff employed all are abandoned, leaving behind a good deal of dissatisfaction and frustration on the part of the staff. Third, some activities carried out by the NGOs/INGOs overlap with each other and also with that of the government, resulting in a waste of resources and poor results. In order to overcome this problem, a sector-wide approach has been initiated under which government is the lead implementer, and the resources from all donor organizations for an individual sector are pooled into one basket. But donors are not compulsorily required to join the pooled fund, and some have earmarked funds for specific activities through the preferred NGOs. Fourth, the high difference in the salary structure between the government and the INGO employees at comparable positions has generated inferiority feelings and demotivation on the part of government employees. Fifth, the INGOs' sources of funding and financing mechanisms are not transparent and many INGOs refuse to provide annual income-expenditure statements to the SWC, despite the legal requirement.

Detailed studies on the effect of the proliferation of the NGO sector in rural development, community participation, self-reliance, enhancement of equitable development or a shift in policy are lacking. Also, there has been no study on whether the increased funding, both governmental and foreign, to the NGO sector has fulfilled the expectations of reaching the poor and vulnerable people and ingrained the ethos of self-help, cooperation and brotherhood in rural society. In this regard, a study remarks,

> Despite the plethora of Nepali non-governmental organizations (NGOs) that has emerged over the last decade, few of these have been able to establish an effective field presence as far as the poor and vulnerable are concerned. For many in Nepal, including the rural and urban poor and many of the intelligentsia, the international and other development agencies (both governmental and non-governmental) are (at worst) the instruments of imperialism or of the oppressive ruling elites or (at best) ineffective and largely irrelevant to the lives and livelihoods of ordinary villagers and urban dwellers.
>
> (Seddon and Hussein, 2002: 5)

The activities of some NGOs/INGOs in the wake of the 15 April 2015 earthquake bear testimony to the misappropriation of a substantial amount of funds raised from donors for relief and humanitarian assistance to the victims of the earthquake. The earthquake prompted many NGOs/INGOs and individuals to raise a huge amount of money by creating crowdfunding sites across the internet. An investigative article reveals that billions of rupees were raised from different sources and through crowdfunding, with INGOs being the frontrunners, in the name of earthquake victims of Nepal, but there is no record of where so much money has gone (Bhandari and Adhikari, 2016). According to the report, the government of Nepal also raised this issue at the UN World Humanitarian Summit held in Istanbul, Turkey, on 23 and 24 May 2016. The Office of the Auditor General's report for 2016 shows that 145 NGOs were given permission to carry out reconstruction and rehabilitation works (75 for school building construction, 15 for health post construction, 15 for house construction and 40 for construction, training and livelihood activities) involving Rs. 40.75 billion for 2015/16. The report says,

> As there was no monitoring of works accomplished by these NGOs, it was not possible to conduct performance audit. However, discussion with concerned stakeholders revealed that the NGOs did not submit the progress report to the District Development Committee on quadrimester basis as required and concentrated training programmes only in accessible places. It appeared that the targeted individuals and groups were deprived of rehabilitation and livelihood support meant for them.
>
> (OAG, 2016: 13)

3.14 Outcome of Nepal-Donor Meetings

Nepal started a process of regular meetings with donors, representatives of multilateral aid organizations and, in some cases, civil society, with the objective of enhancing mutual understanding and discussing issues and constraints in the effective utilization of aid. However, the intrinsic motive appears to be soliciting larger and even larger volumes of bilateral as well as multilateral aid by presenting a pathetic resource crunch to meet the development needs of the country and resolve the emerging political challenge. The political challenge was none other than the then Maoists' armed insurgency that prevailed for a decade (1996–2006), presenting insurmountable threats to the royal institution, prevailing political order and mainstream political parties of Nepal. Meetings with the donors are organized by Nepal both at a broader and narrower level. The broader scale meeting involves a larger number of donors, aid agencies and civil society, while the narrower level meeting involves a smaller number of donors represented by diplomatic missions and representatives of donor agencies based in Nepal in the MOF. Initially, the broader level aid meeting was known as Nepal Aid Group (NAG), which was later christened as Nepal Development Forum (NDF), and donors were also labelled as 'development partners' in order to camouflage the relationship between Nepal and donors not as donors and beggar, but as concerned partners sharing the same vision for Nepal's development. The major objectives of the NDF were as follows:

- i Charting Nepal's development roadmap along the path of sustained peace and resulting socio-economic transformation with support from the development partners;
- ii Committing to create reforms agenda through reviewing the progress made and challenges encountered during the implementation of high priority projects;
- iii Developing a new FAP (i.e. Foreign Aid Policy) of Nepal and the National Action Plan for Aid Effectiveness in consultation with the Development Partners;
- iv Building roadmap for trade, investment and private sector development through creating a conducive environment and increasing competitiveness.

(Pyakuryal, 2012: 202–4)

The subject of donors' involvement in designing Nepal's development policy and strategy has neither been an issue of discussion in the government nor in the academic circle. The objectives of NDF indicate the involvement of donors in charting the country's development roadmap and policy reform for their acceptance and assurance of aid. Even the design of the foreign aid policy of the country, which should have been purely a national endeavour, depended upon consultation with donors, which virtually implied their acceptance.

The first wider-level meeting with donors was organized in 1976 in Japan as the 'NAG' Meeting under the auspices of the World Bank. Subsequent NAG Meetings were held at two-year or four-year intervals, mostly in France until 2000, but from 2002, the meeting was held in Nepal not as a NAG Meeting, but as an NDF

Table 3.7 Nepal Aid Group/NDF Meetings (1976–2009)

Date	*Type*	*Country*	*Date*	*Type*	*Country*
December 1976	NAG Meetings	Japan	October 1990	NAG Meetings	France
May 1978	NAG Meetings	France	April 1992	NAG Meetings	France
January 1980	NAG Meetings	France	April 1996	NAG Meetings	France
December 1981	NAG Meetings	France	April 2002	NAG Meetings	France
December 1983	NAG Meetings	France	February 2002	NDF	Nepal
January 1986	NAG Meetings	Japan	May 2004	NDF	Nepal
April 1987	NAG Meetings	France	February 2008	NDCM	Nepal
November 1988	NAG Meetings	France	May 2009[a]	NDF	Nepal

Source: Pyakuryal (2012: 205).

a Means cancelled.

Meeting. The second NDF Meeting was held in 2004, which was followed by the Nepal-Donor Consultative Meeting in 2008, and the NDF Meeting scheduled for 2009 was cancelled owing to the unstable political situation in the country (Table 3.7). There has been no NDF Meeting after 2008.

In the beginning, donor participation at NAG Meetings was poor but increased with the passage of time, and by 1987, participation in NAG increased to 16 countries and 6 international agencies. Following the devastating 7.8-magnitude earthquake on 25 April 2015, the International Conference on Nepal's Reconstruction was hosted in Kathmandu on 25 June 2015 to garner foreign aid for reconstruction and rehabilitation. The outcome of the conference was a pledge of $4.1 billion in grants and loans by 24 foreign governments and multilateral lending institutions, like the Asian Development Bank and the World Bank, to help Nepal's reconstruction.

At the MOF level, there are three different mechanisms to hold dialogues and discuss the issues and problems standing in the way of aid harmonization and effective use of aid between the government and donors. First, local donor meetings are held periodically in the MOF for coordination and dialogue between donors and the government on economic policy issues and donors' concerns. Second, the MOF organizes the 'Nepal Portfolio Performance Review (NPPR)' meeting for dialogue between the government and the development partners based in Kathmandu on an annual basis to discuss and review issues and problems in implementation, aid harmonization, project deliverables and overall public financial management. The NPPR meeting has been in place since 2000. Third, an online web-based system called the 'Aid Management Platform' system is set up in the MOF for regular reporting of progress in portfolio management by the development partners.

Despite periodic NAG and NDF Meetings and regular interactions with the development partners at the MOF, in the past two decades, progress in the harmonization of aid, use of the country's system to deliver aid and effectiveness of aid have still remained abysmally poor. Such meetings have not gone beyond the ritual of repeated discussion of the same problems and issues and expression of commitments to improve aid management policies and practices in the coming days by both the government and donors. In this context, it would be worthwhile to quote a pungent remark by the government,

> Despite the repeated high-level commitments made by donors to use the country systems, majority of them tend to seek safeguard measures to ensure that the country systems are up to the mark of international standards. Such concerns regarding fiduciary risks stand on the so called capacity constraints in the recipient countries, which normally become a good escape to bypass the country system and end up with reverting to the donors' own structure.
>
> (MOF, 2008b: 1)

The donors usually retreat, putting the blame on Nepal for not developing the necessary capacity and institutional arrangements, having weak results-based management systems, making frequent transfers of officials or project chiefs, conducting unsound public financial and procurement management, allowing political interference in the management of aid-financed projects/programmes, etc. There may be some truth in these allegations, but Nepal cannot be solely blamed for the ineffective results of aid. The donors are equally or even more responsible for what the aid has delivered. They also have the responsibility to abide by the declared principles of mutual accountability and transparency, enhancing country ownership and reducing aid fragmentation and avoiding unnecessary interferences.

3.15 Donors' Political Fiddle

Donors and international aid agencies often place the blame for the failure of aid in enhancing growth and reducing poverty on the recipient countries. The recipient countries are accused of weak governance, inconsistent policies, fragile institutions and uncanny attitudes of the bureaucracy for the poor performance of aid. So since the early 1980s, international aid agencies started persuading poor countries to bring about a more favourable environment for growth through conditionality-based structural adjustment lending and tying release of aid installment on fulfillment of certain conditions and change in policies. Findings of research studies based on cross country as well as individual country data were construed to show that aid has a positive effect on economic growth when the recipient country has good policies, good economic management and governance (Burnside and Dollar, 2010; Collier and Dollar, 1998). But poor countries adopting good policies prescribed by donors did not experience any better outcome; rather, they became the victims of counterproductive influences and pressures. When conditionality-based lending failed to deliver the results and aid was subject to increasing scrutiny for impact and value for money, the donor countries and aid agencies attempted to bind together donors acting as a group and aid recipients as individuals in shared responsibility in enhancing aid effectiveness by organizing HLF, conferences and announcements of joint declarations. The first in this series was the Monterrey Consensus (2002), which was focussed on mobilization of domestic as well as international financial resources for development. The first HLF on aid effectiveness was held in Rome in 2003, which made commitments to facilitating aid harmonization, working within partner country systems and streamlining donor procedures and practices. The Monterrey Conference on Financing for Development was followed by the Doha Declaration in 2008, which called upon countries to maintain their commitment to devote 0.7 percent of Gross National Product (GNP) to ODA. The Rome HLF on aid effectiveness was followed by three HLFs in Paris, Accra and Busan, respectively in 2005, 2008 and 2011. The major principles that were agreed upon at these international forums include encouraging country ownership, alignment with the national budget, harmonization to reduce transaction costs, avoidance of fragmented efforts and the creation of results frameworks. However, 17 years have passed since the first HLF and neither aid effectiveness has been enhanced nor uncoordinated or bad aid practices ended. It is an irony that the donor countries and international aid agencies are themselves reluctant to abide by the key principles agreed upon in various HLFs and Conferences.

First, on the issue of finance for development, the Monterrey Consensus (2002) and subsequent Doha Conference (2008) stressed the need for substantial increases in ODA to enable the poorest countries to cut poverty by half and achieve other internationally agreed-upon development goals. A major step in increasing assistance to poor countries would have been the compliance of 0.7 percent of GNP by the advanced countries as ODA to developing countries.[2] It has been half a century since the 0.7 percent ODA/GNI target was first agreed upon in the UN General Assembly in 1970 and later repeatedly re-endorsed at the highest level international aid and development conferences, but except for a handful of Northern European countries, most donors, including the United States, have still not been able to meet this long-standing pledge. While the United Kingdom met the 0.7 percent target only in 2017, the United States has still ignored this because its ODA/GNI was only 0.17 percent in 2018. It is certain that poor countries would get more aid if 0.7 percent of the GNP target were met by the advanced countries. This should not, however, be taken as a suggestion for increasing aid flow from the developed countries to the less developed countries for their development. It is just to point out how honest the developed countries are in keeping up their pledges. This is evident in other issues too.

Second, no one can dispute the importance of having good policies for development, but would good policies for underdeveloped countries mean one-size-fits-all policies prescribed by donors and international aid agencies irrespective of particular country characteristics? Moreover, no thought is given to what makes it more likely that a country will have good policies. It could be just that good policies are inhibited because aid-reliant governments do not feel the need for growth-promoting, revenue-raising, expenditure-regulating and inequality-reducing policies. Good policies are generally homegrown, which gets undermined when there are external interferences. Instances abound where the IMF imposed fiscal tightening policies that had adverse consequences on the well-being of the people including health. Stiglitz (2002) documented Thailand's AIDS increase as a result of IMF-forced cutbacks in health expenditure. Stiglitz had been rather vocal on the ulterior motive of supporting or toppling a particular ruler under the veil of World Bank assistance, which cost him his job as chief economist at the Bank in 1999 at the behest of the US Treasury (Sogge, 2002). Third, one of the key principles agreed upon in various HLFs from the Paris Declaration (1975) to

Busan (1988) is the 'country ownership' for enhancing aid effectiveness.[3] But this is a misleading concept, and questions may be raised on its relevance and usefulness when referring to a country. As Willem Buiter (2007) questions, 'Under what circumstances and how can the concept of country ownership be relevant to a country with a myriad of heterogeneous groups with diverse, often divergent and conflicting views, interests, policy objectives and programmes?' And he further remarks that programmes have been designed and implemented that served the interests of an unrepresentative few at the expense of the unrepresented many. Moreover, country ownership requires a proactive role from the recipient country's government in determining how aid is allocated and managed and how it is to be used. But the donors often tend to undermine ownership by maintaining various types of controls over the design and implementation of reform policies and programmes. Similarly, the Paris Declaration adopted a blueprint for donor harmonization in order to increase aid effectiveness. effective donor harmonization largely depends on a genuine commitment and collective effort between donors and the governments of recipient countries. Furthermore, donors have continued to stress the need for disbursement through the country's budgetary system while at the same time they continue to disburse about one-fourth of aid outside the budgetary system to fulfil their covert interests.

The HLFs have been criticized not only for donors retaining control of aid but also for poor compliance of pledges and for weak progress in delivering results the Paris Declaration has been criticized for its technocratic approach and unequal power relation between donors and developing countries. Kelegama says that the PD has not been able to address development goals of human rights, social justice and equity and quotes from the Reality of Aid Report (2008), 'The PD springs from a technocratic depoliticized vision of development, with no accountability for intended beneficiaries. The power in aid relationships is still heavily weighted on the side of donors, and the Declaration does nothing to check this imbalance. The aid effectiveness being promoted remains essentially donor centred' (Kelegama, 2012: 3). Similarly, Whitfield (2009) says,

> [T]he Paris Declaration has not yet had a significant impact in terms of rectifying bad aid practices, such as uncoordinated donor projects, setting up project implementation units, donors driving the designs of projects, spending lots of money on consultants, high transaction costs for recipient governments, micromanaging implementation, not evaluating projects or learning from evaluations, rotating donor staff in country offices frequently, poaching civil servants to work in aid agencies, among others.
>
> (p. 13)

Similarly, the Paris Declaration adopted a blueprint for donor harmonization in order to increase aid effectiveness. But, effective donor harmonization required a genuine commitment and collective effort among donors on the one hand and between donors and the governments of recipient countries on the other. But this has not happened. The Accra Agenda for Action is criticized for not addressing tied aid, donor conditionality and institutional framework to monitor implementation (Tandon, 2009). As demonstrated by the MCC issue in Nepal and also in other countries, bad aid practices are still there; aid stills remain uncoordinated and fragmented; donors still drive the design of projects; there is still micromanagement of implementation by donors, particularly the TA; and expenditure on expatriate consultants is still very high.

3.16 Exit from Aid

After decades of massive foreign aid inflow, some developing countries have achieved success and graduated from low-income countries (LICs) and have made an exit from or reduced dependence on aid, whereas a large number of countries have continued to show abysmally poor performance and perpetual dependence on aid.

A study by Engen and Prizzon (2019) for Overseas Development Institute notes, 'Over the past 15 years, 35 LICs have joined the ranks of the world's MICs: a reflection of the strong and sustained economic growth achieved in most parts of the developing world' (p. 1). And some of these countries have significantly reduced dependence on aid. Of the eight countries (Egypt, Ghana, the Lao People's Democratic Republic, Nigeria, Pakistan, Papua New Guinea, Sri Lanka and Vietnam) selected for case studies, three have already graduated from the IDA window: Egypt in 1998, and Sri Lanka and Vietnam in 2017.

In the case of some countries, donors initiated the phase-out of their aid programme. For example, in Vietnam, the Netherlands stopped bilateral support in 2012, followed by Sweden in 2013, Denmark in 2015, the United Kingdom (Department for International Development) in 2016, Switzerland (Swiss Agency for Development Cooperation); the State Secretariat for Economic Affairs in 2016 and Finland in 2017/18. Similarly, smaller donors left Pakistan, and the United States announced major cuts in its aid programme in early September 2018. In Sri Lanka, the Swedish International Development Cooperation Agency left the country in March 2010 and wound up its office in 2015. In Ghana, the Netherlands, the United Kingdom and Japan have cut their ODA significantly since 2011.

Other countries successful in ending aid dependency, according to an Action Aid study, were Botswana, Korea and Taiwan, which were all highly aid dependent in the 1960s and 1970s, as were European countries and Japan after the Second World War, but they all graduated from aid dependence. Action Aid says that all three countries reduced dependence gradually over 15 to 25 years. In two decades (between 1975 and 1995), Botswana cut aid/GNI from 30.0 percent to 2.0 percent, and aid/expenditure from 60.0 percent to 6.0 percent. The success of these countries in reducing dependency on aid is attributed to their

> policies and strategies which included strong leadership and clear policies for national development, combining centralized strategic planning with protection of local industries and market based growth. Furthermore, aid was used to develop their own national institutional capacity and skills from weak initial levels and to investing in infrastructure such as roads, education, and in

> supporting increases in tax revenue. All three countries determined their own strategies with relatively little interference from external sources. They used aid until they had put infrastructure, and higher tax and savings in place. In other words, one of these countries' key routes to reducing aid dependence over the longer-term, was using real aid to promote development. And 14 of the 30 most aid dependent countries in 2000 reduced their dependence by more than 20.0 percent of expenditure by 2009, and the average dependence of these 30 countries fell by 36.0 percent of expenditure over the same period.
>
> (Action Aid, 2011: 23)

Korea presents a unique case of transition from an aid-dependent country to a major donor country during a period of four decades. Similarly, India, while being dependent on aid but with a substantial reduction in aid volume since 2003, has come a long way towards strengthening its position as an emerging donor. It would, therefore, be worthwhile to briefly look at these cases so as to gain some insights for Nepal on how an exit from aid could be made.

(a) **Korea**: Korea relied heavily on foreign assistance to rebuild its economy, which suffered severe damage from the Korean War (1950–3). The OECD report of 2008 states, 'Part of its success was due to its effective use of official development assistance (ODA) – the government estimates that it received USD 12.7 billion in the post-war period, which helped spur economic development and decrease poverty' (OECD, 2008: 9). Consequently, Korea made a miraculous transition itself from one of the world's poorest aid-dependent countries half a century ago to now one of the world's developed and largest aid-donor countries. It became a member of the Organisation for Economic Co-operation and Development on 12 December 1996 and a member of DAC, which is known as the 'donors' club' in 2010. This placed Korea among the most developed nations in the world. It began modestly as a donor country in 2009 and gradually emerged as an advanced donor. A comparison of Korean aid in 2011 and 2019 clearly indicates its dominant position among the developed donor countries. In 2011, Korean net aid flows reached US$1,248.32 million (or 0.12 percent of Korean gross national income) to the extent that it has almost matched DAC traditional members, such as Japan (0.18 percent) and the United States (0.20 percent) in 2011. In 2019, Korean aid amounted to US$2.5 billion, which corresponded to 0.15 percent of its GNI, making South Korea the 25th-largest donor in proportion to the size of its economy (Donor Tracker, 2021). The amazing transformation of Korea was mainly due to the judicious utilization of foreign aid to overcome various domestic challenges and constraints through state-led policies and projects designed to accelerate economic development and reduce poverty.

(b) **India**: Unlike Korea, India is both a recipient and a donor of foreign aid. The Indian government still receives billions of dollars in foreign aid each year and at the same time provides billions of dollars in foreign aid to less developed countries. But over time, it reduced dependence on aid substantially and emerged as a major donor.

> Between 1951 and 1992, India received US$55 billion in foreign aid, becoming the world's largest recipient (although when translated into per capita terms it appears much less reliant on aid). From being one of the world's largest recipient of foreign aid in the mid-1980s, India has become a net donor.
>
> (Bijoy, 2013: 65)

A similar picture was drawn by another study:

> The size of external assistance was for some time around 10.0 percent of the total public-sector investment per annum. Total external aid as percentage of GDP fell from 1.4 percent in 1991/2 to 0.5 percent in 2001/2, amounting to USD 3.57 billion. Total bilateral aid disbursed in 2001–2 from 31 donor countries was USD 1.14 billion.
>
> (de Groot et al., 2008)

There are two main factors that helped India transit from a heavily aid-dependent country to a net donor. First, consequent to India's nuclear test on 11 and 13 May 1998, several developed countries terminated or suspended aid to India (like the United States, Japan and many European countries). Wadhva (1998) states that Japan, the single-largest donor of aid to India with an annual commitment of around US$1 billion annually, temporarily froze most of it. Germany suspended its US$300 million aid package. Sweden and Denmark, whose combined aid amounted to US$200 million, did the same. So did the United States by suspending all its aid to India. The Reserve Bank of India estimated the total loss of foreign exchange to India due to the suspension of foreign aid at US$2.8 billion (Wadhva, 1998). The United States not only suspended its aid but also asked other G-8 countries to impose their own sanctions and withhold aid worth US$143 million to India.

Second, in the 2003 budget speech, the Bharatiya Janata Party (BJP) government expressed its determination to reduce the country's dependence on aid. The minister of finance announced,

> A stage has come in our development were we should now, firstly, review our dependence on external donors. While being grateful to all our development partners of the past, I wish to announce that the Government of India would now prefer to provide relief to certain bilateral partners.

In response to government's budget speech, the National Assembly decided to phase out foreign aid within a three-year period, starting in 2004 and closing in 2006/7. What the BJP government said in the 2003 budget, they really meant, and the successive governments, irrespective of their party ideologies, stood firmly by the mission of ending dependency on aid and continued projecting India as an economy which was not 'aid dependent'. This was demonstrated by the United Progressive Alliance government in the aftermath of the tsunami, which hit the Indian coast on 26 December 2004. The offer of aid by donors was not accepted, as the government considered that it had the required resources to manage the devastations (de Groot et al., 2008).

The study by de Groot et al. shows that the 2003 budget speech triggered a gradual phase-out of aid programmes in India by Denmark, the Netherlands, Norway and Sweden: Denmark decided to conduct a gradual phase-out from India over a time period of ten years and closure of all projects by the end of 2008; the Dutch government decided for an accelerated phase-out of its bilateral development cooperation with India in two years; Norway decided to carry out a natural phase-out of its bilateral development cooperation with India; Sweden suspended aid to India in 1998, and as a consequence, the number of bilateral projects decreased from 11 at the beginning of 1999 to 4 projects in 2002, and it planned a reduction in annual aid volume to a maximum of US$15 million between 2005 and 2008 and a further reduction to less than US$9 million per year from 2008 onwards.

Even as India continues to receive foreign aid, it has been providing more than US$1 billion in aid to neighbouring and other smaller countries since 2012/13. India spent US$1 billion on foreign aid in 2012/13. In 2017, the government declared that India had been a net donor in 2015/16. In 2019/20, India's overseas aid stood at US$1.32 billion, which was 0.3 percent of the overall budget (Wikipedia, 2021).

Nepal has been an aid recipient for as many as seven decades from a variety of sources for a variety of purposes. Instead of pulling the country out of the shackles of underdevelopment and poverty, it is stuck in an aid dependence trap. If the present dependence on aid continues, the situation of Nepal may be like that of Sub-Sahara Africa, where a high level of dependence on aid over an extended period of time had a retarding effect on growth and development due to harmful effects on the overarching governance structure and institutional quality of the recipient country (Abuzeid, 2009).

There is no indication that Nepal would be able to phase out from aid at some future date. We find government foreign aid policy issued in different years replete with sentences such as these: 'While increasing quality and quantity of foreign aid during short and the medium term, the government would try to achieve self-reliance in the longer term by enhancing domestic resource mobilization' (MOF, 2002), '[t]o help build a self-reliant economy through gradually reducing dependency on aid' (MOF, 2014) and '[e]nhancing national capacity through transparent and results-oriented mobilization of international development cooperation so as to gradually reduce aid dependency' (MOF, 2019b). From the first aid policy, 18 years have elapsed, and governments of political parties of right, left and centre have been formed, but reducing dependency on aid has been confined to government documents only. The dependency on aid has become more entrenched, as each government, rather than making real efforts to reduce the quantum of aid, seems to be bent upon mustering more aid than the previous government to show its success. The US$500 million MCC grant controversy between the prime minister and his supporters and the other faction of the ruling NCP government is an illustrative example of government's diehard attitude towards receiving aid, even if it carries donors' strategic and security interests. The NC also supported the government in tabling the MCC in the parliament for endorsement. The MCC issue subsided for some time because of political wrangling for power among the major parties but came into intense debate when Sher Bahadur Deuba, president of NC became prime minister with the support of Maoists, Unified Socialist and other smaller parties. Eventually, the MCC was ratified from the parliament after US warned the government of severe repercussions on Nepal-US relation if not rectified. One can discern three types of vested interests that have fostered foreign aid dependency in Nepal. First, strong interest groups exerted heavy pressure on the respective donor governments to keep Nepal under their political and strategic orbits and the pressure groups within the country that stand to gain from aid programmes. Second, the politicians and policy makers in Nepal find aid as an easy source of money to fiddle with and keep intact interest groups for political support. Third, the government and the bureaucracy desire foreign aid to meet the revenue deficit of an unsustainable large budget. As it appears unlikely that Nepal would move away from aid by itself, its dependency on foreign aid would be minimized or brought to zero only if donors themselves start exit planning, as in the case of countries mentioned earlier. This is because even the Nepal Communist Party–led government with a nearly two-thirds majority which prepared the national budget for three consecutive years (2018/9 to 2020/1) and brought out the Fifteenth Plan showed no concern towards reducing dependence on aid in line with the spirit of the government's foreign aid policy. The foreign aid policy documents mention 'achieving or building a self-reliant economy', but achieving this will never be possible unless Nepal plans for an exit from aid more seriously. If the word 'exit' was not acceptable, the Fifteenth plan should have contained some discussion on 'phasing out' or 'scaling down' of aid. The contrast between what the government policies state and what the government itself and bureaucracy practice makes one believe that those who are in power are not prepared to reduce dependence on aid, as they continue to benefit from it. It appears that Nepal may have to wait many more years for another 'mass movement' or 'uprising' that would place the real people in power committed to a policy of self-reliance with ideology and strategy to free the country from donors' high-handedness on Nepal's development discourse and policy orientation.

Notes

1 Point Four Program announced by Harry Truman:

Point 1: The United States would back UNO
Point 2: The United States would support European Reconstruction (the Marshall Plan)
Point 3: NATO would be created to counter Soviet Union
Point 4: 'We must embark on a bold programme for making the benefits of scientific advances and industrial progress available for the improvement and growth of underdeveloped areas'.

The old imperialism has no place in our plans. What we envisage is a program of development based on the concepts of democratic fair-dealing.

2 The UN General Assembly adopted a Resolution on 24 October 1970 which included the goal that each economically advanced country will progressively increase its official

development assistance to the developing countries and will exert its best efforts to reach a minimum net amount of 0.7% of its gross national product at market prices by the middle of the decade.

("International Development Strategy for the Second United Nations Development Decade", UN General Assembly Resolution 2626 (XXV), 24 October 1970, paragraph 43)

3 Four HLFs on Aid Effectiveness sponsored by the DAC Working Party on Aid Effectiveness have been convened since 2000 to assess and meet the ambitious targets set by the MDGs; in Rome (2003), Paris (2005), Accra (2008) and Busan (2011). The following is a brief summary of the principles adopted at these forums.

HLF1 (Rome, 2003)

The Rome forum resulted in the adoption of the following priority actions, embodied in the Rome Declaration:

that development assistance be delivered based on the priorities and timing of the countries receiving it.
that donor efforts concentrate on delegating cooperation and increasing the flexibility of staff on country programmes and projects.
and that good practice be encouraged and monitored, backed by analytic work to help strengthen the leadership that recipient countries can take in determining their development path.

HLF2 (Paris, 2005)

The Paris Declaration, a product of HLF2, outlined the following five fundamental principles for making aid more effective:

1 Ownership: Developing countries set their own strategies for poverty reduction, improve their institutions and tackle corruption.
2 Alignment: Donor countries align behind these objectives and use local systems.
3 Harmonization: Donor countries coordinate, simplify procedures and share information to avoid duplication.
4 Results: Developing countries and donors shift focus to development results and results get measured.
5 Mutual accountability: Donors and partners are accountable for development results.

HLF3 (Accra, 2008)

This forum convened in order to strengthen and deepen implementation of the Paris Declaration. The Accra Agenda for Action (AAA) centred on capacity development and proposed improvement in ownership, partnerships and the delivery of results. The key points agreed as part of the AAA are as follows:

Predictability – donors will provide three to five years forward information on their planned aid to partner countries.
Country systems – partner country systems will be used to deliver aid as the first option, rather than donor systems.
Conditionality – donors will switch from reliance on prescriptive conditions about how and when aid money is spent to conditions based on the developing country's own development objectives.
Untying – donors will relax restrictions that prevent developing countries from buying the goods and services they need from whomever and wherever they can get the best quality at the lowest price.

HLF4 (Busan, 2011)

The Busan Partnership for Effective Development Co-operation reinforced the principles that were adopted in the three earlier forums and specifically reemphasized the following:

Ownership of development priorities by developing countries.
Focus on results.
Inclusive development partnerships.
Transparency and accountability to each other.

4 Nature of the State and Underdevelopment in Nepal

4.1 Concept of Nation State

The problem of economic backwardness and growing inequality in Nepal cannot be interpreted as an initial stage or a natural transitional stage in a spontaneous process of economic development, as mainstream economists argue. On the contrary, they need to be analyzed from the perspective of internal politico-economic dynamics which are embodied in the nature of the state and the causative links with the world-capitalist economic order, especially the Indian hegemony on Nepal's economic and political matters. This chapter takes up the first issue for analysis, while the second issue, which requires a detailed analysis of the detrimental effects of Nepal's interrelationship with the capitalist nations and the complex dynamics of many-fold channels through which the Nepal-India relationship operates is not discussed.

At the most general level, the nation state is defined as a form of political organization in which a group of people who share the same history, traditions or language live in a particular geographical territory under one government. In other words, the nation state connotes a form of government or a political regime or a system which has some authority network to enforce its activities. Lipton defines the state as a set of institutions with three main activities: government or political decision-making, administration and enforcement (Lipton, 1991). The Marxists view the state as consisting of (a) a ruling class, e.g., bourgeoisie or proletariat, and (b) a state class or bureaucracy. States are categorized into different forms based on a socio-economic system (slave, feudal, capitalist, communist), or content or substance (monarchy, aristocracy, democracy), or form (absolute, constitutional, parliamentary). In any country, the state mediates in enlarging, transferring and extracting surplus products and reinvesting them for further accumulation. This mediation takes place through two key policies: (a) the rules governing the social relations of production, which critically affect the allocation of surplus value, and (b) the rules governing the flow within and across frontiers of the factors of production – capital, commodities and labour – which critically affect the price structure of the market (Wallerestein, 1986).

4.2 Nature of the State during the Shah Regime

The present state of Nepal was the result of territorial expansion by Prithivi Narayan Shah, king of Gorkha, who conquered tiny principalities, popularly

DOI: 10.4324/9781003359777-4

known as *'baise-chaubise rajyas* (22–24 states). He fought open, as well as guerrilla-type, wars for nearly 30 years against these small states and by 1769 AD annexed them into a greater geographical space, which has come to be known as Nepal. Prithivi Narayan Shah's drive for territorial expansion was primarily aimed at gaining control over a large area of land, which included the productive land of Kathmandu Valley as well as the terai plains, for laying a solid foundation of a greater centralized feudal state. He, however, pursued a self-reliant strategy by debarring entry of foreign traders into Nepal on the ground that they would cheat the country in the name of trade. Furthermore, Prithivi Narayan Shah wanted to keep Nepal equidistant from northern and southern neighbours, as reflected in his saying 'Nepal is like a yam between two boulders'. The early Shah rulers after Prithivi Narayan also pursued the drive for territorial expansion, but a defeat in a war with the British East India Company led to the signing of the Sugauli Treaty of 1816 AD and halted their expansionary drive. This treaty, recorded as a notorious treaty in Nepalese history, stripped Nepal of one-third of its territory (Shrestha, 2005). The successive Shah rulers and members of the royal family spent most of their lifetime hatching conspiracies and feuds for seizure of the throne and power.

The Hindu Brahminical social order of four hierarchical castes traditionally inscribed in ancient Hindu scriptures and formalized by Jayasthithi Malla, the ruler of the valley towards the end of the 14th century, established the base for the social division of labour and exploitation of the people at the lower strata by those at the higher strata. The hill Brahmins were on the top, who acted as priests and advisors to the kings, followed by the Chhetris, who were the rulers and warriors; the Vaisyas, who were engaged in trading and business activities mainly consisted of Newars of Kathmandu Valley; and the Sudras who were the untouchables and outcastes, such as tailors, cobblers, blacksmiths, goldsmiths and sweepers, and those who served the first three castes by performing menial works. Such social stratification by caste and ethnic character was indispensable for exploitation of the lower caste by the upper caste and the feudal lords, but at the same time, it carried the risk of class conflicts and social unrest. Prithivi Narayan Shah camouflaged this stratification and the growing income inequalities among these social/professional groups by labelling the country as 'a garden of four castes and thirty-six ethnic communities' for social harmony and class coordination for reinforcing a caste-structured form of feudalism for many years to come. Furthermore, Prithivi Narayan Shah established the system of hereditary kingship for his successors as the supreme ruling authority of the country but also laid the foundations for the supremacy of the bourgeoisie class (royal families, and higher castes attached to the place and warrior class) over lower castes, poor people belonging to upper castes, small farmers, artisans and petit bourgeoisie.

Traditionally, land was considered state property, and state landlordism was sanctified both by law and tradition. Using state authority over land, four different types of land tenure systems – Raiker, Birta, Guthi and Jagir – were created (Regmi, 1976) land rights were assigned to individuals or institutions for sustaining the feudal regime and for territorial expansion. Large plots of land were assigned as Birta to warriors (Chhetris, Gurung and Rai) for exemplary bravery in the war and for upholding their readiness to fight the war and conquest the enemy states;

members of the royal family and nobility, courtiers and rural aristocrats and the upper layers of bureaucracy, including the judiciary and the clergy, for keeping them loyal to the palace and mobilizing them to garner peoples' support to monarchy as a holy institution; and palace priests (exclusively Brahmins) for engaging them in religious and holy activities. Such practices of the land tenure system in Nepal resembled the relationship between the lord (king), nobles and warriors (vassals) and the land (fief) that led to the development of feudalism in Europe, particularly France in the medieval period. The size of land granted by the kings reflected the degree of economic as well as social power and intimacy of the beneficiaries with the palace. The Birta-owning class wielded a high level of economic, social and political power throughout the course of Nepal's post-1768 history, even after the abolition of the Birta system in 1959. The Birta system established the base for higher income, education and employment of children of Birta owners, and this cumulated to a growing differentiation between Birta landowners and the tenants who cultivated the land.

The hardships and sufferings of the lower castes and poor people were explained as punishments ordained by the deity for their misdeeds in their previous lives to be salvaged by religious acts for a more favourable rebirth after death. Inculcation of such passive and fatalistic feelings in the minds of lower caste people provided strong leverage for maintaining the traditional exploitative social structure and semi-feudalistic production relations for extracting maximum surplus from the labour of the working class by the ruling class and its appendage.

The religiously sanctioned caste and land-based class relations continued to be reinforced in the course of state activities and conduct of development policies and programmes, mostly benefiting the feudal and bourgeoisie class, who wielded the power or were aligned with the ruling class. The toiling masses had no idea how they were exploited under the religious garb for the lavish living of the feudal class and their parasites. The historically designed social structure and the land rights and tenancy system that exploited the common people and the toiling mass to benefit the royal families, ruling class, upper caste and bureaucracy was carried forward and reinforced by the successive Shah and Rana rulers, which subsequently led to huge wealth and income disparities between the rich and the poor.

What Prithivi Narayan Shah and successive kings did until the Ranas took power was to geographically unify fragmented territories for a unified feudal state, but this was not used as an aide for social and economic unification of the country. The geographical unification was not used for the integration of markets and utilization of production potentials of different areas to build Nepal an economically stronger nation. On the contrary, Shah Rulers had no interest in making the nation economically strong; they were mainly concerned with reinforcing the landed oligarchy and extracting maximum surplus from the peasantry, acquisition of wealth of conquered states and strengthening the hegemony of the feudal Shah dynasty.

With the spread of education and awareness among people and internal as well as external migration starting from the late 20th century, the traditional caste distinctions which determined which castes undertake which occupation was significantly eroded, and the boundaries limiting activities between upper and lower caste have become much more porous. Along with this change, the class formation also underwent significant changes, resulting in the emergence of new, specific classes or new attributes or specific features to the existing classes.

4.3 Nature of the State during the Rana Regime

King Prithivi Narayan Shah's successors failed to keep up the nationalist ethos and uphold the objective he fought for. Instead, they languished in luxurious life, detached themselves from the people and involved themselves in conspirational politics and internecine feuds for power among the royal families and palace courtiers. Taking advantage of the fluid situation in the palace, Jung Bahadur Rana, an army officer and his brothers through a brutal massacre on 14 September, 1846 (Kot Massacre), not sparing even close relatives, civilians, palace relatives and guards including the prime minister and rose to the position of prime minister in 1846. He seized power, reduced the status of king to a mere figurehead and established a powerful Rana dynasty of hereditary prime ministers that continued for over a century till the regime was dismantled in 1951. During the Rana regime, the kings were kept as 'prisoners of the palace', and the Rana prime ministers ruled the country as de facto kings with absolute power in all state affairs. In the words of Chatterji,

> In Nepal's system of polity, the king was a mere figurehead whose writ did not run beyond the palace compound. The hereditary Rana prime minister ruled and ruled absolutely. Also, he enjoyed the unheard privilege of being sole custodian of the state's entire revenue. What this meant to the people of Nepal was nothing but unrewarded toil and unmitigated tyranny. Nepal looked like a gigantic prison house, where darkness prevailed even at noon.
>
> (Chatterji, 1967: 4)

The revenues of the state and those of Ranas were not distinguishable and the entire treasury surpluses were regarded as the personal income of the Ranas. The Rana rulers gave continuity to the agrarian system that Prithivi Narayan Shah and his successors had established and continued exploiting the peasantry. Summarizing the land system in Nepal at end of the Rana regime, Regmi states, 'The Rana regime encouraged social and economic differentiation in the agrarian community and a trend toward the concentration of landownership and toward absentee landownership' (Regmi, 1976: 195).

The Rana prime ministers spent money on building their residences in British style with all decorative materials imported from the European countries and lived ultra-luxurious lives, and whatever was left was used in the purchase of gold and deposited in foreign banks, particularly in Bengal Bank, Calcutta (Chauhan, 1989). The Ranas maintained close ties with the British because appeasement of the British made their position secure as de facto rulers, and in so doing, they made the country a semi-colony of British India. Jung Bahadur Rana established a good rapport with British India through the policy of supporting the British in suppressing the 'Quit India' movements by the Indians and in wars against other countries. He sent a Nepali troop to assist British India in suppressing the Indian uprising of 1857, and the British returned a few districts of the western terai

(Naya Muluk) which were previously annexed through the Sugauli Treaty. This established the basis for recruitment of Nepali soldiers (Gurkhas) in the British army, and hundreds of thousands of Gurkhas fought for the British during the First and Second World Wars. Excepting the special relationship with the British, the Ranas kept Nepal isolated from the rest of the world in order to restrict external influences, suspecting that these would make people aware of their authoritarian rule and pose a threat to the regime. The Ranas also entered into matrimonial alliance with the Shah family members in order to quell the potential revolt by the palace against their rule and for strengthening the Rana–Shah alliance for a unified stronger feudal class. This was essential to expropriate and exploit the country and the people in an unhindered manner. Even after the downfall of the Rana regime, King Mahendra gave continuity to this tradition of a matrimonial alliance by having his three sons married to three daughters of a Rana occupying a high post in the army to consolidate and strengthen the king-Rana feudal class. The Ranas occupied the top positions in the army, while their close relatives and persons from the warrior class filled the lower-level positions. Thus they created a huge parasitic class of military and civilian bureaucratic forces mostly composed of persons of their own clan or relatives as an aid to them and as a medium to expropriate the state resources and the peasantry to build their personal fortunes. Rana prime ministers in the later years initiated certain social reforms like the introduction of a written national legal code (Muluki Ain), opening of a couple of educational institutions and initiation of some programmes of development. However, these were just to show the outside world that they were not feudalistic and authoritarian but were reformists and concerned with the development of the country.

4.4 Nature of the State during the Panchayat Regime

The independence of India from British rule in 1947 stirred the Nepali Congress (NC) Party to intensify resistances and insurgencies that were going on for the past few years against the autocratic Rana regime. This led to the capture of districts and towns one by one by the rebel groups. Meanwhile, King Tribhuvan and his family sought asylum in the Indian Embassy, from where he was flown to Delhi. As India also had no interest in preserving the Rana autocratic rule in Nepal, and expecting that the NC would yield to its strategic and economic interest, it mediated a tripartite agreement on power sharing between the king, political parties and the Ranas in February 1950 in Delhi (Delhi Accord). This ended the feudal Rana regime, and the monarchy was reinstated as the supreme authority of the country, which was expected to pave the way for introducing a democratic system in the country. The Indian mediation in the tripartite agreement, however, had serious implications in legitimizing Indian hegemony and interference in Nepalese political and economic activities throughout the future and until now. For several years during Tribhuvan's rule, an Indian Civil Service official became a key figure in the palace secretariat, and the Indian ambassador in Nepal attended the cabinet meetings with decisive influence in policy matters, while the junior officers of the Indian Embassy dictated the important correspondence in the Foreign Office (Dangol, 1999). Many mainstream intellectuals label the 1950 uprising as a 'revolution', but in essence, there was no revolutionary overthrow of the Rana regime resulting in the establishment of a peoples' democracy. It was an uprising directed towards replacing the feudal Rana regime with a feudal monarchical regime. As Riaz and Basu mention,

> [T]he 1950 uprising was an elite rebellion with the potential for establishing a popular accountable government. It was a product of anti-colonial nationalism and emerged victorious due to the collapse of colonial rule in India. Yet in reality this victory was a compromise between the monarchy and the emerging party political apparatus. King Tribhuvan's reluctance to intervene and the Indian government's attempt to retain a weak and divided authority in Nepal allowed this power sharing to continue.
>
> (Riaz and Basu, 2007: 41)

The promise of the election of a national constituent assembly made by King Tribhuvan under the pressure of political parties that would restore the kingship to power was never kept by his successors or by the NC and United Marxists–Leninist (UML) parties that held the reins of the government from 1991 to 2007. This issue was raised four-and-a-half decades later by the Maoists when they waged the 'Peoples' War', which continued for more a decade (1995–2005). Even though the first ever general election was held on 18 February 1959 in which the NC own more than two-thirds of the total seats (74 out of 109 seats) and the first democratic government was constituted by the NC with Bishweshwar Prasad Koirala as prime minister, this was only a drama by King Mahendra (son of King Tribhuvan, who died on 30 June 1955) to fool the people of Nepal and the political leaders. Not even two years of democracy had elapsed when Mahendra, by using his sovereign power, staged a coup d'état on 15 December 1960, truncating the baby democracy and all its norms. This included outlawing political parties, suspension of elected parliament as well as the government, imprisonment of Prime Minister Bishweshwar Prasad Koirala and all prominent political figures, ban on civil society organizations and suppression of civil liberties and press freedom, etc. This was justified on the grounds that the NC government fostered corruption, promoted partisan politics above national interest, failed to maintain law and order and encouraged anti-national elements. A new Constitution was promulgated by King Mahendra on December 1962, vesting all sets of power – executive, legislative and judicial – on the king and treating people as subjects to be ruled over. The palace remained the nucleus of power, and anyone daring to go against the palace desires and directives or indulge in opposition political activities risked his life not to talk of loss of career and even property. The Panchayat system was defended as something indigenous and suited to the Nepalese soil against the parliamentary system, which was denounced as alien and incompatible with the Nepalese history and ground reality. The Constitution reinforced the hill Brahmin–Chhetri domination in all spheres of the society.

The Constitution provisioned a four-tier (village, district, zonal and national), partyless Panchayat system in which people could elect their representatives. Corresponding to four tiers, there were government-sponsored classes and professional organizations for peasants, labourers, youths, students, women, ex-soldiers and college graduates. Created as substitutes for the prohibited political parties' sister organizations, these class organizations were basically meant for supporting the Panchayat system. These organizations were strictly prohibited from engaging in political activities and expressing verbally anything derogatory about the Panchayat system.

According to Dangol, King Mahendra initiated different strategies in order to establish a feudal monarchical system on a firm basis and consolidate his autocratic rule (Dangol, 1999). First, consolidation of state apparatus under firm control by expanding and modernizing the army and the police forces by granting them land and other benefits so as to keep them always loyal to the king. Second, direct contact with ordinary people by touring different rural or semi-urban areas of the country and listening to their grievances and dispensing justice on the spot in order to project his image as a popular king and endorse the divine right of the king to rule the country. Third, repression and fragmentation of opposition forces led by banned political parties by imprisoning, torturing and confiscating properties of political parties advocating multiparty democracy. Fourth, disintegration of communist forces by appointing their leaders in key political and administrative posts in order to build a counter-force against the NC. Last, stationing the Nepali Army along the Indian borders to counter the insurgent activities by the self-exiled leaders of NC from across the Indian borders against the Panchayat regime.

King Mahendra wanted to project himself as a modernizer so as to veil his absolute rule through the single-party Panchayat system. Taking the lesson from the inability of Ranas to move troops swiftly to different parts of the country to put down the armed insurrection against their regime, Mahendra gave high emphasis on the development of transport and communication in the name of economic development and political unity of the country (Blaikie et al., 1980). Nepal's neighbouring countries, India and China, supported road projects which had strategic importance for road connectivity from their borders to Nepal's capital city. As a result, considerable achievement was made in the construction of all-weather roads, accelerating from 376 km in 1952 to 4940 km in 1980 and further to 7262 km in 1990 (Skerry et. al., 1991). Even after Mahendra's death in 1972, expansion of the road network continued to receive high priority, and by the time the Panchayat regime fell, the total length of roads in the country was 7,330 km (NPC, 1992).

When Nepal initiated development efforts in the mid-1950s, the lack of roads was often cited as the major constraint to growth, but even with the considerable expansion of road networks in the later decades, growth did not occur. Expansion of road networks was not used as a means to expand the productive base of the areas opened by roads. Rather, it was used as reinforcement of the domination of the feudal class and the privileged groups in the rural economy by facilitating their movement and strengthening linkage with the rulers and the government bureaucracy in the centre. Besides, their children could easily move to city-based bourgeoisie educational institutions for education and training. The rulers and the government bureaucracy had ease of access for swift deployment of security forces to crush insurgent activities against the regime and an opportunity for revenue extraction in the form of tolls and user taxes for financing state expenditure. The merchant class found an opportunity to start merchandising and trading, hotel and catering businesses along the stoppage points of roads. To the general public and the small holder peasants, roads carried no enthusiasm except easy movement from one place to another. A study made in the context of Kathmandu–Pokhara road (Prithivi Highway) showed that the road, rather than breaking out the low and stagnant levels of production, led to the decline of small-scale indigenous crafts, i.e., blacksmithery, tailoring and shoemaking, by facilitating the inflow of cheap manufactured goods from India (Blaikie et al., 1980). Even certain agricultural products, such as rice and vegetables, which could be abundantly produced in the country, decelerated and an increasingly larger quantity of such items started to be imported to meet the domestic requirements.

King Mahendra was in a dichotomy of opting for political development or political survival but chose political survival. So he did not push fundamental reforms for the development of the country, which would have made Nepal a modern nation state and also a more politically conscious middle class. The middle class was seen as a potential threat to the Panchayat regime that could undermine the king's position (Gaige, 2009 [1975]). So he focussed on capability strengthening of the army and absorbing some potentially restive educated young men in high positions in the bureaucracy.

On the insistence of a Ford Foundation American adviser that foreign aid would have no utility if not accompanied by land reform, King Mahendra introduced land reform laws in 1964. However, the land reform laws were not really meant for changing the agrarian base of wealth and power but were meant to formalize the existing skewed landownership pattern. Not only was the land ceiling higher (4.9 ha in hills, 3.1 ha in Kathmandu and 18.4 ha in terai), but also the landowners were permitted to transfer the same amount of land to each son over 16 years of age and each unmarried daughter over 35 years of age. Many tenant families cultivating large landholders' land were evicted or replaced by owner cultivators or using labourers on a daily wage basis to deny sharecroppers their tenancy rights. Because of various escape ways in the laws, the large landholders retained excess land above the ceiling as homesteads or registered it in the name of relatives. Various studies undertaken in the past reveal that the land legislations, as these were introduced by the feudal rulers and executed by bourgeoisie class-dominated bureaucracy, had hardly any impact on changing the highly skewed distribution of land holdings and the prevailing inequitable land tenure practices (Poudyal, 1983).

Birendra, who ascended to the throne on 31 January 1972, also continued the authoritarian rule like his father, King Mahendra. He tried to give the posture of a developmental king like his father by undertaking a royal entourage of different parts of the country every year with the purpose of understanding the state of local development and the problems faced by the people and issuing on-the-spot directives to initiate needful actions to the attending band of noblemen that included a minister, NPC vice-chairman/member, top-level officials of the palace and bureaucracy and trusted officials. But development did not take place in the areas visited by the king because the band of noblemen and the officials had no interest in development except impressing the king with the demonstrations of splendid development activities that did not exist. The king was shown fake scenes of developmental activities taking place in areas of his visit. For example, at the inauguration of a water tap the king performed, the tap gushed with a high flow of water, but the moment passed, no water dripped from the tap again and people were left to continue their hardships in accessing drinking water. Likewise, there were demonstrations of big-size cauliflowers sprouting in the field, but these were temporarily planted there the night before the royal visit. In Kavre, an adjoining district of Kathmandu Valley, big-size potatoes were harvested in the presence of the king, but these were buried beneath the potato plants the night before the arrival of the royal entourage.[1] Thus the king was made a fool, as there was no innocent child as in Hans Christian Anderson's 'Emperor's New Cloth' to say that there was nothing in the field.

King Birendra endorsed the development strategy of regional specialization of agricultural production with livestock development in the mountains, horticulture in the hills and cereals as well as cash crops in the terai, but the palace officials and the bureaucracy did not pursue it further. In 1985, the king announced the national economic goal of raising the living standard of the Nepalese people to the 'Asian Standard' in the next 15 years. This announcement was highly applauded as something unparalleled in Nepal's development history and a boon to the Nepalese people to enjoy the Asian Standard of living in the near future. But the noblemen, planners and policymakers surrounding the king did not even describe what was meant by the Asian Standard and how it was going to be achieved. There was no description of whether the standard to be achieved was the average standard of diverse Asian countries that varied not only in terms of geo-physical setting but also in terms of level of development or the standard of a single Asian country. Given Nepal's profile as having the lowest socio-economic status among Asian countries, the attainment of the standard of even Burma on the low side by 2000 was just impossible (Poudyal and Sharma, 1985). As there were no further thinking and exercises, the royal proclamation did not go beyond the rhetorical speeches of politicians, ministers and planners. It is hard to believe that King Birendra, who was educated at Eaton College and Harvard University, was not aware of such deceptions, but he remained a passive observer of the lack of or virtually no execution of his proclamations and directives. Instead of taking action against those flouting his commands, Birendra continued appreciating them by awarding medals and promotions to higher posts or providing grade increases in salaries every year on his birthday.

During his two-decade rule (1972–91), King Birendra could have used his absolute power for directing state investment towards making Nepal economically self-reliant, introducing administrative and institutional reforms and instituting and enforcing a strong reward and punishment system to compel the bureaucracy committed to the achievement of growth and development targets set in the periodic plans. He could also have obtained candid advice and comments on development policies, programmes and the implementation process from the intellectuals not aligned with the Panchayat politics. But he preferred to rely on loyal bureaucrats and palace coterie occupying top positions in the bureaucracy and the palace secretariat. All such persons had feudal and aristocratic lineage, as they were the sons of landowners, feudal lords, palace priests and high-ranking officials and wanted to maintain the status quo. The state and the bureaucracy functioned under the patronage or clientele system in political appointments and promotions, which blocked good governance and fostered corruption of public resources. These people eulogized the monarchy as a symbol of national unity, factor of stability, patronizing factor of development and source of nationalism. Furthermore, the king's position was made religiously unparalleled in the world by evoking the phrase 'the only Hindu King/Kingdom in the world' in order to appease the king, maintain the status quo, rise to higher level administrative posts and cover up their clandestine activities. A powerful palace-aligned notorious group known as 'Mandale' was groomed for carrying out acts of oppression, terrors and violence against the critics of the Panchayat system, leaders and supporters of outlawed political parties tagged as 'anti-national elements' by the government, be they individuals or press, and government officials not complying to their demand for unfair decisions. Quite often, such activities were carried out under the patronage of royal family members, palace courtiers and power elites with a stake in the fund thus garnered, often at the cost of national interest and national treasury. Because no mechanism which would act as a countervailing force to the misdoings of the government existed, the state machinery and the bureaucracy often protected by the ruling class and the royal family members were absolutely free to indulge in all forms of self-aggrandizing acts in the forms of commission, fees and presents and even misappropriation of public resources. The king could not be said to be unaware of this reality, but he was circumscribed to take any stern action against such activities, as this would alienate him from the palace coterie and supporters of the regime.

During King Birendra's regime, the palace secretariat was expanded and made more powerful than the government secretariat in order to exercise control over government activities and decisions. In the words of Dangol,

> During King Birendra's time, the palace secretariat played a very dominant role in the politics and administration of Nepal. At this time each and every major issue of the country was determined by the palace secretariat. The central secretariat of the government remained simply as an instrument to carry on the orders of the palace secretariat. Thus Nepal was made to face a kind of double governments – one run by the palace secretariat and the other run by the HMG (His Majesty's Government). In the process of running the government, the palace secretariat remained behind the screen without bearing any responsibility or accountability to the people.
>
> (Dangol, 1999: 176)

The palace secretariat was 'a state within a state' as it had the patronage of kings and royalties, while the state bureaucracy was subordinated to it. As such, the government had virtually no choice in making major policy decisions independent of palace directives, even if these did not comply with the existing laws and rules.

The Panchayat regime laid emphasis on public enterprises as 'the commanding heights of the economy' and between 1960 and 1990 public enterprises grew to 61 with a dozen built under Chinese and Russian aid in order to make Nepal self-reliant in some construction materials and consumption goods. But these public enterprises were not directed for the development of state capitalism which required, in Marxian terminology, enlarged reproduction or capital accumulation, but were used as a ploy to serve the self-interest of rulers and bureaucrats. The nature of the state and class configurations that existed did not promote a capitalist mode of reproduction, which required steady conversion of surplus into real capital for expanded reproduction. Rather, it perpetuated the historically rooted semi-feudal mode of production with surplus value appropriated by the royal class, courtiers and bureaucrats. The appropriated surplus was transferred not only into private property and bank balances in foreign countries but also into the conspicuous consumption of the ruling and the bourgeoisie class. Poor people and the disadvantaged community were subjected to various forms of exploitation by the landed class, particularly hill Brahmin–Chhetri and terai Brahmin through highly discriminatory tenancy relations (either highly unequal share-cropping or low daily wages), usury and various other mechanisms. This resulted in the rising affluence of minority groups patronized by the regime amidst growing unemployment, poverty and hunger of the majority of people in the rural and remote areas.

The situation of Nepal thus presents a failed case of the authoritarian monarchy in pursuing modernizing efforts. This is contrary to the generally held view that centralization of power in the monarchy was necessary to promote social, cultural and economic reform. The failure to modernize the country could be attributed to the king's interest not to displease monarchical forces to make the fullest and most effective use of political tools for promoting the traditional elites and the coterie for the sake of accommodating the emerging demand for modernization. Hayes aptly describes the situation as the king being caught in a dilemma. If he attempts to modernize certain elements of the system in order to accommodate emerging elites, he alienates the only durable base of support for the regime of the monarchy. But if he does not pursue modernization in the face of social change, he draws the hostility of new elites, who would be increasingly oriented towards the regime transformation, i.e., elimination of the monarchy (Hayes, 1974: 617). But the king gave priority to the first option and only symbolic expressions were made for modernization and development.

In the later years of his rule, there were mounting public dissents and demonstrations against the atrocities of the Panchayat system, curbs on the freedom of political parties and deprivation of a large number of people from employment opportunities and other state facilities. The regime launched rampant arrest, imprisonment and torture of a large number of dissenting people and also execution under a veil, but the anti-regime activities continued unabated. Sensing a danger ahead, King Birendra tried to pacify all such resentments by announcing a referendum on 23 May 1979 calling people to vote either for a reformed Panchayat system or a multiparty system. In the referendum held on 2 May 1980, the reformed Panchayat system got a narrow victory (54.8 percent against 45.2 percent of total voters), which the agitating left forces and independent intellectuals alleged the government of rigging, while the NC leader BP Koirala accepted it as the peoples' verdict. However, some prominent leaders of NC, such as Ganesh

Man Singh and Krishna Prasad Bhattarai, remarked that the result would further accentuate the political conflict in the country. Following the Referendum, the 1962 Panchayat Constitution was amended by introducing certain democratic elements, such as the election of a prime minister by the Rastriya Panchayat, the Council of Ministers would be accountable to the Rastriya Panchayat and not to the king and freedom of speech and limited freedom of political activities. An 11-member Constitution Reform Commission was also constituted to amend the Constitution by introducing certain features of democracy. Despite acceptance of the referendum result, the political parties boycotted the Panchayat elections held in 1981.

The reforms introduced in the Constitution towards greater democratic practices did not, however, quell peoples' demand for the end of the Panchayat regime and a full-fledged democratic system. The movement against the regime, which had remained sporadic and weak in the past, gained momentum in February 1990 with the NC and the United Left Front,[2] a conglomerate of left parties, joining hands to mount a fatal assault against the Panchayat system and restore multiparty democracy in the country. The urban mass including human rights activists, professionals, students and artisans also came down to the street with violent strategies demanding the end of the system, notwithstanding the brutal physical assaults, arrests and indiscriminate firing by the royal police. The deployment of the army and shooting at the mob by the government only contributed to escalating the movement. At around the same time, relations between Nepal and India, which were already strained because of Nepal's arms deal with China and the introduction of a work permit system for Indian nationals to work in Nepal, worsened. India showed its resentment by refusing to renew two separate treaties on trade and transit and insisted on a single treaty. India closed all but two transit points and imposed a trade embargo on Nepal. This not only paralyzed peoples' lives owing to acute shortages of basic necessities like kerosene, machinery, petrol, diesel, coal, baby food, etc., but also laid off a number of industries for lack of basic raw materials, spare parts and chemicals imported from India. Some prominent leaders of India also came to Nepal and spoke against the Panchayat system and argued that democracy was at hand. The system also lost its external manoeuvrability of the China and India cards, which it had been cashing to keep the regime secured in the past. Scared of the collapse of a nearly two-and-a-half-century-old monarchy, King Birendra squashed the Panchayat regime and introduced multiparty democracy that was truncated by his father 30 years ago. People rejoiced this as a great victory with the expectation that the democratic political representation would bring a golden dawn and open up better prospects for the country and the people.

4.5 Class in the Nepalese Society

The concept of class draws many ambiguities over its definitions. Class is a social category and may be divided along income, gender, education, skill, caste, culture and other attributes. Class is also defined as a way of life and used as a basis for the identification of a group of people by their dress, attitude, beliefs, morals and values (Dasgupta, 1998). According to Marxian theory, class is defined not in terms of status, social esteem or income level but in terms of a person's ownership of productive factors and his objective interests rooted in production relation and sharing of return. Marx postulated two classes, capitalists and labourers with conflicting interests, capitalists interested in securing power and expanding profits and labourers in higher wages, better working conditions and job security. In his later writings, Marx envisaged three dominant classes – wage-labourers, capitalists and landowners that, respectively, derived income in the form of wage, profit and ground rent (Fischer, 2008). Writers attempting to analyze class divisions in a specific country context have taken up the Marxian concept of class divisions as the starting point and made classifications presumed to reflect the reality of the country concerned. In the Indian context, Bardhan identifies three proprietary classes – the industrial capitalist class, the rich farmers and the professionals in the public sector – which constitute the top two deciles, while the bottom half of the population lives in abject poverty (Bardhan, 1998). On the other hand, Sau delineates classes in India in terms of the agrarian sector and the rural sector. In the agrarian sector, the classes consist of substantial landowners, moderate landowners, poor peasants and landless labourers, while in the urban sector, these are the industrial and commercial bourgeoisie, petty bourgeoisie, urban proletariat and semi-proletariat (Sau, 1986). A more general approach is to classify the classes in terms of rich class, middle class and poor class on the basis of income level or wealth possession. The rich category includes wealthy people that include politicians, senior civil servants, businessmen, lawyers, accountants, doctors, engineers, managers and owners of factories and firms, who derive their power and wealth from the semi-feudal socio-economic structure and production relations as well as connection with the comprador capital. On the other hand, the poor category includes wage workers, subsistence farmers, artisans, lower-level civil servants and honest politicians who are compelled to live a subsistence life. The middle class falls in the middle of the rich class and the poor class but holds aspirations to climb to the position of the rich or bourgeoisie class. Included in the middle class are the professionals (emerging lawyers, doctors, engineers, teachers, accountants, etc.) corporate managers and civil servants who possess significant human capital and earn reasonably high incomes.

A basic feature of the Nepalese social, economic and political structure has been the dominance of well-to-do Brahmin and Chhetri castes at the central as well as local levels. These two castes have always been nearer to the power circle whatever may be the type of political regime. The main decisive factors that have placed these two castes at higher political status from the early years have been the control of land, high-caste status and identification with the hill culture since 1950, and education has also become an important determinant of success in national politics (Gaize, 2009 [1975]). As the hill Brahmins and Chhetries were the ones to possess all four of the prerequisites for successful participation in national politics, they occupied dominant positions in national politics as well as in the bureaucracy. The Baisya caste, mainly consisting of Newars of Kathmandu Valley and primarily engaged in trading and business activities, built a close rapport with Brahmin and Chhetri, and with educational attainment, they gradually gained proximity to the power circle and obtained appointments to higher administrative posts. These three castes were often competitive and rivals with each other in appointments to higher administrative posts, and during the Panchayat regime, the kings often had a hard time maintaining balance among these castes in the higher posts in the palace as well as the central secretariat. The hill Janajatis (Gurung, Magar and Rai) were largely recruited into the security forces, while the Dalits were totally alienated from government jobs. The terai as a whole, except for appointments of a handful of Madheshi belonging to the affluent upper caste (terai Brahmin and Rajputs) and business community (Marwari) in higher administrative posts, were ignored by the Brahmin–Chhetri–Newar coalition dominated power centre. Other low-caste Madheshi people, such as Dalits and ethnic, were not even recruited into the military, not to speak of government bureaucracy. The voices of the Madheshi people against their exclusion, discrimination and inequality vis-à-vis Pahade (hill people) were compressed during the Panchayat regime but started to surface in the political scene after the dawn of the democratic regime in 1991 and went full-blown as a powerful political force beginning in early 2007 with Maoist party joining the national politics.

Over the past hundred years, the rulers of the country created an uneven pattern of development between the small urban centre, mainly Kathmandu Valley, and the vast periphery, mainly the rural areas. The concentration of development activities and administrative functions in Kathmandu Valley led to its faster modernization, while the periphery, where two-thirds of the total population resided, was bypassed in the process of development. The polarization between the urban centres and periphery led to increasing migration of relatively well-off families from the hills and terai to urban and metropolitan cities. As a consequence, caste-based class division gradually lost its relevance, and wealth and income gained prominence as the basis of class division, giving rise to the formation of a rich class, a burgeoning and aspirational middle class and a poor class. In the class formation process that occurred over time as a result of the semi-feudalistic mode of production and the expansion of the market economy, new classes were formed or a new, specific character was added to the existing classes. Differences in income and wealth within the high-class category were often so high that certain strata belonging to this class may be at a much lower income level than the upper strata of a lower-class category. Therefore, certain generalizations and simplifications are unavoidable, if the heterogeneous class groups are to be categorized into certain homogenous categories. With this caveat, we broadly categorize the classes in Nepal into four strata each at the centre as well as at the periphery as is schematically presented in Figure 4.1.

By ruling class, we mean the hereditary kings, selected members of royal and Rana families, urban aristocrats, politicians and persons at the top positions of bureaucracy. For about two centuries and a half until the dethroning in 2008, the king remained head of the state in theory and practice, and the royal family members became the centripetal and centrifugal forces around which the political leaders, the urban as well as rural bourgeoisie, the military and bureaucracy revolved. The politicians of the Panchayat era were mainly the defectors of the NC Party and the communist parties, and they joined the Panchayat politics to make it a full-time occupation motivated either by the lure of power or by personal gain or by both. Others who were involved in Panchayat politics were the persons from the landed aristocracy, bourgeoisie class and middle-class educated persons who desired to be a

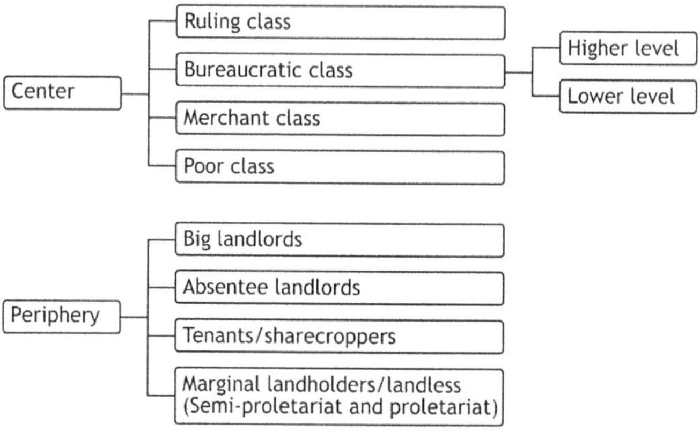

Figure 4.1 Classes in the Centre and the Periphery.

part of the power circle headed by the king and the royal family members. Such persons were all rooted in feudal lineage and found the new regime an opportune source to acquire state power and serve their self-interests under the patronage of the king and the royal family. The king's brothers and close relatives were involved in business and trading activities, while the queen and other female members of the royal family controlled various social organizations, such as the Social Welfare Council, Nepal Red Cross Society and Family Planning Association, where foreign aid was funnelled from many sources. The king bestowed higher bureaucratic as well as diplomatic positions to a limited number of favoured persons and also moved them from one to another lucrative higher post to keep them dedicated to the monarchy and the Panchayat system and allure others to move on the same path.

During three decades from the mid-1950s, consequent to the initiation of planning, increasing inflow of foreign aid and rapid increase in government functions, there had been a proliferation of several government offices, departments and agencies resulting in the phenomenal expansion of government bureaucracy and growth of the middle class. During the same period, the number of educated persons also increased phenomenally owing to the expansion of educational institutions within the country and the offer of scholarships for higher education and training by a number of foreign countries under their aid programmes. However, a large majority of educated persons belonged to three main caste and ethnic groups – namely, Brahmin, Chhetri and Newar. As shown by the 1991 population census, of 96,977 persons with graduate and above degrees, 38.3 percent were Brahmin, 23.7 percent were Newar and 12.4 percent were Chhetri (CBS, 1993). And these three caste and ethnic groups were the ones to occupy higher posts in civil services and security forces since the time of Junga Bahadur Rana. In 1854, these groups occupied 98.0 percent of top civil service posts, and 115 years later in 1969, these groups still held 93.0 percent of the posts (Seddon, 1987). The situation did not change for many years since then. A study report of 1973 revealed that Brahmin, Chhettri and Newar, which constituted 22.8 percent of the total population, occupied 92.8 percent of under-secretary and above positions, and other castes, which constituted 77.2 percent of the total population, occupied only 7.2 percent of such positions (Beenhakker, 1973). In the army too, in 1967, Chhetri occupied 74.0 percent of high-ranking posts with Brahmin, Newar and Gurung occupying 6.5 percent each (Gaige, 2009 [1975]). Nepal's bureaucracy has thus always remained under the control of three dominant castes. At the same time, university graduates from other castes as well as from the lower stratum of dominant classes who succeeded in entering bureaucracy formed a new genre of bureaucrats, what could be best termed as 'modern bureaucrats' in high positions in the administration (Seddon, 1987). Even though the modern bureaucrats knew that various forms of semi-feudalistic production relations inherited from the past were inimical to the country's growth and development and even though they could initiate efforts to alter or fight against these, a large majority remained silent and started working as henchmen to the people connected with the palace and the ruling class to fulfil their interest of rising to a higher income class. With the increasing inflow of foreign aid and foreign-funded projects in the country, the modern bureaucrats occupied a special place in the administrative machinery and started enjoying benefits along with the so-called comprador bourgeoisie that served as an agent of foreign capital and helped it to penetrate into the economic affairs of the country. As a consequence, a strong power nexus was formed among the politicians, top-level bureaucrats, modern bureaucrats and commercial or trading mafia for fulfilling their immediate and strategic interests. The immediate interest meant amassing a disproportionate share of the surplus social product by using public office for private gain even at the cost of national interest, gaining access to positions of political power and maintaining its social well-being within the existing order. On the other hand, the strategic interest meant the creation of necessary conditions for the perpetuation of existing semi-feudal order so that they could give continuity to their power as a state class and expropriate the social surplus for personal benefit. In the Marxian view, bureaucracy rarely creates new wealth by itself, but rather controls, coordinates and governs the production, distribution and consumption of wealth. And it is in this regulatory process that politicians, ministers and bureaucrats find an opportunity for bribery and corruption through policy changes, policy circumvention and partisan decisions.

In the agrarian sector, land constituted the most significant asset, and the size of land ownership determined the economic and political power that permeated beyond the local level onto the central level. The rural economy was basically under the grip of big landlords and absentee landlords, who mostly belonged to upper castes/ethnic groups, such as Brahmin and Chhetri because these were the beneficiaries of state granted land in the form of Birta and Raiker from the early Shah rulers. These landlords rented out the land to the marginal or landless farmers at rent as high as 75 percent of the paddy crops. In addition, the tenants were forced to mandatory labour contributions of various chores for the landlords. Moreover, most of the tillers and landless farmers had deficient income/production to meet even their bare consumption needs and hence were forced to take loans both in cash or in kind from the big landowning class as well as village money lenders at exorbitant interest rates. As can be seen from the data presented in Table 4.1, the dependence of subsistence farmers, including tenants for loans from the village moneylenders as

Table 4.1 Dependence on Village Moneylenders and Interest Rate

Description	*1969/70*	*1976/7*
Farm families borrowing from private credit agencies (percent)	48.5	76.0
Interest rate (percent)	10.0–100.0	10.0–150.0

Source: Agricultural Credit Survey Vol. I, 1972 and Agricultural Credit Review Survey, Vol. I, 1980, Nepal Rastra Bank, Kathmandu.

well as landlords, increased in 1976/7 as compared to six years before. Along with the increase in the percentage of borrowing farm families, the interest rate increased from 100.0 percent to 150.0 percent at the highest starting from 10.0 percent. As a consequence, borrower farmers accumulated debt which they could not repay and were dispossessed of their meager land or homesteads.

The landowners and absentee landlords who rented out land to the tenants for cultivation appropriated the bulk of the production from the direct producers through high tenancy rates but did not invest even a single rupee for land improvement, nor did they invest the surplus value in establishing or expanding industrial enterprises leading to further accumulation; rather, they used the funds for conspicuous consumption or invested in real or other non-productive assets (gold and jewellery) or used it as merchant capital, which hardly added to the expansion of productive potential.

4.6 Nature of the State in the Post-democracy Period

Democracy was reinstated in 1990 as a result of a long struggle by the NC culminating in a joint assault with the United Left Front against the Panchayat regime in April 1990. The assault turned into an unprecedented mass movement with civil society groups, academics, students, middle class, working class and peasantry joining the movement, which eventually forced King Birendra to dissolve the Panchayat system and announce a multiparty democratic system. This movement was, however, basically a bourgeois-democratic movement against the repressive Panchayat regime that was imposed upon by King Mahendra in 1961 by crushing the short-lived democracy that emerged in 1951. The parties took the dissolution of Panchayat structures and the reinstating of the multiparty system by the king as something bestowed upon them and made the mistake of giving space to the king in the democratic system. The institution of monarchy was allowed to exist as one of the major constituents of state power, while political parties and bureaucracy constituted the two other constituents to rule over the country and extract the surplus value generated in the economy. The NC embodied the characteristics of a bourgeoisie party, even though it often referred to 'democratic socialism' in its official documents and public statements. Prior to the formation of the UML party through the merger of Marxist–Leninist (ML) and Marxist parties, the former was a revolutionary party which conducted armed activities against the rural landlords and exploiters of peasants, even resorting to their execution in the eastern terai districts (Jhapa and Sunsari), resembling the Naxalite Movement in India. The main objective of the ML party was to establish 'peoples' democratic new socialism and emancipate the toiling peasants and workers from the exploitation of landlords and feudal elements. However, the unified communist party gradually abandoned the Marxist–Leninist ideology and assimilated itself with the mainstream politics and neo-liberal economic paradigm. As a consequence, there was no change in the nature of the state or the class configurations of Nepalese society in the post-democracy period. Neither was the political agenda of the constituent assembly election agreed upon in the 1950 tripartite agreement evoked, nor was the position of the king reduced to a figurehead of the nation.

An 11-member coalition Interim Council of Ministers was formed under the premiership of NC president Krishna Prasad Bhattarai with three principal mandates: (i) investigate and punish the Panchayat ministers, security officers and top bureaucrats who had carried out inhumane atrocities, oppressions and indiscriminate shooting of demonstrators during the mass movement, (ii) write a new Constitution and (iii) hold a general election for the legislative body.

Regarding the first mandate, the government constituted a high-level Commission (Mallik Commission) headed by a retired Supreme Court Justice Janardan Mallik to investigate the atrocities, oppressions and killings conducted by both the Panchayat rulers and the security forces and suggest actions against them. The Commission implicated ministers, senior army and police officers, high-level government bureaucrats and several other persons linked to the palace for the atrocities and killings of innocent people. However, neither the interim government nor the governments formed after the first general election of 12 May 1991 made any attempt to execute the recommendations of the Mallik Commission. The interim government, which had the peoples' mandate and the representation of the left party, as well as the human rights activists in the cabinet, remained passive on this issue. On the contrary, the government opted for reconciliatory rather than confrontational politics with the king, leaders of the Panchayat regime and the security forces by not executing the recommendations of the Commission.

Second, a new Constitution was written and promulgated on 9 November 1990, but it was a product of a compromise between the NC, United Left Front and the monarchy written by the nominated representatives of three forces. The new Constitution made the king intrinsically as powerful and as pervasive as during the Panchayat regime with military and other constitutional powers vested in him. Not only was the king made constitutional head of the state but his control over the national army as the supreme commander-in-chief was also preserved, along with emergency power. The king was also provided authority to nominate 10 members in a 60-member National Council (Upper House). Even in the interim government, the king was given the privilege to nominate two persons and was allowed to nominate a few Nepalese envoys to foreign diplomatic missions abroad.

Third, a general election was held on 12 May 1991 which placed NC as the major political power with majority seats (110 out of 205), while UML gained 69 seats and the rest were claimed by other parties.

The interim government, founded on the basis of the mass movement that displaced the Panchayat regime and the people's unprecedented support, did not dare to break the inherited feudal structure and stranglehold of the bourgeoisie and privileged class in the bureaucracy, as well as in the wider political economy, or initiate bold measures for setting the course of the economy in the right direction. Rather, the government forged an alliance with the ruling class, the bourgeoisie and the reactionary remnants of the Panchayat regime. As Houften says, 'The interim cabinet under the leadership of Krishna Prasad Bhattarai may have been the most powerful government for over one hundred years, but it did not seem to exercise these powers' (Houften, 1994: 19). The government required ministers and bureaucrats up to the section officer level to declare property ownership and also submit additions or deductions in their assets during the year at the beginning of each fiscal year and also stated that property of known corrupt officials was to be evaluated and culprits were to be brought under legal action. However, during the interim government period, not a single corrupt person in the regime was brought to trial nor were actions taken against them. Although the ministers declared their property, this became only a routine practice, and several ministers in the interim government were charged during the year with corrupt practices and illegal activities, but there was no action against them (Seddon, 1994).

Following the results of the 1991 election, NC came to power, and Girija Prasad Koirala became prime minister. The government was no different from the interim government in its activities to uphold the spirit of the mass movement. Despite the strong public demand to implement the Mallik Commission report, the government did not show any interest in this. Consequently, former Panchas, as well as feudal and reactionary classes, got an opportunity to consolidate themselves under the umbrella of the Rastriya Prajatantra Party (RPP), contest elections and hold the rein of power. The government also sought to accommodate the bourgeoisie class and maintain close ties with the palace and the elements of feudalism to consolidate and strengthen anti-communist forces. Even though the country was under democratic rule, the king remained powerful owing to political parties' soft attitude of opting for monarchy as an indispensable institution for nourishing the 'baby democracy'.

The NC had a majority government for about 43 months and also remained either in the helms or as a powerful coalition partner party in the government several times thereafter until 2007, except for a brief spell of nine months of the UML minority government during 1994–5 (Table 4.2). Prime Minister Koirala resigned after losing the support of 36 lawmakers of his own party led by Sher Bahadur Deuba ('Group of 36') when a 'vote of thanks' was to be passed on the royal address in the House in July 1994. Along with resignation, Koirala asked the king to dissolve the parliament and call fresh elections. This step of Girija Prasad Koirala ensued political instability and uncertainty in the country for the next 30 years, altering the government every nine to ten months with a coalition of different political parties until the first general election in 2017 which gave a stable government of Nepal Communist Party (resulting from the merger of UML and Maoist party) for three years but the 2022 election results show that future governments will also be instable.

In the mid-term election of 15 November 1994, the UML occupied the first position with 88 seats, just 5 seats more than the NC, which gained 83 seats and was degraded to second position. Surprisingly, the pro-royalist RPP mustered 20 seats against a gain of only 4 seats in the 1991 election and became the third major political party. For the RPP, the candidates of which were pelted with stones and bricks in the 1991 general election, this was an unprecedented bonanza, which

Table 4.2 Prime Ministers of Nepal during the Constitutional Monarchical System (1990–2008)

SN	*Prime Minister*	*Parties*	*Days*	*Period*
1.	K. P. Bhattarai (1/2)	NC-ULF-Palace-Independents Coalition	402	19/4/1990–26/5/91
2.	G. P. Koirala (1/5)	NC (Majority)	1284	26/5/91–28/11/94
3.	Man M. Adhikari	UML (Minority)	286	29/11/94–12/9/95
4.	Sher B. Deuba (1/5)	NC-RPP-Nepal Sadbhavana Party (NSP) Coalition	547	11/9/95–12/3/97
5.	Lokendra B. Chand (1/2)	RPP-UML Coalition	209	12/3/97–7/10/97
6.	Surya B. Thapa (1/2)	RPP-NC-NSP	190	7/12/97–15/3/98
7.	G. P. Koirala (2/5)	NC-CPN(ML)-UML-NSP Coalition	411	15/3/98–31/5/99
8.	K. P. Bhattarai (2/2)	NC	296	31/5/99–22/3/2000
9.	G. P. Koirala (3/5)	NC	491	22/3/00–26/7/2001
10.	S. B. Deuba (2/5)	NC	435	26/7/2001–4/10/02
11.	Gyanendra Shah (1/2)	Direct rule	7	4/10/2002–11/10/2002
12	L. B. Chand (2/2)	RPP	237	11/10/2002–5/6/2003
13.	S. B. Thapa (1/2)	RPP	364	5/6/2003–3/6/2004
14.	S. B. Deuba (3/5)	NC-UML	243	3/6/2004–1/2/2005
15.	G. Shah (2/2)	Direct rule	448	1/2/2005–25/4/2006
16.	G. P. Koirala (4/5)	NC	764	25/4/2006–28/5/2008

Sources: https://en.wikipedia.org/wiki/List_of_prime_ministers_of_Nepal (accessed on 21/2/2018).

Table 4.3 Caste/Ethnic Composition of Members in the House of Representatives (Total Seats 205)

Caste/Ethnicity	*Year*					
	1991		*1994*		*1999*	
	No	*Percent*	*No*	*Percent*	*No*	*Percent*
Brahmin/Chhetri	114	55.6	129	62.9	122	59.5
Madheshi	42	20.4	40	19.5	41	20.0
Ethnic and Indigenous	48	23.4	36	17.6	42	20.5
Dalits	1	0.5	–	–	–	–
Total seats	**205**	**100.0**	**205**	**100.0**	**205**	**100.0**
Women	7	3.4	7	3.4	12	5.9

Source: Computation based on the election results of 1991, 1994 and 1999 made public by the Election Commission. https://en.wikipedia.org/wiki/List_of_prime_ministers_of_Nepal

would have been impossible three years before. 'Moreover, its 18 percent share of the vote was significantly higher than the 12 percent won by the parties of the former Panchas in 1991. Two former Panchayat prime ministers, Lokendra Bahadur Chand and Surya Bahadur Thapa, both routed in an embarrassing fashion in 1991, were returned to parliament in 1994' (Brown, 2010: 195). Even more embarrassing was their comeback as prime ministers of the coalition governments in a March 1997 to March 1998 and October 2002 to June 2004 (Table 4.3). Obviously when in political power, the RPP was in a position to strengthen its stranglehold of former Panchas in and outside of state bureaucracy and promote the concerns and interest of bourgeoisie and feudal classes.

The political change of 1990 offered an opportunity to overhaul the administrative machinery inherited from the Panchayat regime for breaking the vicious circle of underdevelopment, poverty and unemployment and creating conditions for the development of a self-reliant economy. However, for the next three decades, neither the NC nor the UML, despite their slogan of 'democratic socialism' and 'peoples' democratic new socialism', respectively, initiated any effort towards this direction when they were seated in power. The NC government continued with the existing semi-feudalistic socio-economic structure and pushed the country towards neo-liberal and world-capitalist order. This was in contravention of Bishweshwar Prasad Koirala's (the founder of NC) philosophy of 'democratic socialism' and the 'socialistic pattern of society'. The UML, despite its Marxist–Leninist tag, became content to operate in the terrain of bourgeoisie politics and discarded its original commitment to revolutionary politics for social and economic transformation. It deviated from its professed Marxist–Leninist philosophy and got swayed by the mainstream advocacy of reliance on market forces and deregulation as necessary conditions for growth and efficiency, in tandem with the NC. However, the political parties became the victim of their own act of retaining the king as 'constitutional head of the state' with emergency power and the final authority to endorse the bills passed by the parliament as well as 'commander in-chief of the national army', when King Gyanendra sabotaged democracy on 1 January 2005, replicating what his father Mahendra had done some four decades ago.

In a democracy, the sovereignty ultimately lies with the people, and this is expressed by the adoption of universal adult franchise. This means that all individuals should have the opportunity to exercise their voting rights freely without any pressure or threat, and the elections should also be free and fair. However, the democracy and the associated electoral system, as it was practiced in Nepal from 1991 to 2006 and even thereafter, did not ensure the participation of all or the majority of people in the political process and effective representation in the legislature. People got political freedom, but this freedom was curbed by the highly unequal distribution of wealth and income. Free and fair elections became a far cry, and democratic politics and political participation depended on money and muscle power. The electoral system was monopolized by the upper castes and privileged sections of the society by using money for contesting and winning the elections. This becomes evident if one examines the caste/ethnic composition of the persons elected in the three Legislative Assembly elections held during the democratic system in 1991, 1994 and 1999 (Table 4.3).

The high-caste groups (Brahmin and Chhetri) had a predominant position in all three Legislative Assembly elections. The hill Dalit had only one elected member in 1991 and none in the next two elections, while the terai Dalit had none elected in three elections. The Dalits are those communities who, by virtue of atrocities of caste-based discrimination and untouchability, are most backwards in social, economic, educational, political and religious fields and are deprived of human dignity and social justice. Although women constituted half of the total population, their representation in the parliament was limited to only 3.4 percent each in the 1991 and 1994 elections and 5.9 percent in the 1999 election. This demonstrates that the 'feudal' political culture and state power dominated by politicians belonging to the Brahmin/Chhetri caste and upper-middle class have remained intact even in the post-democracy period.

The political scenario of Nepal in the post-democracy period is characterized by party splits, mergers and renaming; defections and counter-defections; politicization of the civil service bureaucracy; and growth of corruption. In 1990, when the interim government was formed, politicians and the civil service bureaucracy were engaged in a power game, each trying to overshadow the other, but eventually, politics influenced the administration, and the administration learnt to be receptive to the politicians. Politicians' need for money and bureaucrats' desire for placement in lucrative positions led to the building and strengthening of collusive ties between the two. This becomes evident if one examines Wade's 'transfer model' in which politicians are seen as compelling the bureaucracy to acquiesce in their nefarious activities by controlling a system of rewards (appointments to 'cushy jobs') and punishments (transfer to remote areas) (Wade, 1982). This sort of nexus between the politicians and the bureaucracy has resulted in two deleterious consequences for the economy and the polity of Nepal.

First, there has been a heavy politicization of civil service bureaucracy, which has created various types of distortions in the administrative system and made the achievement of national goals an elusive task. The political parties initiated a culture of placing 'our men' rather than 'appropriate men' in important posts so as to make them subservient to their overt or covert interest in the course of formulation as well as the implementation of state policies and programmes. One aspect of Nepal's administrative system that has led to the politicization of bureaucracy is the promotion system to the post of secretary. The promotion rule requires the Promotion Committee chaired by the public service commission chairman to recommend three times larger numbers of joint-secretaries than the vacant posts of secretary. The vacant post is divided among the parties in government on the basis of their strength, and promotion is made by the cabinet as per the concerned party's recommendation. This gives space to the political parties in power to pick up those who are aligned with the party and can be relied upon to work in the interest of party leaders by manipulation of policies and misuse of discretionary power. And the senior bureaucrats are often compelled to comply with the demands of the politicians or else they have a constant threat of transfers and harassment from the minister of the concerned ministry. The non-complying secretaries and joint-secretaries are transferred to another ministry or office carrying lower significance. Those wanting to be picked up to higher bureaucratic positions or political appointments in constitutional bodies and diplomatic missions abroad have tacitly maintained affiliation with the political parties of their leaning. In so doing, they could influence the politicians in power or get influenced by them for garnering commissions, bribery and other means of earning undue money. In this context, an earlier report says,

> The past seven years of democratic exercise has completely demoralized civil service. Instead of giving support to the bureaucracy as a permanent institution of the state, it was and is being fully politicized by the ruling parties. Politicians oblige and exploit bureaucrats for personal gain and give all protection and patronage to corruption.
>
> (Pro-Public, 1999: 18)

In a similar tone, Mage says, '[T]he parliamentary governments of the post-1991 period quickly discredited themselves by crude lust for the profits of office' (Mage, 2007: 1835).

Second, post-democracy has witnessed the growth of large-scale systematic corruption in the country. A key factor causing the growth of corruption has been electoral politics, which has become a matter of money and muscle power rather than the political and economic agenda. Contesting and winning elections has become a very expensive affair, as the candidate has to indulge in all sorts of unfair activities, such as capturing polling booths and carrying out all kinds of tricks and fraud, in addition to huge campaigning expenses. Obviously, they do not spend a large amount of money just for the prestige of becoming a member of parliament (MP). Rather, they do it in anticipation of the money they will be able to earn as MPs or as ministers. So those who join politics stay there for life and hardly retreat unless convicted for civilian or other crimes, or they become very old, or physically or mentally unfit.

In the drive to collect funds for elections, the contestants and political parties have also resorted to the practice of seeking donations from business houses, industrialists, comprador capitalists and big contractors. In return, the politicians, when elected to power or when they become ministers, interfere with the system in various ways, such as manipulation of tariff and customs duties on certain imports and production, providing undue concessions and facilities and awarding public contracts in a partisan manner. Such kinds of unholy alliances between the politicians and the business houses were unprecedentedly high on certain occasions when a large amount of money was needed for horse-trading of MPs in order to provide a vote of confidence in the house for continuing as prime minister. This has given rise to a unique phenomenon of 'corporatization of politics'. Another phenomenon of 'criminalization of politics' has emerged because of the inclusion of criminals, notorious underworld figures and private contractors, as well as businessmen, into political parties to work as political adjuncts for serving their interests. Most of them of them are grafted into the parliament through a proportional election system.

A well-documented study of corruption is lacking in Nepal, but an extensive reading of newspapers of the past three decades shows that many people involved in corruption have been caught now and then, but many have managed to escape. The corruption cases investigated and probed by the Commission on Investigation of Abuse of Authority (CIAA), which is the apex constitutional body for corruption control in Nepal, show that corruption has become part and parcel of everyday political-administrative structure from top to bottom. Over the last three decades, since the restoration of the multiparty democratic system, bribery, embezzlement of government resources or other kinds of corruption have become rampant among politicians, lawmakers, ministers and decision-makers and in all hierarchies of government bureaucracy. There were various shocking cases of corruption in which even Prime Minister Girija Prasad Koirala, influential ministers of NC, CIAA chiefs and members, the Internal Revenue Department chief and members of the Tax Settlement Commission were implicated for large corruption, embezzlement of public funds and illegal activities. Some of them were sentenced to jail for several months and a penalty of a large sum of money and some top political leaders of NC were banned from entry into politics for life. These instances of corruption and fraud reveal what some of our politicians of high stature, high-level tax authorities and CIAA members are up to. A survey report by the daily newspaper, *Nagarik*, shows that politicians are the most corrupt persons, followed by bureaucrats with almost the same status. Others in descending order of rank are police, lawyers, judges, non-governmental organization workers, corruption control agencies, engineers, businessmen/industrialists, doctors, bank staff, army, journalists, teachers and drivers (Nagarik, January, 2016).

4.7 Maoists and the Nature of the State

The 1990 mass movement was a bourgeois-democratic movement that transferred the bureaucratic machinery from the king to the political parties. Democracy was granted by the king, and the political parties felt obliged to him. As a consequence, there was little change from the Panchayat regime, except for the partial transfer of power from the king to the political parties. Contrary to what people expected of a democratic polity, the state did not function as a non-partisan instrument without any consideration to the vested interest of different feudal and bourgeoisie classes for the sake of development, equality and the welfare of the people. The democratic system failed to grant equal rights and opportunities to the oppressed and disadvantaged classes, women and minority groups. As there was neither the restructuring of the institutions of the feudal monarchical state nor a change in the bureaucratic machinery, the state remained virtually a bourgeoisie state and functioned as a ploy of different powerful feudal classes and succumbed to the interest and interplay of the forces reinforcing patronage and clientelism. Consequently, there was neither a break from the persistence of underdevelopment nor real progress in the upliftment of the downtrodden and deprived class or community.

The template of Nepalese politics took a dramatic turn with the Maoists joining mainstream politics in April 2007. The events that developed following the coup d'état by Gyanendra, who ascended the throne after the cold-blooded palace massacre of 1 June 2001 (that killed his brother King Birendra along with his entire family), brought together the warring Maoists and the Seven Party Alliance (SPA)[3] to launch a joint assault against the monarchy, primarily based on the backing of the army. Prior to this, Gyanendra had sacked the elected prime minister Sher Bahadur Deuba on 4 October 2002 on charges of failure to maintain peace and order in the country, and incompetency to conduct the general elections on the stipulated date in accordance with the Constitution. From October 2002 to October 2004, Gyanendra maintained proxy control by changing three caretaker governments at his whim. In this process, Gyanendra restored Deuba as prime minister on 2 June 2004, which the latter claimed was a correction of earlier injustice towards him. Eventually, on 1 February 2005, in an act resembling the coup d'état of his father Mahendra in 1960, Gyanendra sabotaged multiparty democracy through the dissolution of parliament and seized all state powers through the support of the army. Imposing a state of emergency for 90 days, he dismissed the Deuba-led government, suspended all constitutional liberties, incapacitated the political parties and put senior politicians under house arrest. A puppet Council of Ministers with two old Panchayat prime ministers, who had also helped his father in 1960 to crush the parliamentary democracy, was constituted under his chairmanship. This was a big jolt to the political parties, particularly the NC and the UML, which as ruling parties had enjoyed power and privileges all through 15 years since 1991. These were the parties which had retained monarchy as the constitutional head of the state, bestowing emergency power and control over the army to the king in the 1991 Constitution after the demise of the Panchayat regime.

The first six years of democracy in Nepal remained heydays for the NC and the UML, which as ruling parties enjoyed state power and privileges without any threat to the system from any internal dissident force. As a consequence, the bourgeoisie class continued its stranglehold over economic and political power and garnered most of the benefits of development. However, a grave political crisis was instilled when a 40-point memorandum on issues concerning 'nationalism, democracy and livelihood' submitted by Baburam Bhattarai of United People's Front (Samyukta Janamorcha), the electoral front of the underground Maoists, to the Sher Bahadur Deuba–led coalition government on 4 February 1996 went unheeded. The memorandum included, among others, the abrogation of existing treaties with India, the drafting of a new Constitution by a constituent assembly, nationalizing the properties of capitalists, declaring Nepal a secular country and a number of social reforms (Annex 4). They had given the ultimatum of adopting armed struggle against the existing state if their demands were not addressed by 17 February. But the Deuba government and the political parties took the warning of armed rebellion as childish and not worthy of any consideration. Their calculation, however, proved wrong as the Maoists initiated an armed insurgency, which they named the 'Peoples' War', against the existing state with the objectives of ending monarchy and establishing people's republic.

The Maoist armed insurgency acquired unprecedented support in the rural areas and among the left not aligned to UML as well as independent intellectuals and was sustained for over a decade. There were four main reasons for the triumph of Maoists to emerge as a powerful leading political force, defying the state crusade against them. First, a large majority of people from all walks of life were swept up by a 'revolution of rising frustrations' against the NC and the UML, which governed the country from 1991 onwards, for rampant corruption, violation of rule of law, poor economic performance, regional disparities, growing unemployment and poverty of the mass, widening income inequality and ignoring the needs and concerns of deprived and marginalized communities. The country was kept in a tragic paradox of economic backwardness, poverty and unemployment amidst nature's unlimited endowments and blessings. The Maoists advocated representation of ethnic groups, Dalits and women in the legislative as well as constitutional bodies and other high-level offices and an end to all types of exploitation and repression of a large mass of people on the basis of caste, creed, race, sex and geographical region. This attracted the frustrated mass, particularly the youths, the deprived communities and the ethnic minorities towards Maoists as an alternate political force to work on their behalf. Second, Maoists' call to dethrone the 238-year-old feudal monarchy, writing a new Constitution by peoples' representatives, restructuring of state and transfer of power centralized in Singha Durbar (Central Secretariat) to the local levels gained wide support among certain sections of the intellectual community and the rural articulated groups. Prior to Maoists, the UML, which was the dominant communist party in the country and was also in the government several times, never expressed the need to root out the feudal monarchical institution, to write a new Constitution by the people's representatives or to declare Nepal a federal state. The UML leaders had earlier demonstrated their faith in monarchy by bowing to Gyanendra placing coins on his feet when he was declared the new king of Nepal following the massacre of King Birendra and his family. Third, the social reform activities of Maoists in the rural areas, such as Kangaroo courts in which on-the-spot justice was given to the victims by penalizing the culprits whether these be landlords or village merchants who exploited the peasants and the poor, alcoholic husbands who assaulted wives and men who indulged in physical, sexual, psychological and economic violence against women were greatly applauded by the poor rural people. Fourth, establishment of 'peoples' communes' for collective production and sharing of output was taken as an innovative scheme by the rural community.

The rapid rise of Maoists frightened the ruling political parties, who feared losing their positions, and so deployed every possible state measure, such as the use of the latest military hardware and night vision aircraft to keep vigil over trans-border movements of rebels, deployment of the army and the big price tag on the head of Maoist top leaders as means to crush the rebels. However, all these were of no avail, and the mainstream political parties were forced to concede the Maoists were an emerging political force to be quelled only through dialogues. However, several rounds of peace talks between the Maoists and the Deuba, as well as the Chand government during the period between August 2001 and August 2003, failed because of disagreement on the Maoists' demand for a Round Table Conference regarding election to the Constituent Assembly (CA), writing a new Constitution, dethroning of monarchy and declaring Nepal a federal republic country. The adamant stance of the government on multiparty democracy and constitutional monarchy as non-negotiable items did not, however, last very long. Their failure to reverse Gyanendra's takeover through nonviolent efforts compelled them to join hands with the Maoists to launch a joint assault against the monarchy. So they came around to accepting the same demands of the Maoists that had been rejected earlier, eventually culminating in a 12-point Comprehensive Peace Agreement (CPA) between the Maoists and the SPA in New Delhi on 21 November 2005 (Annex 5). The agreement had three prime objectives: (i) termination of the 'Peoples' War' by the Maoists and the end of the Gyanendra's coup d'état through joint assault, (ii) convening of CA elections with more inclusive representation to draft a new Constitution and (iii) declaring Nepal a republic country and restructuring of the state. The agreement offered the political parties the possibility of retrieving lost ground, while the Maoists had the opportunity to get their demands enforced.

Following the CPA, the people's uprising of April 2006 gained nationwide momentum, and finally, the high-intensity urban insurrection of 19 days forced King Gyanendra to restore the multiparty democracy and reinstate the dissolved parliament. This was followed by the formation of an Interim Constitution Drafting Committee in June 2006, chaired by a retired Supreme Court justice with seven prominent lawyers, including former presidents of the Nepal Bar Association as members. The Interim Constitution announced on 15 January 2007 provisioned an interim legislature of 330 seats that would consist of all 209 members of the then Lower House and Upper House, except those who opposed the April Movement; 73 members from the Maoist Party; and 48 members from professional organizations, political figures and persons from underdeveloped communities and regions.

The Interim Constitution set the path to managing the transition of the country from a decade-long conflict to democracy, peace and progress by implementing and institutionalizing the CPA. The Interim Constitution vested the sovereignty and the state authority of Nepal on the people of Nepal and pledged to accomplish progressive restructuring of the state in order to resolve the existing problems relating to class, ethnicity, region and gender. It stripped the king of all formal powers and made the prime minister elected by the legislature the chief executive and the president the figurative head of the state. Furthermore, it committed to declaring Nepal as a secular, federal, democratic republic upon duly abolishing the monarchy (inserted by the Fourth Amendment). The Interim Constitution provisioned for a 601-member CA (240 to be directly elected from 240 constituencies under First-Past-the-Post (FPTP), 335 through a proportional system where voters vote for political parties and 26 to be appointed by the Council of Ministers) for writing the new Constitution within two years. The provision of appointed persons was made in order to incorporate prominent individuals who could contribute to writing the new Constitution and representatives of ethnic minority (*Janajati*) communities.

The persons nominated by the NCP Maoist to the interim legislature reflected a wider representation both in terms of geography and gender as well as ethnic communities repressed by the earlier rulers. Geographically, legislative members nominated by the Maoist Party represented 52 of Nepal's 75 districts, and 39.7 percent were women (29 of 73). By community and ethnicity, of 73 persons, Madheshi constituted 30.2 percent, Dalits, 15.1 percent and ethnic/indigenous communities, 30.1 percent. The Maoists thus made a head start towards altering the centralization of state power within a small high-caste and privileged circle to a more diversified representation. The Maoist Party also joined the interim government formed on 1 April with NC president Girija Prasad Koirala as prime minister. However, the Maoist ministers withdrew from the government in September 2007 in order to apply pressure for the termination of the monarchy. In December 2007, the Interim Constitution was amended to include the statement, 'Nepal shall be a federal democratic republic country. The Maoists re-joined the government and the parliament.

For the first time in the history of Nepal, the long-awaited elections to the CA were held on 10 April 2008 to write a new Constitution by the people's representatives. To the utter dismay of mainstream parties (NC, UML, RPP), the Maoists emerged as the largest political party, side-lining the dominant parties, the NC and the UML. The Maoists won 220 seats consisting of 120 out of 240 FPTP seats and 100 seats out of 335 proportional seats. The NC had the second position with 110 seats consisting of 37 FPTP and 73 proportional seats, while the UML was in the third position with 103 seats consisting of 33 FPTP and 70 proportional seats. The unparalleled wave in support of the Maoists reflected people's faith in this party as the only political force which could go for radical solutions for freeing the country from the elements of feudalism and uplifting the socio-economic condition of people and politically empowering the deprived and discriminated class. They saw in 'Prachanda' (Puspa Kamal Dahal), the Maoist chairman, a charismatic personality and a saviour who could liberate the people from the oppressive, exploitative, corrupt and chaotic system groomed by the rulers for over two centuries. This was also a reflection of a 'revolution of rising frustrations' with the activities of mainstream political parties obsessed with personal gains even at the cost of public money.

The concept of proportional seats proposed by the Maoists and accepted by other political parties was designed for three purposes: (i) representation of oppressed and marginalized sections of the society, the indigenous and ethnic communities as well as women in the writing of the new Constitution but was not possible to be represented through the FPTP elections. This was believed to offer the needed mechanism to change the nature of the state by incorporating the interests and concerns of oppressed and marginalized sections of the society in

Constitution writing and lawmaking. (ii) nomination of persons whose participation was essential in writing the new Constitution but who had the least chance of being elected through FPTP election. (iii) representation of smaller political parties which failed to win even a single seat in the FPTP election to nominate their representatives in the CA. The proportional seats are allocated to the parties based on the percentage of total votes each owns for the party in the election. However, this system was misused by the political parties to nominate politically favoured persons even of lower quality posture and kith and kin of powerful leaders of the parties or on the basis of pecuniary offerings to the parties.

The caste/ethnic composition of 240 FPTP members in the first CA election held in April 2008 shows a significant break in Nepalese politics, which had long been virtually monopolized by high caste and largely hereditary class. Even though Brahmin/Chhetri still occupied the first position, their relative strength declined to 40.0 percent compared to 55.6 percent in 1991, 62.9 percent in 1994 and 59.5 percent in 1999 (Table 4.3). On the other hand, the Madheshi, ethnic and indigenous groups and Dalits had greater representation than in the past. Similarly, the representation of women also increased from 5.9 percent in 1999 to 12.6 percent (Table 4.4).

It was the Maoist Party that was at the forefront with regard to the representation of Dalits, ethnic and indigenous communities and women in the CA. The high representation of Madheshi (45 FPTP seats) as shown under 'Other Parties' category reflected increased consciousness among the Madhesh-based political parties for participation in national politics. Regarding women representation, 24 out of 30 (80.0 percent) women were Maoist Party members of which nine belonged to ethnic and indigenous communities and one was Dalit. The women members of both the NC and the UML were from high-caste families.

The CA, at its first meeting on 28 May 2008, voted to abolish the nearly two-and-a-half-century-old feudal monarchical system and declare Nepal as a federal democratic republic. This was a historically unprecedented political breakthrough in demolishing the centuries-old feudal nature of the state and bringing to an end the misappropriation of state resources under the veil of a monarchy. This change was made possible largely because of the dominant position of Maoists in the CA with the support of NC and the UML, which were earlier not willing to abolish the monarchy. The new Constitution that was to be written was expected to restructure the state and make the country federal with decentralization of political, administrative and financial rights to the provinces and local bodies so that the obstacles which stand in the way of the full utilization of the latent potential of the regions, as well as the people residing there, would be eliminated and higher levels of development would be achieved.

Even though the Maoists emerged as the largest party, they did not get a clear majority to govern and had to form a coalition government with the UML, Madheshi Janadhikar Forum (MJF) and other parties with Maoist chairman 'Prachanda' as the prime minister. The sitting together of two major communist parties in the government along with the MJF, the main force of terai having some

Table 4.4 Caste/Ethnic Composition of FPTP Members in the First CA Election, 2008

Caste/Ethnicity	*Maoist*		*NC*		*UML*		*Other Parties*		*Total*	
	No	*Percent*	*No*	*Percent*	*No*	*Percent*	*No*	*Percent*	*No*	*Percent*
Brahmin/Chhetri	56	46.7	21	56.7	17	51.5	2	4.0	96	40.0
Madheshi	14	11.7	6	16.3	4	12.1	45	90.0	69	28.7
Ethnic and indigenous	43	35.8	9	24.3	11	33.3	3	6.0	66	27.5
Dalits	7	5.8	1	2.7	1	3.0	-	-	9	3.8
Total seats	**120**	**100.0**	**37**	**100.0**	**33**	**100.0**	**50**	**100.0**	**240**	**100.0**
Women	24	20.0	2	5.4	1	3.1	3	6.0	30	12.6

Source: Computation based on the election results of 2008 made public by the Election Commission, Kathmandu.

shared aims with the Maoist Party, made the government the strongest one in the post-Jana Anadolan II period. However, the Maoist government would remain in power only for nine months from 2008 August to 2009 May because of the hypocrisy of the UML, the major coalition partner, which was supported by the NC, the main opposition party, on the issue of the government's decision to fire the army chief Rookmangad Katwal, who was known for royalist stance and unwillingness to integrate Maoist ex-rebels into the army. The Maoists accused Katwal of defying government orders in three incidents: pulling athletes from the army out of national games in April to protest the participation of Maoist ex-rebels, retaining eight brigadier generals for whom the government refused to extend tenure and not stopping the intake of 3,000 fresh recruits in the army when Maoist ex-rebels needed to be integrated into the government army. The last defiance was taken more seriously by the Maoists as grounds for the removal of Katwal, as this was in contravention of the peace process, which had a component of the integration of Maoist 'Peoples' Liberation Army' with the Nepalese army. President Ram Baran Yadav, who was earlier an NC leader, at the request of NC, UML and other political parties, intervened to retain Katwal in the post.

Given the situation, Prime Minister Prachanda had the option of either continuing as the passive executive of the state or quitting the post. Prachanda and his party chose the second option and reigned as prime minister, denouncing the president's action as unconstitutional and undemocratic and asserting the need for civilian supremacy over the army. Public opinion was divided on the president's action, with some saying that Prachanda overstepped by firing the army chief without justifiable reasons and others saying that the president's move was an abuse of authority, as he had the right to ask the government to correct its decision in case it was in contravention of the Constitution. The Katwal episode, however, cannot be seen in isolation of the deep-rooted intention of the major mainstream political parties backed by the reactionary groups as well as some sections of the international community that did not want the Maoists to hold state power and go to the extent of interfering with the prevailing bourgeoisie governance structure. They alleged that the Maoist move to sack the army chief was an attempt to take over the state. Among the foreign community, India appeared as the prominent counter-force in pulling down the Maoist government, as the Indian establishment expected the Maoists to serve its interests and also the loyalty of other political parties for the role it had played in bringing the Maoists and the SPA to a 12-Point Agreement for ending the Maoists' insurgency, as well as Gyanendra's coup d'état. The Indian interest is well expressed by Muni:

> India, which played a key role in bringing the Maoists and the mainstream parties together during the *Jana Andolan II*, became disenchanted with the Maoists during their nine months in power from August 2008 to May 2009 on issues of India-Nepal bilateral relations and the Maoists' political conduct. Since then there has been a concerted effort by the mainstream parties and sections of the international community, especially India, to keep the Maoists politically marginalized in order to weaken them in the long run.
>
> (Muni, 2012: 330)

When Prachanda resigned, the government had just completed nine months, and many of the programmes of economic and social transformation stated in the budget of 2008/9 remained unexecuted. The budget of 2008/9 had set the vision of building a 'New Nepal' through four main strategies: (a) transformation of Nepalese agriculture, which had basically remained subsistence-oriented and entangled, into semi-feudal production relations; (b) promotion of national industrial capitalism leading to the development of a self-reliant and independent economy; (c) developing big infrastructure projects of strategic and long-term significance as 'Projects of National Pride', such as big hydropower projects, Kathmandu–Terai fast track road, mid-hill highway, north-south highway and east-west railway; and (d) youth self-employment scheme to enable the unemployed youths to start income generating activities with the financial support of up to Rs. 200,000.0 without collateral at concessional interest rate.

People had expected that the Maoists and the political parties operating in the new political milieu based on the Maoists' insurgency and mass movement would write the new Constitution within the mandated time of two years and speedily carry out the tasks of state restructuring, socio-economic transformation and establishment of a secular federal democratic republic. However, the CA failed to write a new Constitution even in four years (two-year mandated timeframe and two-year extension) because of the failure of major political parties to reach agreement on various key issues: the state restructuring and federal structure (name and number of federal states and their boundaries), the form of government, independence of the judiciary and protection of preferential rights. Following the resignation of Prachanda, the government was changed three times headed, respectively, by Madhav Nepal, Jhala Nath Khanal (both UML) and Baburam Bhattarai (Maoist) (Table, 4.5), but all failed to make a breakthrough in resolving the key issues and writing the Constitution.

Baburam Bhattarai, vice-chairman of NCP Maoist and an academically pronounced visionary person, became prime minister on 29 August 2011 with the support of Madheshi and other smaller parties, while the NC and the UML remained as the opposition parties in the CA. However, the writing of the new Constitution did not progress because of uncompromising stand of major parties, including the Madheshi parties, on the same issues as in the past. With the rejection of the government proposal to extend the term of the CA by three months by the Supreme Court, Prime Minister Bhattarai dissolved the CA on 27 May 2012. This further delayed the process of bringing out the new Constitution and restructuring the feudal unitary state into various autonomous states so as to empower them politically, administratively and economically. On the consensus of four major political parties, an interim non-political government led by Chief Justice Khil Raj Regmi with eight retired secretaries of the government as ministers, nominated equally by four major parties (Maoist, NC, UML and MJF), was formed to carry out the executive activities and perform the next election of the CA that would continue the writing of new Constitution.

The second CA election held on 19 November 2013 reversed the power equilibrium of parties in the CA. The Maoist Party, the largest political party in the first CA election, came in third with only 26 FPTP and 54 proportional seats.

Table 4.5 Prime Ministers of Nepal after Peoples' Movement II

SN	*Prime Minister*	*Party*	*Days*	*Period*
1.	G. P. Koirala (5/5)	NC-Maoist	83	28/5/08–18/8/08
2.	Prachanda (1/2)	Maoist-UML, MJF-N and other smaller parties	280	18/8/08–25/5/09
3.	Madhav K. Nepal	UML-NC-MJF-N	622	25/5/09–6/2/11
4.	Jhala N. Khanal	UML-Maoist	204	6/2/11–29/8/11
5.	Babu R. Bhattarai	Maoist-Madheshi parties	563	29/8/11–14/3/13
6.	Khil R. Regmi	The chief justice of the Supreme Court and eight former bureaucrats	334	14/3/13–11/2/14
7.	Sushil Koirala	NC-UML-smaller parties	608	11/2/14–12/10/2015
8.	Khadga P. Oli (1/3)	UML-Maoist-RPP-Nepal and MJF-D	297	12/10/2015–4/8/2016
9.	Prachanda (2/2)	Maoist Centre-NC	300	4/8/2016–31/5/2017
10.	S. B. Deuba (4/5)	NC-Maoist Centre	253	7/6/2017–15/2/2018
11.	K. P. Oli (2/3)	NCP	1,183	15/2/2018–13/5/2021
12.	K. P. Oli (3/3)	Minority	60	13/5/2021–12/7/2021
13.	S. B. Deuba (5/5)	NC-Maoist Centre-USP-PSP and other smaller parties	531	13/7/2021–26/12/2022
14.	Prachanda (3/3)	Maoist, UML, National Independent Party, RPP and three other Madhesh-based parties	Incumbent	16/12/2022

Sources: http://en.wikipedia.org/wiki/List_of_prime_Ministers_of_Nepal (accessed on 21/2/2018).Updates for later years by the author.

The NC, which was the second party in the first CA election, became the largest party with 105 FPTP and 91 proportional seats, and the UML, the third in the first CA election, became the second-largest party with 91 FPTP and 84 proportional seats. The Madhesh-based parties, because of a split caused by lust for power, lost their strength in national politics. In CA-1, only three Madhesh-based parties contested the elections, and the MJF emerged as the fourth largest party, but in CA-2, there were 13 Madhesh-based parties, and their presence was insignificant. To most peoples' surprise, the RPP (Nepal), which advocated constitutional mon archy and the Hindu kingdom agenda, emerged as the fourth largest party with 24 proportional seats, even though it did not win even a single FPTP seat in the elections.

There was also a reversal of caste/ethnic composition of CA members with Brahmin/Chhetri caste occupying 54.2 percent (130 seats) as compared to 40.2 percent (96 seats) in the first CA election. The representation of Madheshi was reduced from 69 to 62 seats. The representation of ethnic and indigenous communities suffered a large reduction from 66 seats in the first CA to 47 seats in the second CA. The position of Dalits was limited to one seat from nine seats previously. Likewise, only 10 women were represented compared to 30 women in the first CA (Table, 4.6). The second CA thus reverted to a centre-leftist status quo orientation from the previous leftist orientation. This was mainly due to the defeat of the Maoist Party, which fought to have adequate representation of Dalits, ethnic minorities and women in the writing of the new Constitution.

Following the second CA election, the NC president Sushil Koirala formed the government in coalition with the UML and other smaller parties. The government failed to draft the new Constitution by the promised date of 22 January 2015 because the opposition parties were not willing to forge a consensus on issues relating to the federal structure of the country and the form of governance. Rather, the coalition government held an adamant attitude of passing the Constitution by majority votes in the CA. This triggered a rift between the ruling coalition and an alliance of 33 opposition parties consisting of Maoist, Madhesh-based and other smaller parties, which demanded that the draft be passed by consensus and not just by the majority in the CA. The ruling coalition forwarded a proposal of seven federal states and the election of an executive head by two-thirds majority votes in the parliament, while the opposition alliance proposed 10 to 14 federal states along ethnic lines that would reflect the identity of historically marginalized ethnic groups as well as indigenous people and a directly elected executive head of the state.

The voices for recognition of ethnic groups, indigenous and tribal and Madheshi have been the main concern of the state in the post-conflict politics of Nepal. Although some concerns were shown to address the needs and interests of these people by the governments after the restoration of democracy in 1990, but were not in the direction of political and economic empowerment of these people. Rather, these were simply consisted of certain facilities and benefits to pacify these people in order to prevent them from seeking a radical political solution. The domination of hill Brahmin/Chhetri and to a lesser extent Newars of Kathmandu

Table 4.6 Caste/Ethnic Composition of FPTP Members in the Second CA Election, 2013

Caste/Ethnicity	*Maoist*		*NC*		*UML*		*Other Parties*		*Total*	
	No	*Percent*	*No*	*Percent*	*No*	*Percent*	*No*	*Percent*	*No*	*Percent*
Brahmin/Chhetri	12	46.2	60	57.1	55	60.4	3	16.7	130	54.2
Madheshi	9	34.6	26	24.8	13	14.3	14	77.8	62	25.8
Ethnic and indigenous	5	19.2	19	18.1	22	24.2	1	5.5	47	19.6
Dalits					1	1.1			1	0.4
Total seats	**26**	**100.0**	**105**	**100.0**	**91**	**100.0**	**18**	**100.0**	**240**	**100.0**
Women	1	3.8	6	5.7	3	3.3	–	–	10	4.2

Source: Computation based on the election results of 2008 made public by the Election Commission.

Valley continued to prevail in the bureaucracy as well as other power structures, while the ethnics, Dalit, Madheshi and indigenous peoples remained marginalized in all spheres. A study of the leadership patterns of constitutional bodies in the last 64 years from 1950 to 2014 shows that Brahmin and Chhetri absorbed 32.4 percent and 36.6 percent, respectively, followed by Newars with 25.4 percent, while Madheshi and ethnics had only 4.2 percent and 1.4 percent, respectively (Bhatta, 2015). The ethnic issue was pronounced as a serious issue by the Maoist, and the Madheshi issue, which the Maoist also raised, was articulated by the Madheshi parties. The discontent of the Madhesh was so widespread and so severe that the Madheshi parties at one point in time boomed the slogan of 'one Madhesh one Pradesh (province)' to make the entire Madhesh belt a separate autonomous province to end the exclusion of Madheshi in state structures and all types of state discrimination. The non-acceptance of 'one Madhesh one province' by other major parties compelled the Madheshi parties to change their previous slogan to 'larger area of Madhesh as one or two Pradesh'. What all these signify is that the historical process of governance evolved by the ruling elites and the upper castes over the years was to strengthen unhindered economic and political domination over the lower castes, minority groups and Madheshi people in all spheres of state activity. This made the Madheshi people, ethnic groups and indigenous communities feel alienated and develop a sense of indifference to nationalism and national identity.

4.8 Uproar over New Constitution

The Constitution of the Republic of Nepal announced on 20 September 2015 provisioned for three tiers of government – federal, provincial and local – and delineated seven provinces. The federal legislative was provisioned 165 seats under the FPTP category and 110 seats under the PR category, while the provincial assembly of seven provinces were to have 330 seats under the FPTP category and 220 seats under the PR category. The Constitution made it mandatory that at least one-third of the total number of members elected to the federal legislature from each party must be women. The 2017 Act provisioned a threshold of at least 3.0 percent of the total valid proportional votes cast and at least one seat under FPTP to qualify as a national party and nominate persons under the PR seats. The Madheshi parties resented the new Constitution because their demands for electoral constituencies based on population, proportional representation of Madheshi in government bodies, autonomous identity-based provincial demarcation, equal citizenship provision for Indian women marrying Nepali men and Janjati (ethnic) and two Madhesh provinces Mechi River in the east to Mahakali River in the West were not considered.

In protest of the Constitution, the Madheshi parties burnt copies of the document, stirred agitations in most Madhesh district headquarters and declared the closure of Eastern Madhesh districts adjoining India. Besides this, they also erected human barriers at the main border points with India, thereby blocking the movement of vehicles between Nepal and India and from terai to Kathmandu. In the tussle, about 50 persons lost their lives, with many injured, and the country faced shortages of petroleum products and other essential commodities. India also was not happy with the new Constitution, as its deep-rooted interest in making Nepal a Hindu state, citizenship provisions for foreign nationals and separate Madhesh states were not incorporated. In the meantime, a series of Indian envoys came to Nepal to pressurize the government to incorporate their interests in the Constitution. But the government and the Maoist Party ignored their advice including last-minute attempt to defer the announcement of the new Constitution. Instead of welcoming Nepal's historical achievement of writing a new Constitution by the CA, the Modi government of India expressed its resentment by simply stating that it had taken note of the new Constitution. In order to show what this disobedience would cost Nepal, the Modi government of India capitalized on the Madheshi parties' agitation by blocking the entry of Indian carriers loaded with petroleum products, medicine and other essential goods to Nepal. Indian officials justified this action by pointing out the violent threats to the Indian vehicles and the drivers. The blockade continued for four months and the people of Nepal were forced to live in severe hardship due to the shortage of cooking gas, petrol, diesel, medicine and food items. Besides this, the economic blockade severely affected the reconstruction as well as resettlement programmes in the aftermath of the devastating earthquakes of 20 April and 12 May of 2015 that killed 9,000 people, injured many more and destroyed about 80,000 houses. It was ironic that India was the first country to swiftly send rescue and relief support when the earthquake hit the country, but the same India imposed an economic blockade when there was an urgency for the reconstruction of the devastated physical structures and resettlement of thousands of homeless people. Prior to this, back in 1989, India had imposed a 14-month-long economic blockade on Nepal in a display of resentment against Nepal's import of weapons from third countries without Indian permission and King Birendra's unsubmissive attitude to yield to Indian interests. This shows that India can be friendly to Nepal so long as its interests are well taken care of by the government of Nepal. As a consequence of the earthquakes and the Indian blockade, Nepal's GDP growth rate plummeted to a meagre 0.2 percent in 2015/16 and the country's development process was reversed ten years back.

4.9 Electoral Defeat of the Maoist Party

The local-level elections which were held after 15 years were the first milestone in institutionalizing the new Constitution and the federal structure of the country. The elections were held in three phases – on 14 May, 28 June and 18 September 2017. It took two-and-a-half months from the second phase to conduct the third phase of elections because of the agitation of Madhesh-based political parties in Province 2, which consisted of all eight terai districts of the country. Fulfilment of their demands required amendments to the Constitution by a two-thirds majority in parliament which did not exist, as the UML, the main opposition party in the parliament was not in favour of Madheshi demand for amendments.

The local election results placed Maoist into a distant third position showing no improvement over the 2013 CA election performance, while UML gained the first position and NC the second position. Of the total 35,041 local seats, the Maoists won 5,441 (15.5 percent), while the UML won 14,099 seats (40.2 percent), followed by NC with 11,456 seats (32.7 percent) while the rest was own by other parties. The election results were shocking to the Maoist Party, and yet the party claimed that even in defeat, it won by making the local bodies powerful and decentralizing Singhadarbar's (central secretariat) power over the people's courtyards.

The defeat of Maoist in the local elections made the party apprehensive of further weakening of its position in the provincial and federal elections of November and December 2017 if it contested on its own. At the same time, the UML longed to become an even more powerful political force and continue holding the reign of power for a longer period. The political compulsions of the Maoists to regain the lost ground and the desire of the UML to be an all-powerful party brought the two parties together, despite bitter rivalry and differences in ideologies between them, into a political alliance to contest the provincial and federal elections of 2017. Initially, the Naya Shakti Party of former prime minister Baburam Bhattarai was also to join the alliance but detached itself when its demand for electoral seats in the federal parliament and state assemblies was not accepted by the Maoist and the UML. The Maoist and the UML eulogized their electoral alliance as a move toward mustering two-thirds seats in the up-coming federal and provincial elections leading to the unification of two parties to form a single powerful communist party. This sent shockwaves through the NC as well as the Modi government of India as the former saw a spectre of losing elections and the latter saw a challenge to the established order and danger to the Indian hegemony over Nepal. Moreover, Nepal moving towards a strong communist regime meant the total failure of Indian policy in this Himalayan country in keeping communist parties out of power. This also meant that if communists held power in Nepal, there would be further strengthening of Nepal–China relations, which was against the Indian interest. To retaliate the left alliance, the ruling party NC formed a counter-alliance called 'Democratic Alliance' with Rajapa (Mahanta Thakur), Forum (Upendra Yadav), RPP and RPP (Democratic). In the meantime, India also invariably used its economic and political influence to debar the UML-Maoist alliance from forming the new government by bringing together NC, Maoist and Madheshi parties to form the government. But this move was not successful.

Indeed, the UML-Maoist electoral alliance paid unexpected dividend to the UML, placing it in the first position with 121 seats in the federal parliament (80 out of 165 FPTP seats and 41 out of 110 proportional seats). The Maoist with 53 seats (36 FPTP and 17 proportional seats) was in the third position, the same as in the second CA elections. This shows that the electoral alliance with UML was not beneficial to the Maoists to resurrect their past political strength and image (Table 4.7).

The seats owned by UML led by KP Sharma Oli and Maoist led by Prachanda together yielded a nearly two-thirds majority in both the House of Representatives (174 out of 275 seats) and the Provincial Assemblies 351 out of 500 seats). Following the victory of alliance in the 2017 general elections, UML and Maoist was unified in May 2018 to form a single party called 'Nepal Communist Party'.

Table 4.7 Results of Provincial and Federal Elections, 2017 and 2022

2017						*2022*					
Parties	*FPTP*	*Proportional Votes*	*% of total*	*Seats*	*Total*	**Parties**	*FPTP*	*Proportional Votes*	*% of total*	*Seats*	*Total*
NC	23	3,128,389	32.8	40	63	NC	57 (84)	2,715,225	25.7	32	89 ↑
UML	80 (97)	3,173,494	33.3	41	121	UML	44	2,845,641	26.9	34	78 ↓
Maoist	36 (58)	1,303,721	13.7	17	53	Maoist	18 (47)	1,175,684	11.1	14	32 ↓
Federal Socialist Forum	10	470,201	4.9	6	16	Unified Socialist	10 (20)	298,391	2.8	0	10
Rajapa	11	472,254	4.9	6	17	National Independ.	7	1,130,344	10.7	13	20
RPP	1	196,782	2.1	0	1	RPP	7	588,849	5.6	7	14 ↑
Naya Shakti	1	81,837	0.9	0	1	Janata Samajbadi	7	421,314	4.0	5	12
Janamorcha	1	62,133	0.7	0	1	Janamat	1	394,655	3.7	5	6
Independent	1			0	1	Nagarik Unmukti	3	271,722	2.6	0	3
NEMAKIPA	1			0	1	LOSAPA	4	167,367	1.6	0	4
				0		NEMAKIPA	1	75,168	0.7	0	1
						Janamorcha	1 (2)	46,504	0.4	0	1
						Independent	5				5
	165	**9,525,723**	**93.3**	**110**	**275**	**Total**	**165**	**10,560,082**	**95.9**	**110**	**275**

Source: Election Commission, Nepal.
Notes: Figures in parentheses show number of seats contested as per the agreement of allied parties.

This was expected to bring much-needed political stability for the next five years, facilitate movement towards socialism and accomplish economic prosperity. However, unification was dismantled after three-and-a-half years like a house of cards owing to adamant attitude of then prime minister KP Oli.

The second general election held on 20 November 2022 did not also strengthen Maoists' political position, still it held the strategic role in deciding whether the NC or UML would form the new government. Maoists contested this election through a coalition of NC, Unified Socialist Party, People's Socialist Party and Janamorcha, which also joined the Duba led coalition government formed after pulling down the KP Oli government on 13 July 2021. This coalition was meant to give continuity to the government for another five years, but the tussle between Deuba and Prachanda to be the prime minister first eventually led to break up of coalition. This break up was made possible by KP Oli, who fished in a troubled water to dismantle NC-Maoist-Unified socialist coalition by offering UML's support to Prachanda for the post of prime minister. It is to be recalled that Prachanda and Oli had partnered in the parliamentary election of 2017 on the agreement that both would equally share the prime minister's five-year tenure. But this understanding was not kept by PM Oli in order to continue as prime minister for the entire five-year period, which compelled the Maoist ministers to quit the government that pushed Oli government on the brink of collapse. To forestall this crisis and prohibit Maoist, NC and other parties to form alternate government, PM Oli made unconstitutional moves to dissolve the parliament twice and seek the people's fresh mandate with the prompt support of the president, but this was also squashed by the Supreme Court. The result was a Deuba-led coalition government of NC, Maoist, Unified Socialist, Janata Samajbadi and Janamorcha.

Even though Maoists' position in the second general elections was third, the same as in the first, the number of federal parliamentary seats declined from 53 to 32 (18 FPTP and 14 proportional). The NC emerged as the largest party with 89 seats (57 FPTP and 32 proportional), up from the second position in 2017 elections by 26 seats, while the UML held the second position with reduced strength of 78 seats (44 FPTP and 34 proportional) from 121 seats in the previous election. The results show that neither the electoral coalition with NC nor with UML has helped the Maoist Party to garner more seats and enhance its strength in the parliament, on the contrary, the Maoist has shouldered the brunt of placing the other main electoral alliance party to the first position–the UML in 2017 and the NC in 2022 elections. Astonishingly, the National Independent Party, formed just six months prior to election, garnered 20 seats (13 FPTP and 7 proportional) which made it fourth major party in the parliament, and the RPP, the pro-monarchy party, made unprecedented gains with 14 seats (7 FPTP and 7 proportional) as against just 1 FPTP seat in 2017 elections. The Unified Socialist Party, a breakaway faction of UML led by Madhav Nepal, gained only 10 FPTP seats (Table 4.7). Thus the 2022 electoral outcomes provided a mixed picture with law makers representing diverse ideologies and rise of pro-royalist parties and having opposite views on the federal structure of the country.

An analysis of the socio-economic and political profile of 165 directly elected representatives in the 2017 general election shows the dominance of rich, higher caste and seasoned politicians in the House (Nepal Weekly, 2017). It was revealed that more than half of the representatives (54.0 percent) were the ones who had held the position of MP, prime minister and minister several times in the past, and 80.0 percent had no other experience and specialty except involvement in politics. The representation of deprived sections of the society was very poor (3.6 percent), and the remaining 96.4 percent had no problem with existence; in total, about 78.0 percent was made up of well-to-do families (middle and high class). In terms of caste/ethnicity, half of the representatives (50.9 percent) were from the upper castes (Brahmin/Chhetri/Sanyasi), while the aborigines/ethnics accounted for 27.9 percent; the Dalits, which constituted more than 13.0 percent in total population, accounted for only 1.8 percent; and the Madheshi community accounted for 17.6 percent. There was also poor representation of women (addition of one through the election to fill the death of a male elected member) limited to only seven persons (3.7 percent) entirely belonging to upper castes (Brahmin/Chhetri). The parties fulfilled the mandatory requirement of 33.0 percent women representation in the federal parliament from the proportional list submitted to the Election Commission some days prior to election date. However, most of those who were nominated by the political parties were the persons with better education, closer connection with the leaders of concerned political parties by relation, family status in terms of wealth, and power to mobilize people's votes in favour of the party. Hence, it was very unlikely that they would attempt to reform the distorted system and make a break from the prevailing socio-economic order that allowed the powerful groups unhindered space to accumulate wealth, garner more power and suppress the weaker sections of the society. On the other hand, a small minority who were nominated were weak in forcefully arguing for their rights and influencing the decision-making process due to a lack of education, knowledge, exposure and experience. This led Khas-Arya (Brahmin–Chhetri) to continue their dominance in Nepali politics and the state decision-making process.

The 2022 election (FPTP) further reinforced the upper caste (Brahmin–Chhetri/Sanyasi) domination in the federal parliament with 58.8 percent representation as compared to 50.9 percent in the previous election. This meant decrease in the proportion of directly elected ethnics, Madheshi and Tharu in the federal parliament, while the representation of Dalit was limited to only one person. The aborigines/ethnics (including Newars) had 20.6 percent representation, down from 27.9 percent in the previous parliament. The representation of Madheshi declined marginally from 17.6 percent to 15.7 percent and that of Tharu community was 4.2 percent (7 seats). And the representation of women increased by two seats to nine.

4.10 Dwindling Political Space of the Maoist Party

The Maoist armed revolution in Nepal, which can be termed as probably the last revolution of the 21st century in one of the most backward countries of the world, dramatically altered the entire political landscape of the country. Named the 'Peoples' War', this was never ever foreseen by the monarchy and the mainstream political parties that enjoyed unhindered space under the constitutional monarchical system and also different from the one anticipated by Marx. The revolution threw away a two-and-a-half-century-old feudal monarchy and substituted the parliamentary democracy with a federal democratic republic. When the Maoists decided to abort the revolution, they were in a predicament between compromising with the establishment and continuing the revolution with the danger of extinction. They chose the first option and decided to use the parliamentary system for the seizure of state power. But they failed to correctly visualize the deep-rooted prevalence of feudal and reactionary forces that were bent on nullifying the growing popularity of Maoists. The Maoists claimed that by dethroning the monarchy writing a new Constitution through CA and declaring Nepal a federal republic, the first stage of the democratic revolution was accomplished, and by working through the 'federal democratic system', they would move towards the second and final revolution of establishing socialism.

The incorrect judgement of the end of the feudal regime and reactionary elements with the end of the monarchical system cost the Maoists the government constituted after the first CA election. Even though it was not necessary, the Maoists, swayed by their revolutionary overhang, Prachanda resigned as prime minister, and the party decided to struggle by mobilizing people in the road and staging demonstrations against the president's unconstitutional act and infringement of people's sovereignty by retaining the army chief sacked by the government. The struggle did not bring any tangible result to the Maoists but placed the UML and the NC in power for the next three years, which enabled them to consolidate their strength and influence to win future elections.

Ever since the second CA elections, the Maoists' position in the parliament started declining and has had difficulty maintaining its image, not to speak of winning a relatively large number of parliamentary seats to lead the coalition government. Various reasons may be identified for the dwindling political space of the Maoist Party. First, the party was politically weakened by a series of splits and break-ups, and even though there were occasional comebacks of some leaders from the breakaway fractions, this could not resurrect the party's initial image and strength. The first major split was that of Mohan Vaidya 'Kiran', senior vice-chairman of the party and political guru of Prachanda, along with some hardliner factions of the party on 21 June 2012. Vaidya was resentful of the peace process from the very start of the CPA of 21 November 2006, which was signed when he along with CP Gajurel was serving in the Indian prison. His group criticized the Maoist Party that led the decade-long 'People's War' for deviation from its ideology and labelled handing over the cantonments to the Nepal Army as 'surrender and disarmament'. Vaidya charged the party chairman 'Prachanda' for leaving the revolution halfway by terminating the 'People's War' without achieving the avowed goal of capturing the state and deviating from the Marxist–Leninist–Maoist ideology for power and privileges. The group formed their own party, Communist Party of Nepal (Revolutionary Marxists) which included many powerful leaders of the Maoist movement – Ram Bahadur Thapa 'Badal', CP Gajurel, Dev Gurung, Pampha Bhusal, Netra Bikram Chand 'Biplab' and other key leaders. However, two years later in 2014, a more radical faction led by Chand deserted Vaidya to form a new party. In 2016, Thapa, Gurung, Bhusal and a host of other key leaders also broke ties with Vaidya and returned to the mother party.

The second incident was the sudden resignation of Baburam Bhattarai, vice-chairman of the party and one of the architects of the 'People's War', not only as a member of the parliament but also from the primary membership of the party and all responsibilities he had been entrusted a week after the new Constitution was announced. While quitting, he voiced concern over the Madheshi 'being denied a say' in the very Constitution he had endorsed a week ago as chairman of the Constitutional-Political Dialogue and Consensus Committee (CPDCC) of the CA. The CPDCC was constituted to hold dialogues with political parties and forge consensus on the contentious issues to be incorporated into the new Constitution. It was understood that he had some differences with the party chairman 'Prachanda', but quitting the party which he had nurtured and carried over three decades including the 'Peoples' War' for a decade was a conundrum. However, one of the main reasons, as many believed, was his ambition to be the first man in the party as he always was in the academic accomplishments. While quitting the Maoist Party, Bhattarai said that Maoism has become irrelevant and obsolete in today's world. This implied that he had abandoned the communist ideology altogether, but projected himself as a socialist. Some months after breaking away from the party, he announced the 'Naya Shakti' (New Force) party on 12 June 2016, embracing socialist and progressive agendas and constituted his staunchest supporters from the Maoist Party, former bureaucrats, disgruntled political persons from the NC and the UML and some well-educated persons. He justified the new political party as a means to address the country's needs and carry out an economic revolution to drive Nepal towards a developed country status, as he considered the democratic revolution to have been completed with the announcement of the federal Constitution. However, he was left almost isolated when some of his staunch supporters quit the Naya Shakti Party some months before the general election of 2017 to rejoin the mother Maoist Party. The 'Naya Shakti' could not establish its presence in the local political scene, as it could win only two out of 753 mayors/ward chairmen in the local elections of May 2017. Regarding federal parliament, Baburam Bhattarai was the only person to win the election from his home constituency, Gorkha, and that too with the support of NC. In 2019, he merged his party with Federal Socialist Forum, Nepal (led by Upendra Yadav) which after undergoing a series of mergers including six other Madhesh- based parties and then break-up, followed by merger with some other parties, became People's socialist party on 22 April 2020. Bhattarai quit this party also with some leaders to form Nepal socialist party on July 28 2022.

The third breakaway was that of Gopal Kirati and Lokendra Bista who quit the party because of resentment over the unification of the Maoist Party with the UML on 17 May 2018 under the name of 'NCP' with a vow to carry on the revolution to establish true socialism in the country. Kirati accused the party leadership of surrendering the party to UML and clamping down on the objectives of the '21st-century people's democracy' for which the Maoist had fought.

The fourth split was that of Ram Bahadur Thapa, who was made a home minister in KP Oli's government from the Maoist quota but deserted the party to side with Oli. Thapa was followed by Lekh Raj Bhatta who was the industry minister from the Maoist side and thereafter by Top Bahadur Rayamajhi, Prabhu Shah, Mani Thapa and Gauri Shankar Chaudhary, who were appointed ministers by KP Oli for a brief spell and also stayed with UML when the Supreme Court annulled the merger of Maoist and UML as NCP on 8 March 2021 because the name was already allotted to a party led by Rishi Kattel. As a consequence of these break-ups, party members, supporters and general voters were demarcated into various camps, severely weakening the political strength of the Maoist Party.

Third, the Maoists assimilated into Nepal's democratic political mainstream but at the same time wanted to exhibit their revolutionary ethos and commitments. This put them in a dilemma of how to make a fusion between the two and gradually slipped into reformism. When the party was heading or sharing the government it made no attempt to introduce any measure towards socio-economic transformation, which would reflect that the Maoist are more radical than other communist parties of Nepal. This reduced the faith of rural youths, people in general and deprived sections of the society in particular and, left-leaning intellectuals in Maoist Party as being no different from UML or even NC. The party was also not successful in using parliamentary politics and electoral strategies for winning the elections, as the NC and UML had done. The NC and the UML had used their power, influence and tactics and had expanded their institutional base not only in civil service but also in various organizations, such as non-governmental organizations, banks and financial institutions, as well as educational and health institutes over the past three decades with the aim of promoting their own party concerns and interests. But the Maoist Party did not pay attention to strengthening the institutional base, rather remained overwhelmed by the pleasure from its achievements in ending the monarchy, declaring Nepal a federal democratic republic and inclusive representation in all bodies of the state.

Fourth, the party failed to address the needs and concerns of disqualified warriors, who were forced to be satisfied with a small amount of lump-sum monetary compensation, the victims of war and disability and families of disappeared youths. Some of the warriors had to live with bullet fragments in the body, those crippled had a precarious life, and some of those who had gone to Gulf countries for employment were brought back home in coffins. The Maoists did not integrate the party cadres at the grassroots and sister organizations with production from the very beginning when the leaders headed the government or were ministers in the coalition government. The party had advocated and executed the concepts of 'Production Brigade' and 'Village Communes' system as was practiced in the People's Republic of China to increase production and generate employment at the grassroots level during the period of the 'People's War', but when in power these concepts were totally abandoned. A large number of combatants were not eligible for integration into the Nepal Army, and the ones who chose cash settlements were entitled to a meagre Rs. 500,000 to 800,000 for their livelihood and sustenance.

Fifth, intellectuals and professionals aligned with the Maoist party remained passive to champion the cause for which the Maoists had fought, counterattack the opponents' false allegations and remarks and serve as intellectual backstop of the party. Their main concern was to get appointed to lucrative public posts and garner personal benefits by cashing the membership of 'intellectual organization' of the party. The party command did not think of organizing a core group of intellectuals as a think tank of the party for interdisciplinary research on policy issues and problems through the use of specialized knowledge and conducting research on ways of creating theoretical and objective conditions for socialism.

Sixth, the Maoist leaders distanced themselves from the working class and the mass by adopting a lavish lifestyle as soon as they assumed authority in public offices. Furthermore, they started aligning more with the mafia and contractors for accumulating wealth and properties through kickbacks. The party workers were required to wait several days or queue for a long time to explain their grievances to party chairman and top leaders, but the mafia and business people could get easy and direct access.

Seventh, the Maoist Party virtually ended its identity when it decided to unite with the UML after the shock of defeat in the local-level elections (municipalities and village committees) in 2017 elections. The Maoist Party leaders were haunted by a spectre of being reduced to the status of a smaller party and merged with UML on 17 May 2018 to form the 'Communist Party of Nepal'. For unification, the Maoist party even sacrificed its name and flag (red flag with a hammer and sickle engrossed in a circle) and accepted unequal sharing of representation in various hierarchical committees of the unified party. Even though this unification was short-lived and the Maoist party returned back to its earlier status, this damaged its image built in the past.

4.11 Economic Prosperity and Socialism

The government formed under the premiership of KP Oli in 2018 with ministers drawn from both of the two previous parties adopted the slogan of 'economic prosperity and socialism' as its twin goal. Socialism was also enshrined in Nepal's Constitution promulgated through the CA in 2015 as an avowed principle of the nation. Following the Constitution, ministers and leaders started echoing economic prosperity and socialism as the main objective of the party and the government.

There is a plethora of ideas for achieving economic prosperity, but a concrete framework is still lacking for a less developed country like Nepal. Some would say that agriculture and tourism would lead to prosperity; others would say that education and health are the main drivers to prosperity; still some others say that industry and trade are the roadways to prosperity. Some others consider labour as the main driver of production and prosperity. There is also an argument that inclusive economic and political institutions are the factors that create prosperity (Acemoglu and Robinson, 2013). It is also debated whether the prosperity is going to be a socialist prosperity or a capitalist property. There is also the question of whose prosperity. Is it the prosperity of poor and disadvantaged people, who have been historically excluded from the government-initiated development process, or of those who have been all through the ages manipulating the state resources for their personal benefit? There are also other questions to address: how is economic prosperity defined and measured? What are the indicators of prosperity? Is it measured by GDP per capita or some other indicators? All such divergent opinions and questions have added more confusion rather than providing pathways to prosperity. But one thing is certain: there is no single causative factor of economic prosperity, nor is there an easy recipe for achieving prosperity. Nor is prosperity something which can be achieved in ten years, as echoed by PM Oli and some politicians of NCP. Since the days of Adam Smith till now, economists have asked the question, What makes some countries prosperous and others poor? Still, the mystery of prosperity has not been resolved. The prosperity of India, China and the West reveals that it took them several centuries with periods of ups and downs and the interplay of several factors to rise to their current positions. The rise and fall of the richest nations in history from Sung China to modern-day Japan and the United States reveals that nations at different times have found new ways of creating wealth and developed successful economic cultures to achieve economic prosperity (Clydesdale, 2016). In the earlier times, following Adam Smith, specialization was emphasized for raising productivity, and population determined production. But in the later years, population was no longer necessary for wealth, as countries could gain access to external markets for exporting their products. But export and wealth required innovation of new products, new processes, work ethics and culture and new markets. Nepal failed on all these counts owing to the ineptitude of its rulers. It was argued that the country would soon be linked to China by train from Kerung (Nepal–China border point in the north) to Lumbini (mid-west), the birthplace of Buddha, which would free Nepal from India-locked geography that has been a major factor in retarding its development and would convert it into a land-linked country. Furthermore, India is also competing with China in connecting Nepal by train from Birgunj (a Nepalese city adjoining the Indian border). All these would further enhance Nepal's connectivity with the neighbouring countries, but the movement of trains and trucks can only thrive if cargoes exist to be transported, and cargoes are the products of agriculture and industry. But Nepal failed to expand agricultural and industrial production for trade. The country has a long history of adequate road connectivity with India, but trucks bring Indian cargoes to Nepal and return back empty. This has resulted in an ever-expanding and unsustainable trade deficit with India, which multiplied by more than 500-fold in the last decade and amounted to Rs. 865.2 billion (30.1 percent of the total trade deficit) in 2020/1.

Talking about socialism in Nepal, the Panchayat regime (1961–91) advocated 'Panchayati Socialism' which embraced state ownership of major industries and centralized planning, but there was no representation of the excluded and downtrodden sections of the society in the state structure. The NC expounded 'democratic socialism' as the party's political philosophy but did not explain what it really meant. However, when the party had a majority government in 1991, it switched over to liberal economic policy and market-driven, private-sector-led development from the state-led, self-reliant development strategy. The UML advocated 'peoples' multiparty democracy' and followed the NC-initiated neo-liberal economic policy with a human face, as advocated by the World Bank and the International Monetary Fund to mask the devastating effects of neo-liberal reform on the poor and vulnerable people. Comparing the NC and the UML, Hachhethu writes, 'The NC is a liberal democratic party but with a socialist trade mark, and UML is a communist party with allegiance to multiparty democracy' (Hachhethu, 2003: 137). The Maoist party aimed at the establishment of revolutionary socialism through armed rebellion; abandoned the revolutionary doctrine of Marx, Engels, Lenin and Mao with its entry into the bourgeoisie democratic politics; and virtually ended whatever revolutionary spirit it had for three years when it merged with UML. It remains to be seen how the Maoists would define socialism and how it would proceed to achieve this in a country with all the features of semi-feudal society under the grip of crony capitalism.

4.12 Fostering of Crony Capitalism

Rather than moving towards socialism, the three-and-a-half-year regime of NCP under the leadership of KP Oli fostered crony capitalism in the country to a shocking scale. The case of privatization of state-owned enterprises in the 1990s, which involved selling these enterprises (land and factory) at a nominal price to various business groups and financial liberalization that led to granting of licences to commercial banks and other financial institutions, suggests that crony capitalism existed in the past too when the NC headed the government several times and the UML participated as a silent coalition partner. The ten shocking corruption cases of high jurisdictions by the ministers nominated from the erstwhile UML during three and a half years of the KP Oli government show fostering of crony capitalism on an unprecedented scale.

(i) **Tariff Reduction on Chocolate Imports and Hike on Electric Vehicles**: In the 2020/1 budget, Prime Minister KP Oli nominated finance minister, Yuvaraj Khatiwada, slashed the customs tariff on chocolate to 30.0 percent from 40.0 percent and hiked excise as well as customs duty on imports of electric vehicles – 40.0 to 60.0 percent from only 10.0 percent excise duty plus 60.0 percent customs duty. The major beneficiary of the revision in these tax rates was the Vishal Group, a business conglomerate, which is the largest importer and supplier of chocolates of various brands, such as Snickers, Mars, Mounty, Kinder and Milky Way in the Nepalese market and holds a stake in the MG (Morris Garages) Motors that supplies electric vehicles in Nepal. The minister defended tariff reduction on chocolates by saying they constituted food items, while tariff and customs duty hikes on electric vehicles were justified on the grounds that private electric cars were a luxury item and only the rich could afford them. Immediately after the end of ministerial position, Khatiwada was rewarded with an Ambassadorial post in the United States.

(ii) **Gold Smuggling**: A large quantity of gold – 88 kg and 33 kg – was smuggled from the Tribhuvan International Airport, respectively, on 4 September 2017 and 23 January 2019 through government-mediated collusion. While the smuggling of 88 kg gold was nabbed, the 33 kg gold disappeared, and its whereabouts as well as the real owner of the gold remains still unknown. A 752-page report by a government committee stated that it was not possible to smuggle gold into Nepal via the Tribhuvan International Airport without the protection of powerful people, including politicians.

(iii) **Medical Education Mafia**: Collusive corruption between the medical education mafia and the government to permit additional medical colleges in Kathmandu Valley has been a serious issue of public concern against which a senior orthopaedic surgeon, Govinda KC undertook a series of hunger strikes up to death. His demand included a ban on the opening of new colleges in Kathmandu to run bachelor programmes in medicine, dentistry and nursing for ten years; one medical college in each seven federal province; a stronger regulatory mechanism of private medical colleges to maintain quality; phasing out of short-term programmes of Council for Technical Education and Vocational Training; reduction in the fees of medical education, easy access of poor people to health services, etc. The government assured the fulfilment of his demands to break the hunger strike every time, but the time never came to keep the promise.

(iv) **Procurement of Two Wide-Body Jets**: The investigation by a Parliamentary Accounts Committee sub-committee on embezzlement of Rs. 4.4 billion in the procurement of two wide-body jets for the state-owned Nepal Airlines Corporation (NAC) implicated then UML minister for culture, tourism and civil, who later died in a helicopter crash; two former ministers; three secretaries; and the general manager of NAC for their involvement in the scam. Instead of accepting the report, the government constituted a three-member panel to re-investigate the scandal. This raises doubt about the government's intention to take action against the culprits.

(v) **Pappu Construction**: The Pappu Construction Company, owned by Hari Narayan Rauniyar, a lawmaker in the federal parliament, and its joint venture partner companies have bagged 40 construction projects (35 bridges and 5 roads) around the country from various government offices worth Rs. 40.0 billion since 2014 through political power and influence. The company embezzled a huge amount of money by not completing the work on time or completing it with sub-standard materials. Because of the non-completion of a bridge in eastern terai, a boat ferrying people capsized on 15 August 2018, causing the deaths of five persons. The company constructed a 62-metre bridge over the Bishnumati River connecting Teku and Kalimati at a contract of Rs. 201.3 million (financial assistance from the Asian Development Bank) in 2018, but the Department of Roads declared the bridge 'risky' for failing to meet the required safety standards in construction.

(vi) **Baluwatar Land Grab**: A high-level collusive scandal that remained covered up for a long period of time was the Baluwatar land grab by a group of land mafia in collusion with influential political leaders, land revenue officials and business houses. The Baluwatar land (Lalita Niwas) originally belonged to NC leader Subarna Sumsher Rana, but King Mahendra, after the coup d'état of 1961, seized 14 ropani (0.71 ha), declaring Rana as an anti-national element and also acquired 285 ropani by paying compensation. The land was under government ownership until 1990, but the interim government of Krishna Prasad Bhattarai formed after the Jana Aandolan of 1991 decided to return the land to the legal owners who were mostly members of NC. By that time, various parts of the land totalling 172 ropani had already been designated for the Nepal Rastra Bank Central Office building and residences of the prime minister, chief justice and speaker of the house. And the remaining 113 ropani were encroached on by the land mafia by creating fake tenants and transferring the land to individuals with the involvement of land revenue staff and powerful persons. The Probe Committee constituted in April 2019 found that the general secretary of the then NCP belonging to Oli Camp Bishnu Paudel who held the ministerial post several times, was among the individuals who owned a piece of land (eight anna) in the name of his son from one of the two land mafia (Setopati, April 2019). He procured the land at a very low price (Rs. 50,000.0 anna) and had obtained Rs. 4,900,000.0 loan from a development bank against the collateral of this land, which raised serious doubt on his malpractices (Nayapatrika, February 2020). Paudel was also found involved in facilitating cabinet decisions on the transfer of land in the name of individuals and had even arranged a donation of Rs. 40.0 million to the party in return for a government decision (Setopati, 2019).

(vii) **Yeti Holdings**: Prime Minister KP Oli used his enormous and often coercive power to favour Yeti Holdings to garner illicit gains by using state properties. The owner of Yeti Holdings, Ang Tshering Sherpa, who died in a helicopter crash in 2018, had a very strong give-and-take political connection with the UML and Prime Minister KP Oli for a long time back. It was this political link that made it possible for Yeti Holdings to secure several prime public properties, including Nepal Trust property worth billions of rupees, over the last few years at a far lower than fair market price (my Republica, 2019). The series of public properties that Yeti Holdings grasped at nominal lease price included (a) *Gokarna Resort*: extension of the lease period of Gokarna Forest Resort under the ownership of Nepal Trust for another 25 years, 6 years before the expiry of the current lease period at a substantially cheaper price without competitive bidding to operate tourism and business activities. As the Trust Act prohibited the use of trust land for tourism and business purpose, the KP Oli government amended the Act and also reshuffled the Trust Board, replacing government secretaries not yielding to political pressure to grant favour to Yeti Holdings. (b) *Kalimati Land*: lease of 4 ropani of Trust land at Kalimati to Thamserku Trekking, one of the sister companies of Yeti Holdings for 30 years to utilize for commercial construction at Rs. 180.0 million. The decision to lease this land was made in February 2018 but was undisclosed. (c) *Durbarmarga Land*: lease of 1 ropani 14 anna of Trust land located in Durbarmarga (in front of Narayanhiti Durbar) to the Yeti Group for building a business complex for 30 years at Rs. 1.490 billion, as against the suggestion of evaluation committee to lease it at Rs. 6.45 billion. (d) *Kongde View Resort*: transfer of 52 ropani land inside the UNESCO World

Heritage Site of Sagarmatha National Park to Yeti Holdings to establish Kongde View Resort. A decision of the Supreme Court on 21 August 2017 allotted the land to the Yeti Group overriding the CIAA instruction to the Land Revenue Office of Solukhumbu on 7 July 2009 to bring the land under government ownership. (e) *Pathivara Devi Darshan Cable*: lease of land to the Yeti Group by Fungling Municipality of Taplejung to operate a 2.5-km-long cable car joining Pathivara Temple from Kaflepani for 40 years with consent to extend to another 40 years. The municipality granted the land to Yeti Group without publishing it in the local gazette, flouting the Local Government Implementation Act of 2017. It was while flying back from Pathivara Temple that then tourism minister Rabindra Adhikari and Ang Tshering Sherpa died in a helicopter crash. (f) *Land to Sherpa family at Lumbini*: The Sherpa family was granted 14 ropani of land of Lumbini Development Trust at Lumbini by direct instruction of Prime Minister KP Oli, who was the patron of the Trust. This was a clear violation of law, which requires protection and preservation of public and trust property. (g) *Ambassadorial post*: appointment of Dawa Phuti Sherpa, daughter of Lakpa Sonam (sister-in-law of Aang Tshering) as ambassador to Spain on 27 September 2019, despite lack of required diplomatic experience as stated in the 'criteria for ambassadorial appointments' prepared by the government. (h) *Land of Shivapuri National Park*: Yeti World International Private Limited (owned by Ang Tshering Sherpa and Sonam Sherpa) acquired the lease of 216 ropani of land in Shivapuri National Park in June 2018 from Nepal Wildlife Development Company owned by two American citizens at a lump-sum payment of Rs. 6,600,000.0 per annum to the government for 40 years with a provision of extension for another 40 years.

(viii) **Procurement of Security Printing Press**: Involvement of Gokul Banskota, then minister of communication and information, a close aide of KP Oli, in a commission of Rs. 700.0 million from local agent of a Swiss company in the procurement of a security printing press for the government. Banskota was forced to resign from the post when an audio clip negotiating the commission was leaked to different media outlets on 19 February 2020. The audio tape leakage led to the revelation of a string of other projects amounting to Rs. 100.0 billion, in which Banskota had abused his authority to alter the specification, evaluation and even termination of already awarded contracts for receiving off-the-book cash payments.

(ix) **Procurement of Essential Medical Equipment**: The latest scandal that exposed then health minister Bhanu Bhakta Dhakal in KP Oli's government was the award of a contract to the controversial Omni Business Corporate International in April 2020 for the supply of essential medical equipment (masks, RTD kits, PPEs and other logistics) required to safeguard people and health workers from the COVID-19 pandemic prevalent over the whole country. Of the three companies shortlisted, Omni was awarded the contract to supply medical equipment worth Rs. 1. 24 billion from China within a week in three instalments. But the company delivered only18.0 percent of the materials by the deadline of the contract. Moreover, the company had procured questionable RTD kits, and the price quoted was three times higher than the market price. Because of faulty RTD kits, many migrant workers from India initially tested negative against the COVID-19 virus but owing to misleading results, some of them died later from delay in treatment.

(x) **Batas Group**: The Batas Group, which had already infringed on public property in many locations through collusive corruption with high-ranking government officials and political leaders, was brought to public notice by media when the company encroached land in the historical Narayanhiti palace (converted into a museum in 2008 following the abolition of the monarchy and opened to the public) to operate a restaurant. Stretched over an area of 753 ropani (382,704.72 sq. ft.), the Narayanhiti palace was the residence and principal workplace of Shah kings for 122 years, and the palace also witnessed the bloody massacre of King Birendra, along with seven members of his family, including Queen Aishwarya and crown princesses, on 1 June 2001. The collusive corruption between the Batas Group and the UML minister of tourism during the tenure of KP Oli as prime minister came to light after the group was found constructing illegal structures inside the Narayanhiti Palace Museum for running a restaurant. A probe committee established a commission deal in the decision process in awarding the contract to the highest bidder of three companies which all belonged to the Batas Group.

Cases of corruption through collusion between the prime minister and the businessmen reached such a height that the global anti-corruption advocacy group commented, '[T]hough Prime Minister KP Sharma Oli has repeatedly vowed to control corruption, his administration has done little to combat it'. In this context Niti Foundation observes,

> Corruption in Nepal is not a series of disjointed, individual acts. Instead, a range of stakeholders spanning public, private, and criminal spheres operate as one to steal money from the people and ensure impunity thrives. This kleptocratic network is made up of shifting alliances, which span multiple communities that are inter-connected by several powerful businesspersons acting as brokers. The network is vertically integrated. Money flows upwards through the hierarchy while impunity and benefits flow downward. Its strong horizontal linkages across sectors of society enables the network to capture important revenue streams, facilitate the flow of illicit funds through the state apparatus and across borders, and ensure network members are protected.
>
> (Niti Foundation, 2019)

Even the CIAA was made a handmaiden of KP Oli by appointing a former home secretary, Prem Rai, believed to be one of Oli's trusted men, as its chief. Moreover, the appointment of judges to the judiciary was made on the basis of political faith and loyalty to KP Oli.

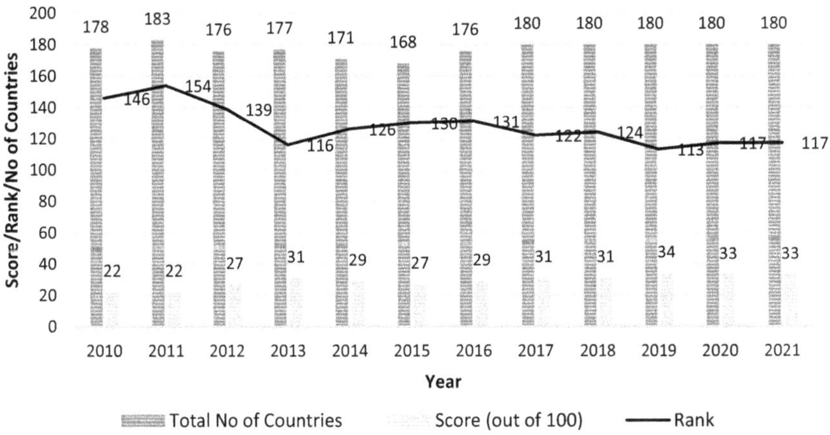

Figure 4.2 CPI of Nepal.

Nepal's higher scores on the Corruption Perception Index (CPI), computed by Transparency International (TI) in the last three years except in 2013, also substantiate fostering of crony capitalism during KP Oli's regime. The score was 34 in 2019, the highest ever so far, and remained almost at the same level at 33 in 2020 and 2021. Even in South Asia, with the exception of Pakistan (28) and Bangladesh (26), Nepal's score was worse than Bhutan's (68), Maldives's (40), India's (40) and Sri Lanka's (37).

The 2020 'Global Corruption Barometer-Asia' published by TI placed Nepal in the top position among 17 Asian countries surveyed in terms of the proportion of people who perceived an increase in corruption in the last 12 months (TI, 2020). It was also revealed that 84.0 percent of people thought government corruption was a big problem in the last 12 months. In terms of institutions, 50.0 percent perceived the office of the president/prime minister as the most corrupt, while 43.0 percent said MPs.

Collusive ties between powerful political leaders and private businessmen have led to the high presence of private businessmen and contractors in the federal as well as provincial legislatures and local bodies (municipalities, village municipalities and wards). An investigative report by *Naya Patrika Daily* (9 February, 2020) shows that a total of 208 representatives including six MPs, mayors, ward chairmen and members are owners of or have business stakes in construction companies. Likewise, in 2022 elections, 19 persons engaged in contracting business were elected in the federal and provincial parliaments – 8 and 11, respectively. Contracting business has its own importance in the society in building physical and social infrastructures, but if the businessmen and contractors hold power in law-making bodies, there will be conflict of interest which may will result in formulation of laws and rules that favour their interests.

4.13 Altering the Nature of the State

Under the prevailing national and international conditions, there is little hope of altering the nature of the state in Nepal in the foreseeable future for transforming the country from an economically backward to a more prosperous nation through another revolution. Revolution is no easy task to initiate and sustain it forward until the semi-feudal elements and compradors are destroyed and a new model of people-oriented, self-reliant development is set in motion. Even though every mass movement/revolution in Nepal has brought a change in 'political system' – the 1950 mass movement ended the 104-year Rana regime and placed the monarchy in power; the 1991 mass movement ended the 30-year Panchayat regime and positioned the democratic political parties in power, while the ten-year Maoist 'People's War' ended the two and half a century monarchical system and made Nepal a federal democratic country, but none were revolutionary in the true sense, with the exception of the Maoist revolution to a great extent. The Maoist revolution was initially meant to smash the semi-feudalistic state and transform Nepal into a socialist state, and when the revolution was gaining height, smashing several police security posts and gaining control over them, as well as the rural areas, the Marxist supporters had the expectation that the revolutionaries would eventually overthrow the old state machinery and replace it with a new government of working class and toiling mass. This required seizure of political power through armed resurrection as had happened in the Russian Revolution of 1917, the Chinese Revolution of 1949 and the Cuban revolution of 1958. But the Maoists aborted the revolution without reaching the ultimate goal, stating that they completed the first stage of revolution – a 'bourgeois-democratic revolution' – and they would carry out the next revolution, the 'socialist revolution', through parliamentary struggle. Nowhere in the world had the parliamentary struggle, even if under the grip of a communist party, been able to establish genuine socialism, i.e., a government of the working class and the poor peasants – and a just society with equal redistribution of wealth and power. However, as Woods argues,

> Under certain conditions, it would even be possible to carry out the socialist transformation of society through parliament. But only on one condition: that the revolutionary socialists, having own a majority in parliament, mobilized the workers and peasants outside parliament to expropriate the landlords, bankers and capitalists.
>
> (Woods, 2009: 335)

He further adds,

> [T]he fundamental issues can never be resolved by parliaments, laws and Constitution, though parliament is one aspect of the class struggle. In the last analysis, the fundamental questions are always settled outside parliament: in the factories, on the streets, in the villages, and in the army barracks. If any proof is required for this assertion, we need only to refer to the events in Venezuela in April 2002.
>
> (Ibid.)

Because the Maoist revolutionaries could not seize power and alter the nature of the state, the prevalent state of affairs and the semi-feudal socio-economic structure continued to exist with all its evils of corruption, scandals and non-performing bureaucratic machinery. With assimilation into mainstream parliamentary politics, the Maoists started working within the terrain of bourgeoisie state apparatus, such as legislatures and judicial systems, security forces (army, police, etc.), elite-oriented educational systems and bourgeoisie institutions. With no change in the nature of the state, there was no shift from the policies which had oriented the Nepalese economy toward an increasingly neo-liberal capitalist, foreign-dominated and dependent development path. The consequence has been a flourishing crony capitalism that in a unified communist party government regime distanced itself from the socialist ideals conceived by Marx, Engels and Lenin. The party talked too much about socialism and prosperity, but the poor and deprived people did not know how they would look, when they would take place or how they would come and what benefit they would get.

On the transition to socialism, Sweezy and Bettelheim, drawing upon Marx and Engels, state, '[T]he state power must first be transferred from the bourgeoisie to the working classes, i.e., the proletariat and peasantry and making the state apparatus, and above all its armed forces loyal and reliable instrument in the hands of the representatives of the working classes. This means not only the leading governmental offices must be occupied by representatives of the working classes: that by itself is not enough, as numerous historical experiences of social democratic and popular-front governments have proved. What is necessary is that the state apparatus and above all its armed forces should be a loyal and reliable instrument in the hands of the representatives of masses. Here it is enough to recall the famous statement of Marx that "the working class cannot simply lay hold of the ready-made state machinery and wield it for its own purposes", and Lenin's interpretation of "Marx's idea that the working class must break up, smash the readymade state machinery", and not confine itself merely to laying hold of it' (Sweezy and Bettelheim, 2010: 124).

The ruling class even if communist in outfits dismisses the idea of the working class occupying power on the logic that the working class would destabilize and ruin the entire economic and social fabric, as they lack knowledge, expertise and skill to exercise state power. This is, however, an erroneous argument that has no basis. The Russian Revolution of 1917, the Spanish Revolution in the 1930s and Venezuela today present examples of colossal creativity, ability and talent that lie dormant in the working class and are set free by revolution to run the administration of society (Woods, 2009). It is the working class, who on taking over state power, would put an end to a tendency to acquire wealth at the cost of the nation. This means that poor peasants and workers of Nepal need to carry out another revolution under a true Marxist leadership hand in hand with the most discriminated against, and powerless people for sweeping out the state apparatus left over from the past and the remnants of feudal and counter-revolutionary elements that always attempt to foil the revolutionary ethos by all means at their disposal. In this context, the remarks by Harry Magdoff, one of the greatest Marxist thinkers of our time, on the armed struggles in the third world are very enlightening.

> I don't think that it is up to the left to judge whether it is warranted or unwarranted when people are in struggle where there is tremendous poverty, misery, and little hope, and in the process either make mistakes, or don't make the best decisions, or are misled by opportunists. It is a natural phenomenon, to be expected. History does not come easy. What we are talking about is a process of liberation which involves not merely a mechanical formula. It involves a way of life, a way of thinking, and there is a great deal of suffering in the process, problems, that cannot be solved. It's very complex, and you're going to get these kinds of problems. It's our job to study and to see and to understand what the forces were. But to judge? It's wrong. Marx at one point says that there will be many revolutions and wars and defeats before the working class learns how to be a ruling class. And that's it. History takes a hell of a lot more work, comes with many more setbacks, than we expect.
>
> (Magdoff, 1999: 63)

Notes

1 When Birendra was to visit Kavre to observe Sanjivini School in 1974, it was decided by the district education officer and local Panchayat leaders to impress the king by demonstration of the good production of peanuts and potato for which the district was known for. There were potato plants in the field, but the product was very small. So it was decided to buy fairly large potatoes from the market by collecting small amounts of money from the students and then burying them underneath the root of the plants. The students of the school were involved in this, and one of the students became vice-chancellor of Kathmandu University, Dr. Ram Kantha Makaju, who was then an eighth-grade student. When the king came in the morning, students pretended they were digging out the buried potatoes, and the king saw good potatoes there. He was happy to see that such good potatoes could be produced in poor soil (narrated by Dr. Makaju in *Reflections on Childhood*, in Kantipur Weekly 'Kopila' Children Souvenir, 7 September 2014).

2 The United Left Front consisted of NCP (Marxist–Leninist), Nepal Workers and Peasants Party, NCP (Fourth Convention), NCP (Marxist), NCP (Burma), NCP (Manandhar) and NCP (Amatya).

3 Seven Party Alliance included NC, (Democratic), UML, Janamorcha Nepal, Nepal Sadbhawana Party (Anandidevi), Nepal Majdoor Kisan Party and Samyukta Bam Morcha (United Left Front).

5 Future Challenges

The challenges that confront Nepal are many, and it is not easy to deal with all these comprehensively in the limited space of concluding pages. From our analysis in the book about the achievements and experiences, the way the rulers have ruled the country, organized the economy and the policy orientation over the last seven decades, one can legitimately gauge that the challenges are there on both the political and economic fronts. It is believed that the causal links run from politics which encompasses the nature of the state, class formations and the interrelations between the two and the representation of class interests in the state structure to economics, which implies economic development, i.e., policies, programmes and activities that intend to improve the economic condition of the country and well-being of the people. However, on certain occasions, the link runs the other way around when economics, particularly mass poverty and inequality-based discontent lead to uprisings, guerrilla insurgencies and civil war, etc., that alter the political regime, as have occurred in Vietnam, Central America and other parts of the world in the past and recently in Nepal in the form of Maoist 'People's War'.

Democracy is considered all over the world as the best political system, as it permits freedom of speech and expression of opposition views and opinions; independent media and civil societies that voice the needs and concerns of the silent, excluded and impoverished people and function as watchdogs of the government; free elections that allow people to choose their leaders; and participatory decision-making and peaceful resolution of internal conflicts. Because of these traits and better allocation of whatever resources are mobilized in investment, democracy contributes to fostering economic growth. However, in Nepal's case, the democratic exercise of three decades and that of a federal democratic republic since 2008 has not yielded the expected fruits of economic growth in terms of growth of 'the right kind' which involves growth in the productive capacity of the country, improvement in the living conditions of the poor, reduction of inequality in assets and incomes across different strata of society and growth of a self-reliant economy. This may be attributed to various flaws in Nepal's democracy which need to be corrected if it is to function as a sound political base for the development of the country. For the realization of the fruits of democracy, just having it is not sufficient; it should be a well-functioning democracy, which is lacking in Nepal. A well-functioning democracy is characterized by various features such as rule of law,

DOI: 10.4324/9781003359777-5

ethical behaviour of politicians, accountability of politicians to the people and holding free and fair elections, political stability, etc. These are the political challenges that confront Nepal in achieving high growth rates and reducing poverty and economic inequality.

The first challenge in making democracy a well-functioning democracy is the ethical purification of political parties and politicians. The major political parties and their leaders are engaged in corrupt politics by maintaining a patronage system to accumulate money. In recent years, the leaders of the major political parties were also engaged in blaspheming each other one after another for holding on to power. In a democracy, parliamentarians have a great role as trendsetters and as key persons not just to alter the given economic and social structure but also to work with a vision supported by commitment and dedication to get the country out of the shackles of underdevelopment and poverty, work for much better governance and practice what they preach. But political leaders of Nepal have side-tracked from evolving suitable policies through the parliament and overseeing their implementation through the government, demonstrating high ethical standards, adhering to the rule of law, exhibiting accountability to the public and delivering promises made to the electorate in return for the votes. Instead, they have used democracy, its privileges and institutions for furthering their self-interest and grooming patron-client relations for abuse of authorities and facilities, often in collusion with bureaucracy for kickbacks in public procurement, awards of public projects, public distribution and delivery systems, revenue collection, security-related decisions, etc. As a consequence, corruption has grown and indicates no signal of diminishing. Despite all such imprudent acts and conducts of political leaders, voters cannot throw them out, and they stay as the people's representatives until the expiry of their five-year tenure or next election, unless convicted by the Supreme Court against corruption and criminal acts. If the politicians engage in constructive introspection of themselves about their conduct and accountability to the people and practice what they preach or promise in their speeches, many of the barriers, issues and policies that have distorted democratic practices and made democracy confined to electoral politics can be rectified, and by applying various objectively designed measures and impulses, a right course of development can be initiated and kept going.

The second challenge of the democratic political system is controlling extravagant elections. Political parties raise vast amounts of money from big business houses, contractors and mafias, and they do not disclose the sources of such funds. Obviously, business people/contractors/mafias do not provide a huge amount of free funds for no return; they want favours in taxation, import licences, contract awards in the procurement of public materials and construction works, etc., and the parties do not want to displease them. Likewise, contestants spend vast sums of money out of their past savings and even property sales, as well as raising vast sums of money from big contractors, mafias and business people, ignoring the limit set by the Election Commission to influence the voters and rigging of votes for getting elected. They need to recover all such expenses, and they do so through a range of corrupt practices, often in tandem with the top officials of the bureaucracy. Among the consequences is the growth of money politics making contesting an election a rich man's prerogative, an erosion in the faith in leaders and delinking of leaders with the people because the electoral victory was not the result of the people's support but the outcome of buying votes like any other commodity.

The third challenge also linked with the second challenge is controlling the growth of crony capitalism which has thrived under the patronage of high-profile political leaders. As the evidences presented in Chapter 4 show, crony capitalism is deeply damaging the economy not only through the wastage of scarce national capital for personal gains but also through suppression of honest entrepreneurial activities. The starting point for controlling the rise of crony capitalism would be the politicians themselves and curb on money politics. Also, there is a need to restructure the CIAA with high power and utmost security to empower its members to investigate high-profile corruption cases without any fear or threat and selection of members not on partisan basis but on quality, integrity and ethical basis. There should also be a system of effective dialogue and coordination between the CIAA and the Supreme Court for convergence in their decisions.

The fourth challenge of the democratic political system is unstable government. Nepal's democracy is not a pure parliamentary system but a mix of parliamentary and presidential systems with a prime minister elected by the parliament as executive head of government and a president elected by the electoral college comprising members of the federal parliament as well as members of the provincial assemblies on weightage system of voting, as head of state. The post-democracy period is characterized by hung parliament most of the years except for the first democratic government of Girija Prasad Kolirala (1991–4) and the Nepal Communist Party government of KP Oli (2018–21), which could have lasted for five years but was truncated in three years owing to internal feuds within the party. With these exceptions, no political party has received a comfortable majority in the parliamentary election in the post-democracy period to complete a five-year tenure. The consequence has been coalition governments which changed 28 times in the last 33 years following the restoration of multi-party democracy in 1990, each averaging a year. The 2022 national election has produced a federal parliament of political parties with diverse beliefs and ideologies and some are not even committed to federalism and secular state and this heterogeneity is also reflected in the coalition government formed in December under the leadership of Maoist chairman Prachanda. Coalition governments are basically fragile opportunistic alliances guided by the lust for power and self-interest rather than ideological affinity and easily fall apart even over small conflicts of interest and divergence in agendas. Political instability infuses uncertainties in economic policies which affect the general climate for investment and industrialization which constitute the growth drivers of the economy and shortens policymakers' horizon to initiate far-reaching policy changes. Even though political instability in Nepal has not led to a visible change in economic policies, rather there has been continuity in policy with regard to liberalization, domestic investment, foreign investment and globalization of the Nepalese economy, the coalition government with a short or uncertain tenure is constrained to initiate long term growth-oriented or redistributive strategies and policies.

There was much hope that the 2017 federal election that produced an almost two-thirds majority in the House of Representatives for the UML and the Maoist party and their unification into Nepal Communist Party would produce a strong and stable government after decades of political instability. But this expectation was tarnished by the unconstitutional decisions by then Prime Minister KP Oli. In an abrupt move and to the utter dismay of major political parties and within a large faction of the ruling party, Prime Minister Oli dissolved the House of Representatives on 20 December 2020, which was promptly endorsed by President Bidya Devi Bhandari. Even though the Supreme Court overturned the prime minister's decision to dissolve the House as an unconstitutional move and reinstated it, the Court later (7 March 2021) nullified the unification of the UML and Maoist party to form the Nepal Communist Party, a verdict which was not sought. As a consequence, three years of unification of the two communist parties was legally ended, and the constitutional status of the KP Oli–led government was reduced from a majority to a coalition government. Still, the coalition of two communist parties could have continued to keep the government intact, but Oli's adamant attitude forced the Maoist to recall its ministers. The prime minister dissolved the parliament a second time on 21 May 2021, but the endorsement by the president was again invalidated by the Supreme Court, which reinstated the parliament. And the Oli government failed to survive the vote of the non-confidence proposal in the parliament owing to the deliberate absence of 14 dissident UML members of parliament led by the former prime minister and senior UML leader Madhav Kumar Nepal and voting in favour of the proposal by the Nepali Congress and the Maoist party. This led to a bitter rift between the Oli faction and the Madhav Nepal faction, ensuing a split in the party. Subsequently, the Madhav Nepal faction formed a separate party named the 'Unified Socialist Party', with Madhav Nepal as its chairman. A new coalition government of Nepali Congress, Maoist Centre, USP and Janata Samajbadi Party was formed on 13 July 2021, with Nepali Congress president Sher Bahadur Deuba as prime minister. But this coalition fell apart after the national election of 2022 due to Deuba's unwillingness to offer the priminstership to Prachanda for the first half of a five-year tenure, as agreed by the two leaders. Consequently, a new coalition government of Maoist, UML, Independent party and RPP was formed.

An alternative to political instability would be a presidential system where the executive head is directly elected through a popular vote or indirectly through the electoral college as in the United States. In the United States, the president also serves as the head of state, and once elected, a president remains in office for a fixed term unless 'impeached for, and convicted of, treason, bribery, or other high crimes and misdemeanours' (Article II, Section 4 of US Constitution). In contrast, in the parliamentary system the prime minister can remain in power till the next election if he enjoys the support and confidence of a majority of members of the parliament. Another factor that distinguishes the parliamentary from the presidential system is the freedom of the president in the selection of cabinet ministers. In the parliamentary system, particularly when it is a coalition government, the ministers must be appointed from the parliament on the recommendation of coalition parties in the government irrespective of their capability, whereas under the presidential system, the president has the power to select cabinet ministers even from outside of parliament on the basis of merit and competency and loyalty to the president. This provides for team spirit and team work which are important for the success of the government.

The need for a stable government for rapid development is demonstrated by the examples of Singapore under Lee Kuan Yew who ruled for 32 years (1959–91) and South Korea under Park Jung Hee who was in power for 17 years (1962–79). Lee governed Singapore under almost one-party rule as a dictator but with a vision, determination and high morals on financial matters. Even though he was disgraced for authoritarianism and being punitive to the opposition, he raised the status of resource-poor Singapore to one of the world's wealthiest economies. Lee believed that discipline was more important than democracy for development. With this strategy, Lee built a competent government, developed a high-functioning and dedicated bureaucracy, adopted stringent anti-corruption measures and rooted out vested interest in administration, which led to amazing prosperity in Singapore. Likewise, Park Chung Hee of South Korea also ruled as a dictator with strong centralized management of the economy to modernize the country. Park concentrated power in his presidential secretariat and the cabinet; distrusted the politicians and kept them away from power; revamped the old administration and established a new bureaucratic system with innovative Western-educated staff, including professors; and maintained tight control on corruption. The economic foundation that Park built during his regime contributed to advancing Korea's economic development, elevating it to the status of a developed country. However, in Nepal's case, despite the stable authoritarian regime for 30 years (1960–90), it was made a poor and impoverished nation with widespread poverty of the masses, while a small segment of the population amassed unlimited wealth and led highly luxurious lives of a Western standard. This suggests that dictatorship is not the solution to underdevelopment but what is needed is a strong government with visionary leadership, right ideas and commitment to make the country and the people better.

The fifth challenge of democracy is moving toward a more inclusive democracy. It has been more than three decades since Nepal became a practicing democracy, but it is still far away from inclusive democracy. The last two national elections show that lower castes, Dalits, Madheshi, aborigines/ethnics still have very poor representation in the federal parliament. Power in all state affairs is still concentrated in the hand of upper castes (Brhamin/Chhetri and to some extent Newars) and elite class. There is a need to change this pattern in order to minimizing further marginalization of historically underrepresented groups for strengthening democratic practices and institutionalizing federalism.

The sixth challenge is overhauling of the entire administrative structure that was developed during the Rana regime and groomed by the Panchayat regime to be loyal to the palace and the top Panchayat leaders and orienting it into a result oriented robust system. During the Panchayat regime, the bureaucracy was bifurcated into palace secretariat controlled and directed by the king and central secretariat of the government under the prime minister simply functioning as an appendage of the palace secretariat. The palace secretariat constituted the nucleus of power in politics and the administrative structure of the country. In the bureaucracy, the role of the junior government officials was imposed by senior officials who were in turn directed by the secretaries, and there was a certain level of discipline in all hierarchies of bureaucracy. However, in matters of promotion, particularly to secretary level, appointment to diplomatic positions and foreign visits, servitude, sycophancy and loyalty to the king, Panchayat leaders and secretaries counted much rather than merit and efficiency in work. Governments formed in the post-democratic period gave continuity to the bureaucratic structure inherited from the Panchayat regime and relied on it to carry out the tasks of promoting economic development. In the democratic political environment gained after three decades of struggles and movements with the sacrifice of thousands of lives, people had newly aroused expectations of an improved way of life different from the past and effective service delivery. Fulfilment of such expectations required a more flexible, adaptive and proactive bureaucracy, which, however, did not exist. The bureaucracy continued to function as in the past and did not go beyond the ruts and routines of writing comments in the files and forwarding these to higher authorities. Even though several Administrative Reforms Commissions were constituted after the political change of 1991 to recommend ways for reforming public administration, no government desired to implement their suggestions. Even the governments of the republic era did not venture to overhaul the administration despite knowing that continuation of the old administrative structure was one of the major causes of Nepal's slow development and inefficient service delivery. This was particularly noticed when Maoist chairman 'Prachanda', during his prime ministerial period (2016–17), expressed dissatisfaction with government secretaries for their lackadaisical attitude in the implementation of his government's decisions and directives. He directed them to get out of their 'old routines' and implement development projects and programmes as they ought to and address people's grievances redirected from the prime minister's secretariat promptly. But these instructions had hardly any effect on the work style of the bureaucracy. The bureaucracy is not even serious about meeting the targets set by their respective ministry, not to talk of achieving the production goals set by the planners. A glaring example of this is the low utilization of capital expenditure year after year despite the fact that the estimated figure of both regular and capital expenditure for the upcoming fiscal year is based on the proposal of each individual line ministry, and the poor progress of national pride projects. The gap has been a persistent problem, and the concern shown by the prime minister as well as the Ministry of Finance to increase capital expenditure has had no effect. The low utilization of the capital budget has also much to do with the inefficiency of the bureaucracy and the lack of systematic performance monitoring of ministerial secretaries by the Office of the Prime Minister and Council of Ministers (OPCM). The OPCM has six secretaries looking after different sectors and the chief secretary, who is the head of secretaries and the entire administration. But the secretaries in the prime minister's office have not gone beyond the assigned routine work and assembling papers and policies sent from the line ministries for approval by the prime minister. They think that they are parked there on partisan basis, which may not be always true.

The last but not the least challenge that needs to be addressed is the heavy politicization of bureaucracy. Even though bureaucracy had the tradition of working as a political instrument since the early 1950s through the Panchayat System, with the restoration of democracy in 1990, it ideologically aligned itself to the Nepali Congress or to the UML for a long period of time and later to the Maoist. It has become the culture of every prime minister and the parties in power to staff senior bureaucrats to key positions, promote to higher posts and appoint chairmen and members of constitutional bodies on the basis of 'party loyalty' rather than competence, technical expertise and experience. The culture of appointing government secretaries immediately after retirement or on the verge of retirement as ambassadors has oriented bureaucracy to submissively carrying out the instructions of ruling parties/ministers rather than providing candid judgement and maintaining political neutrality and impartiality. On the other hand, senior bureaucrats who do not agree with the minister's political preferences or interests are side-lined by transferring them to less important ministries or institutions. This has polarized the civil service along major political parties of the country rather than developing professional competence, dynamism and efficiency.

On the economic front, the main challenge is to resurrect the Nepalese economy from the shambles created by high reliance on neo-classical doctrine, which says that the best way to stimulate growth and control rent seeking is to limit government. However, the experience of South Asia and Japan, South Korea and Taiwan in industrialization and growth offers evidence of the opposite. These countries have achieved high growth performance and industrial transformation through the state playing an active role with the right kind of intervention. In Nepal, there is also a need for an active state for the following reasons.

First, the Nepalese economy is trapped in a low equilibrium trap, which means that the Keynesian theory of the state is still valid for the expansion of the productive capacity of the economy for raising the growth rate and reducing the growing unemployment problem. There is still the need for a proactive state to set the strategic directions of the economy, increase public investment, allocate resources to government-sponsored infrastructure activity and public utilities, review the efficiency of resource use and provide guidance and regulate the private sector. Government has to increase public investment not only for crowding in private investment but also for filling the gaps left by the private sector. Even Joseph Stiglitz, one of the leading advocates of the free-market system, argues that in the United States and the rapidly growing economies of East Asia government played six important roles that spurred development. According to him, much of the role of the government lies in establishing six broad infrastructures – educational, technological, financial, physical, environmental and social safety net – which are beyond the capacity of any single firm but necessary if markets are to fulfil their central role in increasing wealth and living standards (Stiglitz, 1996). The example of the Asian Tigers also reveals that a market-oriented development strategy was not the sole reason for their economic miracle, as is too simplistically claimed by neo-liberal economists. This was made possible largely due to the strategic government interventions that promoted a smooth transition from import substituting to export-led industrialization; egalitarian income distribution; rapid expansion of labour-absorbing, export-oriented manufacturing industries; and agrarian reforms, which complemented and directed rather than negated market forces (Sharma, 1993).

Second, the demographic dividend of Nepal should be used by the country itself for nation building and production increase, rather than allowing it to dissipate to Gulf and other countries. Governments in the past adopted policies encouraging youths to seek foreign employment as an easy source of foreign exchange earning to finance escalating imports. This is suicidal because a sudden fall in labour demand in Gulf and other countries would displace hundreds of thousands of Nepalese workers with two-pronged effects in the economy: (i) adjustment problem of huge mass of youths by engaging them in productive works and (ii) drying up foreign exchange reserves. As this is not the concern of private sector, the government needs to have a strategic plan of shorter, medium and longer duration and attractive incentive packages to retain the increasing number of youths every year in the country and engage them in development and production activities.

Third, the Nepalese economy is still beset with the problems of persistent regional disparities, deep-rooted poverty, rising income inequalities, increasing corruption and growing economic marginalization of deprived communities, ethnic minorities, daily wage workers and poor peasants. Such problems would be further aggravated by the strategy of market-driven and private-sector-led growth. If such problems are glossed and not resolved in time, there is always the danger of the eruption of insurgency or political violence. The evidence is the decade-long (1995–2005) Maoist insurgency in Nepal, which was mainly ignited by the ever-widening inequality between regions, growing gulf between a small group of ruling class including the bourgeoisie and the toiling masses and suppression of poor, deprived and disadvantaged people.

Fourth, the variations in size and economic structure among seven federal states carry the risk of separation and, in extreme cases, disintegration. Hence, it is important that such differences need to be remedied over the course of time through planning and appropriate mechanism of revenue sharing and fiscal transfers. This means that the role of the central government and that of the Planning Commission and other central government ministries would be even more important and perhaps increasingly so. First, each province has a Provincial Policy and Planning Commission which prepares a provincial plan for the overall development of the province. The province plan needs to be coordinated and balanced by a central authority to ensure consistency with the national perspective plan as well as the national periodic plan and also for building complementarities among the states. Second, large projects spanning multiple provinces, such as power generation, irrigation and roads, involve inter-state and inter-ministerial issues relating to sharing of costs and benefits, externalities and spillovers. Such issues cannot be left to be resolved by individual provinces and ministries. So there is a need to strengthen the central-level institutions, such as National Planning Commission and National Natural Resources and Finance Commission for dealing with all such issues and for maintaining and strengthening inter-state operational coordination on issues of infrastructure development, tourism promotion, inter- and intra-province trade, fiscal jurisprudence, etc. The opportunities and challenges of political, economic and administrative autonomy thrown up by federalism to the federal provinces can result in competition among federal jurisdictions for attracting investment and experimenting with new policies and revenue measures. All such complex issues need to be seriously studied and analyzed and appropriate measures and mechanisms worked out in advance to forestall the ensuing dangers to federalism.

Fifth, the new Constitution of Nepal has embraced a three-pillar economy consisting of public, private and cooperative sectors. Debates on development have tended to assume that a country must follow either a 'socialist' or a 'capitalist' path, which implies that resources must be controlled by the state or the private capitalists. The controversy led to the concept of a 'mixed' path wherein both the private and the public sectors would co-exist, and the former would undertake economic activities as defined by the state. Nepal, as India and other countries, adopted the mixed path in which cooperatives also existed but without state priority. But with the promulgation of the new Constitution, cooperatives are given equal space as public and private sectors, and in addition, they are given some additional facilities and support. This has raised some furor in the private sector that the cooperatives would compete against private enterprises performing more or less the same functions, and the former may be propped up by the state through subsidies and other support without regard to how they perform, and they may eventually outpace the private enterprises. There may be some truth in such apprehensions, but it is also equally true that savings and credit cooperatives are competitors of private-sector banks and financial institutions, and they are also competitors to with each other. The same is true with regard to certain production enterprises. It is also true that the pressure of competition may lead to better performance by compelling both the private enterprises and the cooperatives to exhibit managerial efficiency, technological innovation, capacity expansion and diversification in new and risky product lines. However, given the swollen growth of cooperatives in the country, exposure to intense competition and malpractices, a number of them often fall in severe financial crisis entailing huge loss to the depositors. Hence, there is a need to reserve certain areas where cooperatives can perform better, such as irrigation, farming, agro-processing, marketing and social services (particularly education and health care), in rural areas, and there are certainly other areas where private enterprises can show better results, such as infrastructure, large manufacturing and exports. There is thus a need to constantly study and analyze how these three sectors are functioning; the interface between these sectors from historical, political, economic and social perspectives; how a fusion can be made among these sectors so that one sector would complement and supplement the other, rather than instigate unhealthy competition; suggest right policies and programmes; and so forth.

Sixth, the global financial crisis of 2007 has revealed that an unrestrained market may lead to a financial crisis, and there may be market failures and monopoly practices, which may have far-reaching consequences for the economy. Hence the markets need to be made to work the way they should through better regulation, closer oversight, greater transparency and good corporate governance. This calls for a very visible hand of the government, even in the context of liberalized economy. This would be possible only when the government is proactive and the concerned government agencies, Nepal Rastra Bank regulatory authorities and Planning Commission, and concerned ministries work together to monitor the functioning of the market and take prompt corrective actions whenever there are distortions and unfair practices.

Seventh, it would be imprudent to accept the spread of neo-liberalism and globalized capital as an unavoidable global phenomenon and argue that Nepal cannot remain aloof from this. The question is whether the state should remain helpless in the surge of liberalization or it should have the willpower to negotiate, modify, moderate and qualify the rules and conditions associated with it to suit Nepal's interests. Given the structural rigidities and bottlenecks, and consequently a high-cost economy, allowing unrestricted entry of international capital would mean the virtual annihilation of national industrial capital and extinction of numerous petty and small producers. This means that the state has to explore effective ways to counter neo-liberalism and work out policy measures to adapt to the demands of globalizing world capitalism to national needs.

Eighth, there has been a huge rise in the expectations of the people from the state, particularly after the country became a federal republic. But the ordinary people have not found the state where it is needed for the protection of the common good, justice, equality, assistance and provision of basic services during a crisis period. The plight of the poor during the 2015 earthquake and COVID-19 pandemic shows that the state has been the most difficult for them to spot even in a time of crisis. Such discontent carries a serious danger of political crisis, as witnessed in 1951, 1991 and 2006. In a democracy, the elected representatives are accountable to the people, and the bureaucrats are accountable to the representatives, but this is not the case in Nepal. When the representatives are in ministerial positions, it is the bureaucracy which advises them on policy issues, but it has failed to perform well in regard to advising with correct policies, effective implementation strategies and programmes and efficient service delivery. This type of bureaucratic malfunctioning needs to be corrected through fundamental restructuring of the state bureaucracy. And it is this area where studies and comparative analysis of best international practices are needed, and the NPC may be the lead organization for this.

The coronavirus has exposed the emptiness of what was built in Nepal in the name of development over the last three decades under the rubric of neo-liberal economic philosophy that advocates privatization, deregulation, free markets and individualism. What was built was a dependent economy sustained by foreign aid and workers' remittance, and import-dependent production and consumption. The economy was made to reel under a weak state sector that has long shed away the objective of a self-reliant economy, which is what is needed to keep the economy going in times of crisis. On the other hand, the private sector, guided by the 'animal spirit', national concern and community focus, is secondary to them. Therefore, the time has come to change the balance between state and market, free market and regulation and return to 'Keynesianism' as a due correction to neo-liberalism. This would call for a new development strategy, an essential component of which should be self-reliance based on our conditions, needs, problems and experiences, rather than concepts and ideas borrowed from the developed countries of the west. Self-reliance does not, however, mean autarchy. What it means was clearly defined in the Cocoyoc Declaration way back in 1974,

> We believe that one basic strategy of development will have to be increased national self-reliance. It does not mean autarchy. It implies mutual benefits from trade and cooperation and a fairer distribution of resources satisfying basic needs. It does mean self-confidence, reliance primarily on one's own resources, human and natural, and capacity of autonomous goal-setting and decision making. It excludes dependence on outside influences and powers that can be converted into political pressure. It excludes exploitative trade patterns depriving countries of their natural resources for their own development.
>
> (Erb and Kallab, 1975)

To achieve this condition of self-reliance, we need to construct a *socialist national economic plan* based on the principles of socialism and aimed at getting rid of the prevailing system that perpetuates economic dependence. The plan should be guided by the concern of expanding the production base of the economy with the strictest economy of the available resources and increasing production for the home market, thereby replacing imports, instituting robust local value chains, and reducing concentration of wealth and inequalities. This would be the starting point towards achieving the goal of a socialism-oriented economy embraced in the preamble of Nepal's Constitution of 2015.

References

Abuzeid, F. 2009. "Foreign Aid and the 'Big Push' Theory: Lessons from Sub-Saharan Africa", *Stanford Journal of International Relations*, XI: 1.

Acemoglu, D. and J.A. Robinson. 2013. *Why Nations Fail*, London: Profile Books.

Action Aid. 2005. "Real Aid: An Agenda for Making Aid Work", https://actionaid.org/sites/default/files/real_aid.pdf

Action Aid. 2011. "Real Aid: Ending Aid Dependency", https://www.actionaid.org.uk/sites/default/files/doc_lib/real_aid:3.pdf

ADB/DFID/ILO. 2009. *Nepal Critical Development Constraints*, Manila: Asian Development Bank.

Alkire, S. and M.E. Santos. 2010. "Country Briefing, Nepal: Multi-dimensional Poverty Index", OPHI, https://www.ophi.org.uk/wp-content/uploads/Nepal.pdf

American Sociologist. 1974. *Nepal: Helped Down the Drain by Mindless Foreign Aid*, Kathmandu: Mimeo.

Amin, S. 1976. *Unequal Development: An Essay on the Social Formations of Peripheral Capitalism* (Translated by Brain Pearce), England: Harvester Press.

Apodaca, C. 2017. "Foreign Aid as Foreign Policy Tool", https://doi.org/10.1093/acrefore/9780190228637.013.332

ARTEP. 1974. *A Challenge to Nepal: Growth and Employment*, Bangkok: ARTEP.

Bagchi, A.K. 1982. *The Political Economy of Underdevelopment*, Cambridge: Cambridge University Press.

Bardhan, P. 1998. *The Political Economy of Development in India*, Delhi: Oxford University Press.

Bardhan, P. 2017. "The Pattern of Income Distribution in India: A Review" in A.V. Bannerjee, P. Bardhan, R. Somanathan and T.N. Srinivasan (eds), *Poverty and Income Distribution in India*, New Delhi: Juggernaut Books.

Bauer, P. 1972. *Dissent on Development: Studies and Debates in Development Economics*, Cambridge, MA: Harvard University Press.

Beenhakker, A. 1973. *A Kaleidoscopic Circumspection of Development: Planning with Contextual Reference to Nepal*, Rotterdam: Rotterdam University Press.

Berg, E. 1993. *Rethinking Technical Cooperation: Reforms for Capacity Building in Africa*, New York: United Nations Development Programme.

Bhandari, A. and C.S. Adhikari. 2016. "Where Does So Much Money Go?", *The Kantipur*, 20 August 2016, Kathmandu.

Bhatta, B.D. 2015. "Leadership of Three Castes (in Nepali)", *Himal Weekly Newspaper*, 15–21 February 2015, Lalitpur: Himal Media.

Bhattarai, B. 2003. *The Nature of Underdevelopment and Regional Structure of Nepal: A Marxist Analysis*, Delhi: Adroit Publishers.

Bijoy, C.R. 2013. "India: Transiting to a Global Order", https://www.realityofaid.org/wp-content/uploads/2013/02/ROA-SSDC-Special-Report6.pdf

Blaikie, P., J. Cameron and D. Seddon. 1980. *Nepal in Crisis: Growth and Stagnation at the Periphery*, Delhi: Oxford University Press.

Blank, R. 1997. *It Takes a Nation: A New Agenda for Fighting Poverty*, Princeton, NJ: Princeton University Press.

Breiding, R.J. 2019. *Too Small to Fail*, India: Harper Business.

Brown, T.L. 2010. *The Challenges to Democracy in Nepal*, Oxford: Routledge (Special Indian Edition).

Buiter, W. 2007. "A Term Whose Time Is Gone", *Development in Practice*, 17(4–5) August: 647–52.

Burnside, G. and D. Dollar. 2010. "Aid Policies and Growth", *American Economic Review*, 90(4): 847–68.

CBS. 1993. *Nepal-Population Census 1991*, Vol. 1, Part VII, Kathmandu: Central Bureau of Statistics.

CBS. 1997. *Nepal Living Standard Survey Report, V. I & II 1996*, Kathmandu: Central Bureau of Statistics.

CBS. 2004. *Nepal Living Standard Survey Report, 2003/04*, Kathmandu: Central Bureau of Statistics.

CBS. 2006. *Small Area Estimation of Poverty, Caloric Intake and Malnutrition in Nepal*, September 2006, Kathmandu: Central Bureau of Statistics.

CBS. 2008. *Nepal Labour Force Survey*, Kathmandu: Central Bureau of Statistics.

CBS. 2011. *Nepal Living Standard Survey Report*, Kathmandu: Central Bureau of Statistics.

CBS. 2013. *Nepal: Small Area Estimation of Poverty (Summary and Findings)*, Kathmandu: Central Bureau of Statistics.

CBS. 2017/18. *Nepal Labour Force Survey*, Kathamndu: Central Bureau of Statistics.

CEPRUD. 2004. *Impact Evaluation of Micro-Credit Programmes on Poverty Reduction*, Research Report submitted to the National Planning Commission, Kathmandu: Centre for Policy Studies and Rural Development.

CEPRUD. 2007. *Impact Assessment Study of Rural Self-Reliance Fund*, Research Report submitted to Nepal Rastra Bank, Kathmandu: Centre for Policy Studies and Rural Development.

Chakravarti, A. 2005. *Aid, Institutions and Development: New Approaches to Growth, Governance and Poverty*, New Delhi: Oxford University Press.

Chakravarty, S. 1987. *Development Planning: The Indian Experience*, Delhi: Oxford University Press.

Chandra, N.K. 2004. "Relevance of Soviet Economic Model for Non-socialist Countries", *Economic and Political Weekly*, 39(39) (29 May), 2287–305.

Chatterji, B. 1967. *A Study of Recent Nepalese Politics*, Calcutta: The World Press Private Limited.

Chauhan, R.S. 1989. *Society and State Building in Nepal*, Kathmandu: Ratna Pustak Bhandar.

Chenery, H.B. and A.M. Strout. 1966. "Foreign Assistance and Economic Development", *American Economic Review*, September.

Clydesdale, G. 2016. *Waves of Prosperity*, Great Britain: Robinson.

Collier, P. 2008. *The Bottom Billion*, Oxford: Oxford University Press.

Collier, P. and David Dollar. 1998. *Aid Allocation and Poverty Reduction, Policy Research*, Working Paper 2041, Washington DC: The World Bank.

Dahal, M.K. 2004. "Nepalese Economy Towards Building a Strong Economic Nation-State", in M.K. Dahal (ed.), *Nepalese Economy: Towards Building a Strong Economic Nation State*, Kathmandu: Central Department of Economics, TU.

Dangol, S.B. 1999. *The Palace in Nepalese Politics: With Special Reference to the Politics of 1951 to 1990*, Kathmandu: Ratna Pustak Bhandar.

Dasgupta, B. 1998. *Structural Adjustment, Global Trade and the New Political Economy of Development*, New Delhi: Vistaar Publications.

de Groot, A., C.K. Ramachandran, A. Slob, A. Willemsen and A. Morten Jerve. 2008. "Managing Aid Exit and Transformation India Country Case Study", https://cdn.sida.se/publications/files/sida46360en-managing-aid-exit-and-transformation-india-country-case-study.pdf

Desai, M. 2005. *Development and Nationhood: Essays in the Political Economy of South Asia*, New Delhi: Oxford University Press.

Deshar, B.D. 2013. "Squatters Problems along Bagmati Riverside in Nepal and Its Impact on Environment and Economy", *International Journal of Environmental Engineering and Management*, 4(1): 127–42.

Devine, P. 1988. *Democracy and Economic Planning; The Political Economy of a Self-Governing Society*, Cambridge: Polity Press.

Deyshappriya, R. 2018. "Examining Poverty Trends in South Asian Countries: Where Is Sri Lanka among Its South Asian Counterparts?", 31 July, https://blogs.lse.ac.uk/southasia/2018/07/31/examining-poverty-trends-in-south-asian-countries-where-is-sri-lanka-among-its-south-asian-counterparts/

Dhakal, Y. 2019. "Donors' Highhandedness" (in Nepali), *Nepal Weekly*, 10 February, Vol. 19, Kathmandu: Kantipur Publications.

Dollar, D. and L. Pritchett. 1998. *Assessing Aid, What Works, What Does Not and Why*, Washington, DC: The World Bank.

Domar, E. 1946. "Capital Expansion, Rate of Growth, and Employment", *Econometrica*, XIV: April 1946, 137–47.

Donor Tracker. 2021. https://donortracker.org/country/south-korea; https://donortracker.org

Dore, R. 1973. *British Factory-Japanese Factory*, London: Allen and Unwin.

Dostovalov, Y. 1984. "Concepts of Socio-Economic Underdevelopment's", in A.D. Smirnov, V.V. Golosov and V.F. Maximova (eds.), *The Teaching of Political Economy: A Critique of Non-Marxian Theories*, (English Translation) Moscow: Progress Publishers.

Dube, S.C. 1990. *Understanding Poverty: Tradition and Development*, Delhi: Vikas Publishing House.

Easterly, W. 2006. *The White Man's Burden: Why the West's Efforts to Aid the Rest Have Done So Much Ill and So Little Good*, New York: Penguin Books.

Engen, L. and A. Prizzon. 2019. "Exit from Aid: An Analysis of Country Experiences", *Overseas Development Institute*, April 2019, https://cdn.odi.org/media/documents/12662.pdf

EPW. 2014. "Three Articles by D. Nachane, S. Mehrotra and R. Shah", *Economic and Political Weekly*, 14 September 2014 (12–23), Mumbai.

EPW. 2015. "Two Articles by P. Patnaik and G. Rao", *Economic and Political Weekly*, 24 January 2015 (10–16), Mumbai.

Erb, G.F. and Kallab, V. (ed.). 1975. *Beyond Dependency*, Annex -2, 170–77, The Cocoyoc Declaration, Washington, DC: Overseas Development Council.

FEB. 2021. *Repatriation Strategic Plan*, Kathmandu: Foreign Employment Board, Government of Nepal, https://www.feb.gov.np/download#adhyan

Field, G. 1995. *Economic Growth and Political Change in Asia*, London: Macmillan Press Ltd.

Fischer, E. 2008. *How to Read Karl Marx*, Delhi: Akkar Books.

Foster, J., J. Greer and E. Thorbecke. 1984. "A Class of Decomposable Poverty Measures", *Econometrica*, 52(3): 761–5.

Gaige, F. 2009 [1975]. *Regionalism and National Unity in Nepal*, Second Edition, Lalitpur: Himal Books (First published in 1975 by University of California Press, Berkley).
Gallagher, K. 2016. "The Discourse of Power and the Politics of Squatting in Nepal, Crossing the Border", *International Journal of Interdisciplinary Studies*, 4(1), 15 April 2016. ISSN 2350-8752 (Print); ISSN 2350-8922.
Gautam, M.S. and B. Pokharel. 2011. "Influence of Foreign Aid in Policy Process in the Forestry and Local Governance", https://asd.org.np/./foreign aid:public_poli
Ghimire, L.S. 2019. *Inside Out: A Reflections on Development Practices*, Kathmandu: We Read.
Gill, R.T. 1980. *Economic Development, Past and Present*, New Delhi: Prentice Hall.
Gongol, S.D. 1973. *Foreign Experts in the Administration of Nepal*, Kathmandu: Centre for Economic Development and Administration.
Hachhethu, K. 2003. "Nepali Politics: People-Parties Interface", in D.N. Gellner (ed.), *Resistance and the State: Nepalese Experiences*, New Delhi: Social Science Press.
Hancock, G. 1989. *Lords of Poverty: The Power, Prestige, and Corruption of the International Aid Business*, New York: The Atlantic Monthly Press.
Harrod, R.F. 1948. *Towards a Dynamic Economics*, London: Macmillan.
Hasan, P. 2007. "Role of the State in Pakistan's Economy", *Economic and Political Weekly*, 5 May, 1623–30, Mumbai.
Hays, L.D. 1975. "The Monarchy and Modernization in Nepal", *Asian Survey*, XV(7): 616–28.
HIC. 2012. "Habitat International Coalition Urgent Action Appeal NP–DDFE–080512 Forced Eviction and Demolition of 248 Homes in Kathmandu, Nepal", 14 May 2012, http://www.hic-sarp.org/documents/NP-DDFE-080512.pdf
HLLRC. 2020. *Report of the High Level and Reform (Badal) Commission*, 1994, Kathmandu.
Houften, M. 1994. "The Dynamics and Chronology of the 1990 Revolution", in M. Hutt (ed.), *Nepal in the Nineties*, Delhi: Oxford University Press.
Huttington, S.P. 1968. *Political Order in Changing Societies*, New Haven, CT: Yale University Press.
ICIMOD. 2017. *Understanding Multidimensional Poverty in 23 Districts of Nepal*, Kathmandu: International Centre for Integrated Mountain Development.
IDS. 1984. *Foreign Aid and Development in Nepal: Proceedings of a Seminar*, Kathmandu: Integrated Development Systems.
ISACPA. 2003. *Our Future Our Responsibility*, Kathmandu: SAARC Secretariat.
IWMI. 2021. *IWMI in Nepal*", International Water management Institute, https://www.iwmi.cgiar.org/about/where-we-work/asia/south-asia-region/nepal/
Joshi, P.C. 1975. *Land Reform in India, Trends and Perspectives*, Bombay: Allied Publishers.
Joshi, S. 2020. "Famine or Feast in Nepal?", Kathmandu: Annapurna Express, 31/05/2020, https://theannapurnaexpress.com/news/famine-or-feast-in-nepal-2533
Kelegama, S. 2012. "Foreign Aid and South Asia", in S. Kelegama (ed.), *Foreign Aid in South Asia: The Emerging Scenario*, New Delhi: Sage Publications.
Kalegama, S. 2014. "SAARC's Attempts at Regional Poverty Alleviation", https://www.thedailystar.net/saarcs-attempts-at-regional-poverty-alleviation-41818
Kamat, R.K. 2019. "Forced Eviction from Public Land Unlawful: Activists", *The Himalayan*, 25 August 2019, e-paper.
Kanbur, R. 2000. "Income Distribution and Development", in A.B. Atkinson and F. Bourguignon (eds.), *Hand Book of Income Distribution*, New York: Elsevier.
Kappel, R. 2004. "Economic Reforms and the Livelihood of Rural Households: Evidence and Future Prospects", in R. Baumgartner and R. Hogger (eds.), *In Search of Livelihood Systems: Managing Resources and Change*, New Delhi: Sage Publications Pvt. Ltd.

Karma, R. 2019. "5 Myths about Global Poverty", *Current Affairs*, 26 July, 2019, https://www.currentaffairs.org/2019/07/5-myths-about-global-poverty

Kathmandu Post. 2017. "Squatter Settlement Demolished", https://kathmandupost.com/valley/2017/07/16/squatter-settlement-demolished

Kiran, K.C. and K. Pahari. 2012. "A Study on Squatter Settlements of Kathmandu Using GIS, Aerial Photography, Remote Sensing and Household Survey", *Kathmandu: Nepalese Journal on Geo-informatics*, 10: 1–18.

Khandwalla, P.N. 1999. *Revitalizing the State: A Menu of Options*, New Delhi: Sage Publications.

Kirkpatrick, C. 2021 [1811]. *An Account of the Kingdom of Nepaul*, New Edition, Kathmandu: Kathmandu Educational Publishing House (First published in London, 1811).

Kohli, A. 2012. *Poverty Amid Plenty in the New India*, New Delhi: Cambridge University Press.

Krichenko, V.N. 1980. *Socialist Long-Term Economic Planning* (English Translation), Moscow: Progress Publishers.

Krishna, A. 2014. "Poverty Knowledge and Poverty Action in India", in A. Gupta and K. Sivaramakrishnan (eds.), *The State in India after Liberalization: Interdisciplinary Perspectives*, Oxfordshire: Routledge (Indian Reprint).

Kumar, R., G. Gartaula and B. Khadka. 2019. "Maximum Exploitation and Extraction of Poor by Micro-Finance Established for Reducing Poverty through Access to Credit", *Himal Weekly*, 18–24 August 2019.

Kuznets, S. 1955. "Economic Growth and Income Inequality", *American Economic Review*, 45(1): 1–28.

Lipton, M. 1991. "Agriculture, Rural People, the State and the Surplus in Some Asian Countries: Thoughts on Some Implications of Three Recent Approaches in Social Science", in J. Breman and S. Mundle (eds.), *Rural Transformation in Asia*, Delhi: Oxford University Press.

Macfarlane, A. 1994. "Fatalism and Development in Nepal", in M. Hutt (ed.), *Nepal in the Nineties*, Delhi: Oxford University Press.

Magdoff, H. 1999. "An Interview with Harry Magdoff", Interview by Christopher Phelps, *Monthly Review*, 51(1), May 1999, Cornerstone Publications.

Mage, J. 2007. "The Nepali Revolution and International Relations", *Economic and Political Weekly*, 19 May, Bombay.

Mahat, R.S. 2005. *In Defense of Democracy: Dynamics and Fault Lines of Nepal's Political Economy*, New Delhi: Adroit Publishers.

Malla, G. 2012. *Politics of Foreign Aid in Nepal*, New Delhi: Adroit Publishers.

Mandel, E. 1974. *Marxist Economic Theory*, 3rd impression, London: The Merlin Press.

Maxwell Stamp Associates. 1991. *Second Industrial Sector Study*, Report Submitted to Asian Development Bank/Government of Nepal, Kathmandu.

McKinnon, R.I. 1964. "Foreign Exchange Constraints in Economic Development and Efficient Aid Allocation", *Economic Journal*, 74(June): 388–409.

MEP. 1965. *Third Plan (1965–70)*, Nepal: His Majesty's Government, Ministry of Economic Planning.

MFA. 1971. *Farm Management Study in the Selected Regions of Nepal*, Kathmandu: Ministry of Food and Agriculture, Government of Nepal.

Mihaly, E.B. 2002 [1965]. *Foreign Aid and Politics in Nepal: A Case Study*, Lalitpur, Nepal: Himal Books (First published in1965 by Oxford University Press, Oxford).

Mishra, S. 2020. "Walking 3 Days to Get Home", *Nepali Times*, 2 April 2020, e-paper.

MOF. 1992/1993. *Economic Survey*, Kathmandu: His Majesty's Government of Nepal, Ministry of Finance, 1993.

MOF. 2002. *Foreign Aid Policy*, Kathmandu: Government of Nepal, Ministry of Finance.
MOF. 2005. *Economic Survey*, Kathmandu: Government of Nepal, Ministry of Finance.
MOF. 2008a. *Nepal Country Report, Survey on Monitoring the Paris Declaration*, March 2008, Kathmandu: Government of Nepal, Ministry of Finance.
MOF. 2008b. *Nepal Portfolio Performance Review NPPR*, Kathmandu: Government of Nepal, Ministry of Finance.
MOF. 2011. *Nepal Portfolio Performance Review NPPR*, Kathmandu: Government of Nepal, Ministry of Finance.
MOF. 2012. *Development Cooperation Report*, Kathmandu: Government of Nepal, Ministry of Finance.
MOF. 2014. *Foreign Aid Policy*, Kathmandu: Government of Nepal, Ministry of Finance.
MOF. 2015. *Economic Survey 2015/16*, Kathmandu: Government of Nepal, Ministry of Finance.
MOF. 2018. *Development Cooperation Report 2017/18*, Kathmandu: Government of Nepal, Ministry of Finance.
MOF. 2019a. *Development Cooperation Report 2018/19*, Kathmandu: Government of Nepal, Ministry of Finance.
MOF. 2019b. *International Development Cooperation Policy*, Kathmandu: Government of Nepal, Ministry of Finance.
MOF. 2020. *Agreement between Nepal Government and American Aid Institution, Millennium Challenge Corporation (Millennium Challenge Compact)*, Kathmandu: Government of Nepal, Ministry of Finance.
MOF. 2020/21. *Economic Survey*, Kathmandu: Government of Nepal, Ministry of Finance.
MOF. 2021/22. *Economic Survey*, Kathmandu: Government of Nepal, Ministry of Finance.
Morgan, P. 2002. "Technical Assistance: Correcting the Precedents", in S. Browne (ed.), *Development Policy Journal*, Vol. 2, December, New York: United Nations Development Programme.
Moyo, D. 2009. *Dead Aid: Why Aid Is Not Working and How There Is a Better Way for Africa*, London: Penguin Books.
Muni, S.D. 2012. "Bringing the Maoists down from the Hills: India's Role", in S. Von Einsiedel, D.M. Malone and S. Pradhan (eds.), *Nepal in Transition: From People's War to Fragile Peace*, (South Asian Edition), New Delhi: Cambridge University Press.
Myrdal, G. 1972. *Economic Theory and Underdeveloped Countries* (Reprint), London: Meuthen and Co. Ltd.
Nagarik. 2016. "Political Leaders and Civil Servants Are the Most Corrupt", *Nagarik*, 26 January 2016, Kathmandu.
Nagraj, R. 2005. "Industrial Growth in China and India: A Preliminary Comparison", *Economic and Political Weekly*, 21 May, 2163–71, Mumbai.
Nayak, P. 2016. "The State and the Market", *Economic and Political Weekly*, 31(4): 27 January, PE18–PE22.
Nayapatrika. 2020. *Nepali Vernacular Daily*, 9 February 2020, Kathmandu.
Nayapatrika. 2021. *Nepali Vernacular Daily*, 25 September 2021, Kathmandu.
Nayyar, D. 2013. *Catch Up: Developing Countries in the World Economy*, United Kingdom: Oxford University Press.
Nepal Weekly. 2017. "Politics as Profession", *Nepal Weekly*, 31 December 2017, Kathmandu.
Neupane, A. 2020. "Sucide Cases on the Rise, Mental Health Workers Warn of a Grim Reality", 21 May. https://myrepublica.nagariknetwork.com/news/suicide-cases-on-the-rise-mental-health-experts-warn-of-a-grim-situation/
Niti Foundation. 2019. "Nepal's Kleptocratic Network – Mapping Corruption and Impunity", 22 May, Kathmandu, nitifoundation.org>wp-content>uploads>Niti Foundation.

NPC. 1978. *A Survey of Employment Income Distribution and Consumption Patterns in Nepal, 1976–77*, Summary Report, Vol. IV, Kathmandu: National Planning Commission.
NPC. 1987. *Programme for Fulfillment of Basic Needs (1985–2000)*, Kathmandu: National Planning Commission.
NPC. 1992. *The Eighth Plan*, Kathmandu: National Planning Commission.
NPC. 1998. *The Ninth Plan*, Kathmandu: National Planning Commission.
NPC. 2015. *Nepal Earthquake 2015: Post Disaster Needs Assessment*, Kathmandu: National Planning Commission.
NPC. 2018. *Nepal Muti-dimensional Poverty Index: Analysis Towards Action*, Kathmandu: National Planning Commission.
NPC. 2019. *Fifteenth Plan*, Kathmandu: National Planning Commission.
NRB. 1988. *Multipurpose Household Budget Survey*, Kathmandu: Nepal Rastra Bank.
Nurske, R. 1953. *Problems of Capital Formation in Underdeveloped Countries*, Oxford: Oxford University Press.
OAG. 2016. *Performance Audit Report of Earthquake Reconstruction Programme*, Kathmandu: Office of the Attorney General, Nepal.
OECD. 2008. *Development Cooperation of the Republic of Korea: DAC Special Review*, Paris: OECD, http://www.oecd.org/dac/peer-reviews/42347329.pdf
Ohkawa, K. and H. Rosovsky. 2012. "The Role of Agriculture in Modern Japanese Economic Development", in *Economic Development and Cultural Change*, Vol. IX, October, reprinted in K. Eicher and L. Witt (eds.), *Agriculture in Economic Development*, 1964.
Panday, D.R. 1989. "Administrative Development in a Semi-Dependency: The Experience of Nepal", *Public Administration and Development*, 9: 315–19.
Panday, D.R. 1999. *Nepal's Failed Development: Reflections on the Mission and Maladies*, Kathmandu: Nepal South Asia Centre.
Patnaik, P. 2001. *Whatever Happened to Imperialism and Other Essays* (Second Reprint), New Delhi: Tulika.
Patnaik, P. 2014. "End of the Planning Commission", *Economic and Political Weekly*, 19 July 2014 (10–13), Mumbai.
Patnaik, P. 2015. "From the Planning Commission to the Niti Aayog", *Economic and Political Weekly*, 19 July 2015 (10–12), Mumbai.
Pokhrel, M. 2018. "A Revelation of How Political Parties Distrbuted Public Land to Their Kiths and Kins in the Name of Landless Squatters in the Last Thirty Years", *Kathmandu: Centre for Investigative Journalism*, 7 December 2018, https://cijnepal.org.np/landless-squatters-on-the-rise-despite-distributing-46-bighas-of-land/
Poudel, A. 2020. "Over 1200 People Killed Themselves during 74 Days of Lockdown", https://kathmandupost.com/health/2020/06/14/over-1-200-people-killed-themselves during-74-days-of-lockdown
Poudel, D.P. 2008. "Management of Eight 'Ja' for Economic Development of Nepal", *Journal of Comparative International Management*, 11(1): 15–27.
Poudyal, S.R. 1982. *Foreign Aid in Nepal*, (Mimeo), Kathmandu: CEDA, Tribhuvan University.
Poudyal, S.R. 1983. *Planned Development in Nepal: A Study*, New Delhi: Sterling Publishers.
Poudyal, S.R. 1986. *Foreign Trade, Aid and Development in Nepal*, New Delhi: Commonwealth Publishers.
Poudyal, S.R. 2007. "Micro-Finance: A Magic Bullet for Poverty Alleviation", in *Socio-Economic Panoroma: Trends and Issues on Social Aspects of Nepal*, January 2007, Kathmandu: HARD.
Poudyal, S.R. 2016. "Remittance Republic", *Kantipur Daily*: Kathmandu, 30 September 2016.

Poudyal, S.R. and M.P. Sharma. 1985. "Nepal's National Economic Goals: The Asian Standard by 2000 AD". *Strategic Studies Series*, Number 4 and 5 Autmn, Kathmandu: Centre for Nepal and Asian Studies, Tribhuvan University.

Pradhan, B.B. 1976. *Importance and Role of Foreign Aid in Nepal's Economic and Social Development*, (Nepali, Mimeo), December 1976, Kathmandu: Nepal Rastra Bank.

Pro-Public. 1999. *Strategic Review of the Performances of the Commission on Investigation of Abuse of Authority and the Office of the Auditor General*, Kathmandu: Forum for Protection of Public Interest.

Pswarayi-Riddihough, I. 2016. "Fighting Poverty Together in Sri Lanka", https://www.worldbank.org/en/news/opinion/2016/10/17/fighting-poverty-together-sri-lanka

PTI/Kathmandu. 2020. "Business Standard Special on Corona Virus", 17 April 2020, PTI/Kathmandu.

Pun, K. and M. Devkota. 2021. "Nepal's Silent Epidemic of Sucide during Covid-19 Pandemic", 16 January. https://english.onlinekhabar.com/nepals-silent-epidemic-of-suicide-during-covid-19-pandemic.html

Pyakuryal, B. 2012. "Nepal", in S. Kalegama (ed.), *Foreign Aid in South Asia: The Emerging Scenario*, New Delhi: Sage Publications.

Rana, P.S. 1972. *Role of Foreign Aid and Trade in Economic Reconstruction* (August, Mimeo), Kathmandu: Centre for Economic Development and Administration.

Ravallion, M. 2000. "What Is Needed for a More Pro-Poor Growth Process in India", *Economic and Political Weekly*, XXXV(13): 1089–93.

Regmi, M. 1976. *Land Ownership in Nepal*, London: University of California Press.

Regmi, M. 1984. *The State and Economic Surplus: Production, Trade and Resource Mobilization in Early 19th Century Nepal*, Varanasi: Nath Publishing House.

Regmi, M. 1999. *Thatched Huts and Stucco Palaces: Peasants and Landlords in 19th Century Nepal* (Reprint), Delhi: Adroit Publishers.

Riaz, A. and S. Basu. 2007. *Paradise Lost: State Failure in Nepal*, New Delhi: Adarsh Enterprises.

ROA. 2008. *The Reality of Aid: An Independent Review of Poverty Reduction and Development Assistance*, Philippines: IBON International, www.realityofaid.com

Rodan, R. 1943. "Problems of Industrialization of Eastern and South-Eastern Europe", *Economic Journal*, 53(June): 202–11; "Notes on the Theory of Big Push", in Ellis, H.S. (ed.). 1961. *Economic Development for Latin America*, London: Macmillan and Co. Ltd.; Reprinted in Meier, G.M. (ed.). 1976. *Leading Issues in Economic Development*, Third Edition, New York: Oxford University Press.

Rostow, W.W. 1960. *The Stages of Economic Growth: A Non-communist Manifesto*, London: Cambridge University Press.

Ryndina, M.N. 1984. "Theories of Economic Growth", in A.D. Smirnov, V.V. Golosov and V.F. Maximova (eds.), *The Teaching of Political Economy: A Critique of Non-Marxian Theories*, (English Translation) Moscow: Progress Publishers.

Sabina, A. and M.E. Santos. 2010. "Country Briefing, Nepal: Multi-dimensional Poverty Index (MPI) at a Glance", http://ophi.qeh.ox.ac.uk

Sakarweb Wordpress. 2020. "Local v/s Chitwan National Park: Who Is Right?", https://sakarweb.wordpress.com/2020/08/13/locals-v-s-chitwan-national-park-who-is-right/

Samuelson, P.A. 1970. *Economics, 8th Edition*, New York: McGraw Hill Company.

Sanyal, K.K. 1988. "Accumulation, Poverty and State in the Third World", *Economic and Political Weekly*, 23(5) (30 January), 27–30.

Sau, R. 1986. *Economy, Class and Society*, Madras: Universities Press (India) Pvt. Ltd.

Saunders, P. 1988. *Capitalism: A Social Audit* (First Indian Reprint), Delhi: World View Publications.

Seddon, D. 1987. *Nepal: A State of Poverty*, Delhi: Vikas Publishing House.
Seddon, D. 1994. "Democracy and Development in Nepal", in M. Hutt (ed.), *Nepal in the Nineties*, Delhi: Oxford University Press.
Seddon, D. and K. Hussain. 2002. *The Consequences of Conflict: Livelihoods and Development in Nepal*, Working Paper 85, London: Overseas Development Institute, https://cdn.odi.org/media/documents/2682.pdf
Seers, D. 1972. "What Are We Trying to Measure", *Journal of Development Studies*, 8(3): 21–36.
Seligson, M.A. and Passe-Smith, J.T. (eds.). 2004. *Development and Underdevelopment: The Political Economy of Global Inequality*, New Delhi: Viva Books Private Limited.
Sen, A.K. 1982. *Choice, Welfare and Measurement*, New Delhi: Oxford University Press.
Sen, A.K. 2000. *Development as Freedom*, New York: Random House.
Senghaas, D. 1978. "Dissociation and Autocentric Development: An Alternative Policy for the Third World", in *Economics*, Vol. 18, Institute of Scientific Cooperation.
Shah, S. 1988. "Nepal's Economic Development: Problems and Prospects", *Asian Survey*, XXVIII(9): 945–57.
Sharma, S.D. 1993. "Markets and States in Development", *Asian Survey*, XXXIII(9): 894–904.
Shrestha, B.P. 1967. *The Economy of Nepal*, Bombay: Vora and Co. Publishers Pvt. Ltd.
Shrestha, B.P. 1981. *An Introduction to Nepalese Economy*, Kathmandu: Ratna Pustak Bhandar.
Shrestha, B.K. 1992. "Rural Development Projects: Programmed to Forget the Poor", *HIMAL*, March/April 1992, Kathmandu.
Shrestha, B.N. 2005. "What Is Sugauli Treaty?", Paper presented in a Talk Programme, Kathmandu.
Skerry, C.A., M. Kerry and M.C. Kay. 1991. *Four Decades of Development: The History of US Assistance in Nepal, 1951–1991*, Kathmandu: USAID.
Sogge, D. 2002. *Give and Take: What's the Matter with Foreign Aid*, London: Zed Books.
Solow, R.M. 1956. "A Contribution to the Theory of Economic Growth", *Quarterly Journal of Economics*, 70: 65–94.
Solow, R.M. 1957. "Technical Change and the Aggregate Production Function", *Review of Economics and Statistics*, 39: 312–30.
Stiglitz, J. 1996. "The Role of Government in Economic Development", in M. Burno and B. Pelskovic (eds.), *Annual World Bank Conference on Development Economics*, Washington, DC: The World Bank.
Stiglitz, J. 2002. *Globalization and Its Discontents*, New York: W.W. Norton & Company.
Stiller, L.F. and R.P. Yadav. 1979. *Planning for People: A Study of Nepal's Planning Experience*, Kathmandu: Research Centre for Nepal and Asian Studies, Tribhuvan University.
Streeten, P. 1981. *First Things First: Meeting Basic Human Needs in the Developing Countries*, Washington, DC: Oxford University Press (Published for the World Bank).
Suwal, R. and M.P. Dahal. 2014. "Economically Active Population: Dimension and Dynamics", *Population Monograph of Nepal*, Vol. 11, Kathmandu: Central Bureau of Statistics, Government of Nepal.
SWC. 2020. "NGOs Affiliated with Social welfare Council (1977–2019)", https://www.swc.org.np/sites/default/files/downloads/NGOs-affiliated-with-SWC-%20upto%20F.Y.%202075_76.pdf
SWC. 2020. "Brief Information on INGOs working under Agreement with Social Welfare Council (1977–2019)", https://www.swc.org.np/sites/default/files/downloads/total%20INGOs%20list.pdf

Szentes, T. 1976. *The Political Economy of Underdevelopment*, Third Edition, Budapest: Akademiai, Kiado.

Tandon, Y. 2009. *Development and Globalization: Daring to Think Differently*, EPDF, Pambazuka Press, an Imprint of Fahamu Books, https://epdf.tips/development-and-globalisation-daring-to-think-differently.html

Tarnoff, C. and Lawson, M. 2016. *Foreign Aid: An Introduction to U.S. Programs and Policy*, Congressional Research Service Report. http://nationalaglawcenter.org/wp-content/uploads/assets/crs/R40213.pdf

Tayeb, M.H. 1992. *The Global Business Environment: An Introduction*, London: Sage Publications.

TI. 2020. *Global Corruption Barometer Asia 2020: Citizens' Views and Experiences of Corruption*, Transparency International, https://images.transparencycdn.org/images/GCB_Asia_2020_Report_Web_final.pdf

Timilsena, P.C., B. Subedi and A.K. Jha. 2020. "The Lockdown Is Killing the Poor and the Marginalized", https://kathmandupost.com/province-no-2/2020/06/04/the-lockdown-is-killing-the-poor-and-the-marginalised

Thweatt, W.O. 1961. *The Concept of Elasticity and the Growth Equation*, Bombay: Asia Publishing House.

UNDP. 1990. *Human Development Report, 1990*, New York.

UNDP. 1999. *Human Development Report, 1999*, New York.

UNDP. 2004. *Human Development Report 2004*, New York.

UNDP. 2010. *Human Development Report 2010*, New York.

UNDP. 2016. *Human Development Report, 2016*, New York.

UNDP/Nepal. 2009. *Nepal Human Development Report, 2009*, Kathmandu.

USA. 2002. "The National Security Strategy of United States of America", https://2009-017.state.gov/documents/organization/63562.pdf

USA. 2017. "National Security Strategy of the United States of America", December 2017, https://www.whitehouse.gov/wp-content/uploads/2017/12/NSS-Final-12-18-2017-0905.pdf

USA. 2019a. A Free and Open *Indo-Pacific Strategy Report*: Preparedness, Partnerships and Promoting a Networked Region, 1 June 2019, https://media.defense.gov/2019/Jul/01/2002152311/-1/-1/1/Department-Of-Defense-Indo-Pacific-Strategy-Report-2019.Pdf

USA. 2019b. A Free and Open Indo-Pacific – Advancing a Shared Vision, Department of State, https://www.state.gov/wp-content/uploads/2019/11/Free-and-Open-Indo-Pacific-4Nov2019.pdf

Wade, R. 1982. "System of Administrative and Political Corruption: Canal Irrigation in South India", *Journal of Development Studies*, 18(April): 287–328.

Wadhva, C. 1998. "Cost of Economic Sanctions: Aftermath of Pokhran II", *Economic and Political Weekly*, 33(26) (27 June), 1604–7.

Wallerstein, I. 1986. "The States in the Institutional Vortex of Capitalist World Economy", in A. Kazancigil (ed.), *The State in Global Perspective*. United Kingdom: Gower/Unesco.

Whitfield, L. 2009. "Reframing the Aid Debate: Why Aid Isn't Working and How It Should Be Changed", *DIIS Working*, 2009, 34, https://www.files.ethz.ch/isn/111341/WP2009-34Refraiming_the_aid:debate.pdf

Wikipedia. 2021. "Indian Foreign Aid", 14 April 2021, https://en.wikipedia.org/wiki/Indian-foreign-aid

Wildavsky, A. 1972. "Why Planning Fails in Nepal", *Administrative Science Quarterly*, 508–28.

Winterhalt, K. 2018. "Truman's New Deal: Point Four and the Genesis of Modern Global Development", https://researchgate.net/publication/328548675_Truman's_New_Deal_Point_Four_and_the_Genesis_of_Modern_Global_Development

Woods, A. 2009. *Reformism or Revolution*, Delhi: Aaakar Books.

World Bank. 1983. *Nepal: Recent Developments and Selected Issues in Trade Promotion*, Washington, DC: The World Bank.

World Bank. 1989. *Nepal: Policies for Improving Growth and Alleviating Poverty*, Washington, DC: The World Bank.

World Bank. 1990. *Nepal: Relieving Poverty in a Resource-Scarce Economy*, Washington, DC: The World Bank.

World Bank. 1991. *Nepal: Poverty and Incomes*, Washington, DC: The World Bank.

World Bank. 1992. *Nepal: Public Resource Management in a Resource Scarce Economy*, Washington, DC: The World Bank.

World Bank. 2002. *Nepal Financial Sector Study*, SASF, South Asia Region, Washington, DC: The World Bank.

World Bank. 2014. *World Development Report 2014*, Washington, DC: The World Bank.

World Bank. 2018. Washington DC: The World Bank.

Xing, L. 1999. "Socialist Foundations of Market Reforms: Assessing Chinese Past", *Economic and Political Weekly*, 34(49): 3457–64.

Zaman, M.A. 1973. *Evaluation of Land Reform in Nepal*, Kathmandu: Ministry of Land Reform, Government of Nepal.

Annex 1

GDP Growth Rate and Sectoral Composition

FY	GDP Growth Rate (Percent)		GDP Composition (Percent)			FY	GDP Growth Rate (Percent)		GDP Composition (Percent)		
	Current	Constant	Primary	Secondary	Tertiary		Current	Constant	Primary	Secondary	Tertiary
1964/5	–	–	65.2	10.3	24.5	1992/3	14.1	3.3	42.9	20.2	36.8
1965/6	23.3	7.0	69.4	10.0	20.6	1993/4	15.9	7.9	42.6	20.7	36.7
1966/7	–7.2	–1.6	67.0	10.3	22.8	1994/5	9.6	2.9	41.3	21.7	37.0
1967/8	11.9	0.7	68.1	10.7	21.2	1995/6	14.0	5.7	41.0	21.8	37.2
1968/9	11.3	4.4	67.2	11.4	21.5	1996/7	12.6	5.0	40.9	21.7	37.4
1969/70	9.8	3.1	67.6	11.4	21.1	1997/8	7.5	3.3	39.4	21.3	39.3
1970/1	1.9	–1.6	67.5	10.9	21.6	1998/9	13.9	4.5	40.6	20.7	38.7
1971/2	16.0	3.1	68.6	11.3	20.2	1999/00	11.0	6.1	40.1	21.0	38.9
1972/3	–3.9	–0.5	66.0	11.6	22.4	2000/1	7.6	6.1	65.2	10.3	24.5
1973/4	28.5	6.3	69.1	11.5	19.4	2001/2	4.1	0.2	65.2	10.3	24.5
1974/5	24.7	1.5	71.8	8.0	20.2	2002/3	7.0	3.8	65.2	10.3	24.5
1975/6	3.9	4.4	69.4	8.7	21.9	2003/4	8.8	4.4	65.2	10.3	24.5
1976/7	–2.0	3.0	64.1	11.0	24.9	2004/5	9.5	3.2	65.2	10.3	24.5
1977/8	13.3	4.4	63.2	11.8	25.0	2005/6	11.4	3.7	65.2	10.3	24.5
1978/9	34.0	2.4	54.3	20.6	25.1	2006/7	10.6	2.8	65.2	10.3	24.5
1979/80	–11.4	–2.3	62.0	11.7	26.3	2007/8	11.8	5.8	65.2	10.3	24.5
1980/1	16.4	8.3	65.7	5.5	28.7	2008/9	20.4	3.9	65.2	10.3	24.5
1981/2	14.0	3.8	61.2	12.6	26.1	2009/10	19.1	4.3	65.2	10.3	24.5
1982/3	9.0	–3.0	60.6	12.5	26.9	2010/1	15.2	3.6	34.0	14.2	51.9
1983/4	16.9	9.7	61.3	12.3	26.4	2011/2	12.4	5.0	33.3	14.6	52.1
1984/5	20.1	6.2	51.7	14.5	33.8	2012/3	9.8	3.1	32.0	14.5	53.5
1985/6	19.7	4.7	51.4	15.3	33.3	2013/4	13.8	5.7	30.9	14.4	54.7
1986/7	14.9	2.0	50.5	15.2	34.3	2014/5	8.1	3.5	30.0	14.0	56.0
1987/8	19.7	7.0	50.7	15.5	33.8	2015/6	7.1	0.0	29.0	13.5	57.5
1988/9	17.3	5.4	50.1	15.8	34.1	2016/7	16.2	8.6	27.4	14.0	58.6
1989/90	16.2	4.9	51.1	15.5	33.5	2017/8	10.7	7.4	26.2	14.5	59.2
1990/1	16.5	6.4	48.2	17.0	34.8	2018/9	11.0	6.4	25.6	14.4	60.1
1991/2	24.8	4.6	45.5	19.9	34.6	2019/20	3.3	–2.4	26.8	12.8	60.4

Source: Economic Survey, Various Years, Ministry of Finance, Government of Nepal.

Annex 2

Status of National Pride Projects

SN	Name	Scope	Start-End Year	Estimated Cost (Rs. Billions)	Revised cost (Rs. Billions)	Implementation Status (as of 2017/18)	
						Physical (Percent)	Financial (Percent)
1	Sikta Irrigation Project	Irrigation of 42,776 ha of land in 41 VDCs and one municipality and one sub-municipality of the Banke district	2005–15 [a]2020	12.80	25.02	56.7	56.6
2	Babai Irrigation Project	Irrigation of 36,000 ha in Bardiya district	1989–2013 [a]2022	2.87	12.56	59.5	47.2
3	Rani–Jamariya–Kulariya Irrigation Project	Irrigation of 20,300 ha of land in 8 VDCs and one municipality of Kailali district	2008–18 [a]2024	10.16	27.70	36.0	34.8
4	Bheri–Babai Diversion Multipurpose Project	Irrigation of 51,000 ha of land in Bardiya and Banke districts; generation of 48 MW hydro-electricity	2012–20 [a]2022	16.43		35.0	50.0
5	Upper Tamakoshi Hydropower Project	Generation of 456 MW hydro-electricity	2011–16 [a]2020	35.29	70.0	96.4	83.0
6	Budhigandaki Hydropower Project	Generation of 600 MW hydro-electricity	2013–21 [a]2026	250	260	9.9	10.0
7	West-Seti Hydropower Project	Generation of 750 MW hydro-electricity	–			No progress (no feasibility study report yet)	No progress
8	Bhairawa Regional International Airport	Regional airport tourism promotion	2015–17 [a]2019	6.22	9.0	50.0	66.6

(*Continued*)

SN	*Name*	*Scope*	*Start-End Year*	*Estimated Cost (Rs. Billions)*	*Revised cost (Rs. Billions)*	*Implementation Status (as of 2017/18)*	
						Physical (Percent)	*Financial (Percent)*
9	Pokhara Regional International Airport	Regional airport tourism promotion	2008–21	21.60	27.0	15.0	30.0
10	Second International Airport, Bara	Alternative international airport tourism promotion	2015–22	120		39.4	17.6
11	Pashupati Area Development Project	Development of the Pashupati area as a model religious, cultural and eco-tourist spot	2001–18 [a]2019	2.03		40.2	40.2
12	Lumbini Area Development Project	Completion of master plan of birth place of Gautam Buddha	1985–unknown	5.50	6.10	80.0	80.0
13	Mid-Hill Pushpalal Highway	Construction of 1,776 km road along mid-Hills districts (Panchthar to Baitadi)	2008–18 [a]2021	33.37	79.18	45.0	33.9
14	East-West Railway	Construction of 1,318 km rail network from Mechi (Eastern border) to Mahakali (Western border) and 75 km metro in Kathmandfu Valley	2010–19[a]	65.41	69.52	13.7	14.9
15	Terai Hulaki Marga/Postal Highway	Construction of 1,663 km road and 125 bridges (Jhapa to Kanchanpur)	2007–18 [a]2021	20.0	25.0	25.0	41.9
16	North-South Koshi Corridor	Construction of 162 km road (Tehrathum to northern border Kimathanka)	2009–14 [a]2021	2.05	7.50	35.0	40.4
17	North-South Kaligandaki Corridor	Construction of 435 km road (Tanahun, Syanga, Gulmi,Parbat, Myagdi, Mustang)	2009–13 [a]2023	10.0	27.51	10.0	8.4

(*Continued*)

SN	Name	Scope	Start-End Year	Estimated Cost (Rs. Billions)	Revised cost (Rs. Billions)	Implementation Status (as of 2017/18)	
						Physical (Percent)	Financial (Percent)
18	North-South Karnali Corridor	Construction of a 196 km road (Khulalu to Simikot, Humla) and a 88 km road (Hilsa to Simikot)	2009–13 [a]2023	4.10	11.0	12.0	11.7
19	Kathmandu–Terai Fast Track Road	Construction of 76.5 + 18 km fast track from Nijhagad (Bara) to Kathmandu	2008–18 [a]2022	80.0	155.0	-	5.8
20	Melamchi Drinking Water Project	Pure drinking water to 3.0 million people of Kathmandu Valley	2002–8 [a]2019	23.45	35.54	83.7	87.4
21	President Chure Conservation Programme	Sustainable conservation and management of natural resources of the Chure Bhavar and Terai areas for poverty reduction and prosperous Nepal	2011–			92.2	88.2

Source: Brief Introduction and Progress of National Pride Projects, 2015 and 2018, National Planning Commission Secretariat, Kathmandu; Naya Patrika, Daily, June 8, 2019, Kathmandu.

a Revised completion date.

Annex 3

Aid Commitments and Disbursements (Rs. in Million)

Fiscal Year	*Commitment*	*Disbursement*	*Dis/Com (Percent)*
1974/5	438	386.2	88.2
1975/6	1,415.8	505.6	35.7
1976/7	1,911.1	556.9	29.1
1977/8	1,956.2	848.4	43.4
1978/9	2,417.3	989.4	40.9
1979/80	1,911.6	1,340.5	70.1
1980/1	4,012.6	1,562.2	38.9
1981/2	2,886.1	1,723.2	59.7
1982/3	2,959.2	2,075.9	70.2
1983/4	3,099.7	2,547.5	82.2
1984/5	5,991.5	2,676.4	44.7
1985/6	9,504.2	3,491.5	36.7
1986/7	7,523.8	3,314.5	44.1
1987/8	6,449.6	5,078.5	78.7
1988/9	11,254.5	5,666.9	50.4
1989/90	15,830	6,427.1	40.6
1990/1	5,665.5	5,990	105.7
1991/2	21,084.1	7,800.4	37.0
1992/3	20,526.7	9,235.6	45.0
1993/4	13,172.2	11,557.2	87.7
1194/5	12,877	11,249.4	87.4
1995/6	16,537.4	14,289	86.4
1996/7	39,643	15,031.9	37.9
1997/8	32,022.1	16,457.1	51.4
1998/9	18,352.5	16,189	88.2
1999/2000	20,448	17,523.9	85.7
2000/1	31,286.9	18,797.4	60.1
2001/2	33,227.8	14,384.8	43.3
2002/3	43,202.7	15,885.5	36.8
2003/4	23,738	18,912.4	79.7
2004/5	38,152.3	23,657.3	62.0
2005/6	20,924.2	22,041.8	105.3
2006/7	37,022.9	25,854.4	69.8
2007/8	49,186.2	29,300.6	59.6
2008/9	47,975.3	36,351.7	75.8
2009/10	96,609.5	49,769.4	51.5
2010/11	106,096.7	57,997.7	54.7

(*Continued*)

Fiscal Year	*Commitment*	*Disbursement*	*Dis/Com (Percent)*
2011/12	98,178.7	51,893.4	52.9
2012/13	115,156.8	47,199.2	41.0
2013/14	133,445.0	60,204.6	45.1
2014/15	225,819.3	63,901.6	28.3
2015/16	195,598.7	72,772.3	37.2
2016/17	250,244.6	99,841.5	39.9
2017/18	201,998.0	131,551.4	65.1
2018/19	138,256.0	147,271.2	106.5
2019/20	219,883.2	139,704.4	63.5
Total	2,166,009.3	1,152,102.4	53.2
Growth rate (Percent)	28.1	15.1	
CV	3.26	3.23	

Source: Economic Survey, Various Years, Ministry of Finance, Government of Nepal.

Annex 4

40-Point Memorandum Submitted by Dr. Baburam Bhattarai Chairman, Central Committee United People's Front, Nepal

Concerning Nationality

1. All discriminatory treaties, including the 1950 Nepal–India Treaty, should be abrogated.
2. The so-called Integrated Mahakali Treaty that concluded on 29 January 1996 should be repealed immediately, as it is designed to conceal the disastrous Tanakpur Treaty and allowed Indian imperialist monopoly over Nepal's water resources.
3. The open border between Nepal and India should be regulated, controlled and systematized. All vehicles with Indian licence plates should be banned from Nepal.
4. The Gurkha/Gorkha Recruitment Centres should be closed. Nepali citizens should be provided dignified employment in the country.
5. Nepali workers should be given priority in different sectors. A 'work permit' system should be strictly implemented if foreign workers are required in the country.
6. The domination of foreign capital in Nepali industries, business and finance should be stopped.
7. An appropriate customs policy should be devised and implemented so that economic development helps the nation become self-reliant.
8. The invasion of imperialist and colonial culture should be banned. Vulgar Hindi films, videos and magazines should be immediately outlawed.
9. The invasion of colonial and imperial elements in the name of non-governmental organizations and international non-governmental organizations should be stopped.

Concerning People's Democracy

10. A new constitution should be drafted by representatives elected for the establishment of a people's democratic system.
11. All special privileges of the king and the royal family should be abolished.
12. The army, the police and the bureaucracy should be completely under people's control.
13. All repressive acts, including the Security Act, should be repealed.

14. Everyone arrested extra-judicially for political reasons or revenge in Rukum, Rolpa, Jajarkot, Gorkha, Kabhrc, Sindhupalchowk. Sindhuli, Dhanusa, Ramechhap and so on, should be immediately released. All false cases should be immediately withdrawn.
15. The operation of armed police, repression and state-sponsored terror should be immediately stopped.
16. The whereabouts of citizens who disappeared in police custody at different times – namely, Dilip Chaudhary, Bhuwan Thapa Magar, Prabhakar Subedi and others – should be investigated and those responsible brought to justice. The families of victims should be duly compensated.
17. All those killed during the people's movement should be declared martyrs. The families of the martyrs and those injured and deformed should be duly compensated, and the murderers brought to justice.
18. Nepal should be declared a secular nation.
19. Patriarchal exploitation and discrimination against women should be stopped. Daughters should be allowed access to paternal property.
20. All racial exploitation and suppression should be stopped. Where ethnic communities are in the majority, they should be allowed to form their own autonomous governments.
21. Discrimination against downtrodden and backwards people should be stopped. The system of untouchability should be eliminated.
22. All languages and dialects should be given equal opportunities to prosper. The right to education in the mother tongue up to higher levels should be guaranteed.
23. The right to expression and freedom of press and publication should be guaranteed. The government mass media should be completely autonomous.
24. Academic and professional freedom of scholars, writers, artists and cultural workers should be guaranteed.
25. Regional discrimination between the hills and the terai should be eliminated. Backward areas should be given regional autonomy. Rural and urban areas should be treated on par.
26. Local bodies should be empowered and appropriately equipped.

Concerning Livelihood

27. Land should belong to 'tenants'. Land under the control of the feudal system should be confiscated and distributed to the landless and the homeless.
28. The property of middlemen and comprador capitalists should be confiscated and nationalized. Capital lying unproductive should be invested to promote industrialization.
29. Employment should be guaranteed for all. Until such time as employment can be arranged, an unemployment allowance should be provided.
30. A minimum wage for workers in industries, agriculture and so on should be fixed and strictly implemented.

31. The homeless should be rehabilitated. No one should be relocated until alternative infrastructure is guaranteed.
32. Poor farmers should be exempt from loan repayments. Loans taken by small farmers from the Agricultural Development Bank should be written off. Appropriate provisions should be made to provide loans for small farmers.
33. Fertilizers and seeds should be easily available and at a cheap rate. Farmers should be provided with appropriate prices and markets for their produce.
34. People in flood and drought-affected areas should be provided with appropriate relief materials.
35. Free and scientific health services and education should be available to all. The commercialization of education should be stopped.
36. Inflation should be checked. Wages should be increased in proportion to inflation. Essential goods should be cheap and easily available to everyone.
37. Drinking water, roads and electricity should be provided to all villagers.
38. Domestic and cottage industries should be protected and promoted.
39. Corruption, smuggling, black marketing, bribery and the practices of middlemen and so on should be eliminated.
40. Orphans, the disabled, the elderly and children should be duly honoured and protected.

Source: Deepak Thapa, ed., *Understanding the Maoist Movement of Nepal*, Kathmandu, Martin Chautari, 2003, pp. 391, First published in Dr. Baburam Bhattarai, *Barta ra tatkalin rajnaitik nikasko prashna*, Kathmandu: Publication Department, Special Central Command, CPN (Maoist), Fagun 2059 BS.

Annex 5

12-Point Agreement between the Maoists and the Seven-Party Alliance

1. Today, the main desire of most Nepalis is to have democracy, peace, prosperity, social upliftment and an independent and sovereign Nepal. Toward that end, we fully agree that the main obstacle is an autocratic monarchy. Without an end to the autocratic monarchy and establishment of complete democracy we are clear that there will be no peace, progress and prosperity in the country. Therefore, we have reached an agreement that all forces against autocratic monarchy will step up their movement to end the autocratic monarchy and establish complete democracy.
2. The agitating seven political parties are fully committed to the plan to reinstate parliament whose decision will lead to the formation of an all-party government, hold talks with the Maoists and go for an election to a constituent assembly. They identify this as the way to end the present conflict and restore sovereignty to the people. The Communist Party of Nepal (Maoist) has made the commitment to organize a national political convention of democratic forces. The meet should decide on the formation of an interim government and hold elections for a constituent assembly to achieve the agreed goal. The seven political parties and the CPN (Maoist) will engage in dialogue and explore a consensus on procedural matters. It has been agreed that people's power is the only alternative to meet the goals.
3. The country wants a positive solution and a permanent peace. That is why we are committed to these goals and an end to the armed conflict through the end of autocratic monarchy, elections for the constituent assembly and the establishment of absolute democracy. The CPN (Maoist) expresses its commitment to move ahead in a peaceful new political current through this process. There has been an understanding on keeping the Maoists' armed forces and the Royal Nepali Army under the supervision of the United Nations during the elections of the constituent assembly, conduct elections in a free and fair manner and accept the results of the elections – all these after an end of the autocratic monarchy. We also expect the involvement of reliable international interlocutors in our dialogue process.
4. The CPN (Maoist) makes public its commitment to clearly institutionalize the values of a competitive multiparty system, civil and fundamental rights, human rights and the rule of the law.

5. The CPN (Maoist) has made the commitment to let the leaders, activists and the people who were displaced during the armed conflict to be resettled in their homes. It has also committed that all land, houses and property seized unjustly will be returned. This will create an environment where people will be allowed to freely conduct their political activities.
6. Through self-criticism and self-evaluation of the past mistakes and shortcomings, the CPN (Maoist) is committed not to repeat those mistakes.
7. The seven political parties have realized they made mistakes when they were in parliament and in government and have committed that they will not repeat those mistakes.
8. Human rights and press freedom will be respected while moving the peace process ahead.
9. The talk of municipal elections and parliamentary polls is to trick the people and the international community and to legitimize the illegitimate and autocratic rule of the king. We will boycott these polls in our separate ways and urge the people to make such elections unsuccessful.
10. The people and their representative political parties are the real guards of nationalism. We are fully committed to self-reliance, sovereignty, territorial integrity and national unity. It is our common duty to have friendly relations on the basis of the principle of peaceful co-existence with all the countries of the world, especially with our neighbours India and China. We urge all patriotic people to remain alert about Mandale nationalism that the king and the monarchists are preaching to the people. We also appeal to international powers to support the democratic movement against autocratic monarchy through all possible ways.
11. We urge civil society, professionals, people of all castes, communities and areas, the media, intellectuals and general Nepalese to actively participate in the people's movement that will be conducted on the basis of our agreement that has democracy, peace, prosperity, progressive social change, freedom, sovereignty and integrity of the country as the cornerstone.
12. Past misbehaviour of the parties will be investigated, and action taken against those found guilty and the findings made public. Any problem arising will be sorted out at the concerned level or through discussion at the leadership level.

Index

Page numbers in **bold** indicate tables, page numbers in *italic* indicate figures.

For Product Safety Concerns and Information please contact our EU representative GPSR@taylorandfrancis.com
Taylor & Francis Verlag GmbH, Kaufingerstraße 24, 80331 München, Germany

www.ingramcontent.com/pod-product-compliance
Ingram Content Group UK Ltd.
Pitfield, Milton Keynes, MK11 3LW, UK
UKHW020146200926
475702UK00016B/2577

9781032418001